ETHICS

Including the
Improvement of
the Understanding

Additional Volumes in Prometheus's
Great Books in Philosophy Series

ETHICS

Including the
Improvement of
the Understanding

Translated by
R. H. M. Elwes

BENEDICT DE SPINOZA

GREAT BOOKS IN PHILOSOPHY

PROMETHEUS BOOKS
Buffalo, New York

Published 1989 by Prometheus Books
700 East Amherst Street, Buffalo, New York 14215
Library of Congress Catalog Number: 88-63467
ISBN 0-87975-528-8
Printed in the United States of America

BENEDICT DE (BARUCH) SPINOZA was born in Amsterdam, Holland, on November 24, 1632, into a family of Spanish and Portuguese Jewish descent. Given his cultural and religious background, Spinoza was educated in Judaism within the close Amsterdam community. In his mid-twenties, he began to turn away from his religion; after attempting to return Spinoza to the fold, the Amsterdam community expelled him in 1656. To escape these pressures, Spinoza moved to the nearby village of Ouwerkerk in 1660, where he could be close to friends, many of whom belonged to a religious community in the area.

Rather than being schooled at the universities, Spinoza was trained as a skilled craftsman—a grinder of optical lenses. This vocation provided him with a modest living, which permitted ample time for study and for writing on a variety of subjects. One of the early products of these independent intellectual efforts was Spinoza's short work on the philosophy of René Descartes (*Parts I and II of Descartes' Principles of Philosophy, Demonstrated in the Geometrical Manner* [1663]).

Three years after leaving Amsterdam, Spinoza moved to the town of Voorburg, not far from The Hague. Here he wrote and anonymously published his *Theological-Political Treatise* in 1670. It was in this work that he departed from the prevailing religious teachings of his day to argue that the Bible was a source for moral guidance rather than the fountain of philosophical or scientific truth. Spinoza's devotion to freedom of thought was later carried forth in an unfinished work titled *Political Treatise* (1677). Spinoza's skill as a craftsman and as a philosopher gained him so much international attention that in 1673 he was offered the chair in philosophy at the University of Heidelberg.

But Spinoza's desire for solitude and the intellectual freedom that the quiet life afforded, prompted him to decline the post. In 1677, Spinoza moved to The Hague, where a short time later he died on February 21.

By far the greater proportion of Spinoza's work was published after his death: *B. D. S. Opera Posthuma* (1677, which includes the works *Ethics Demonstrated in a Geometrical Manner, Political Treatise, Treatise on the Improvement of the Understanding,* and *Hebrew Grammar*).

CONTENTS

————

ON THE IMPROVEMENT OF THE UNDER-STANDING.

AFTER experience had taught me that all the usual surroundings of social life are vain and futile; seeing that none of the objects of my fears contained in themselves anything either good or bad, except in so far as the mind is affected by them, I finally resolved to inquire whether there might be some real good having power to communicate itself, which would affect the mind singly, to the exclusion of all else; whether, in fact, there might be anything of which the discovery and attainment would enable me to enjoy continuous, supreme, and unending happiness. I say "I FINALLY resolved," for at first sight it seemed unwise willingly to lose hold on what was sure for the sake of something then uncertain. I could see the benefits which are acquired through fame and riches, and that I should be obliged to abandon the quest of such objects, if I seriously devoted myself to the search for something different and new. I perceived that if true happiness chanced to be placed in the former I should necessarily miss it; while if, on the other hand, it were not so placed, and I gave them my whole attention, I should equally fail.

I therefore debated whether it would not be possible to arrive at the new principle, or at any rate at a certainty concerning its existence, without changing the conduct and usual plan of my life; with this end in view I made many efforts, but in vain. For the ordinary surroundings of life which are esteemed by men (as their actions testify) to be the highest good, may be classed under the three heads—Riches, Fame, and the Pleasures of Sense: with these three the mind is so absorbed that it has little power to reflect on any different good. By sensual pleasure the mind is enthralled to the extent of quiescence, as if the supreme good were actually attained, so that it is quite incapable of thinking of any other object; when such pleasure has been gratified it is followed by extreme melancholy, whereby the mind, though not enthralled, is disturbed and dulled.

The pursuit of honors and riches is likewise very absorbing, especially if such objects be sought simply for their own sake, inasmuch as they are then supposed to constitute the highest good. In the case of fame the mind is still more absorbed, for fame is conceived as always good for its own sake, and as the ultimate end to which all actions are directed. Further, the attainment of riches and fame is not followed as in the case of sensual pleasures by repentance, but, the more we acquire, the greater is our delight, and, consequently, the more we are incited to increase both the one and the other; on the other hand, if our hopes happen to be frustrated we are plunged into the deepest sadness. Fame has the further drawback that it compels its votaries to order their lives according to the opinions of their fellow-men, shunning what they usually shun, and seeking what they usually seek.

When I saw that all these ordinary objects of desire would be obstacles in the way of a search for something different and new — nay, that they were so opposed thereto, that either they or it would have to be abandoned, I was forced to inquire which would prove the most useful to me: for, as I say, I seemed to be willingly losing hold on a sure good for the sake of something uncertain. However, after I had reflected on the matter, I came in the first place to the conclusion that by abandoning the ordinary objects of pursuit, and betaking myself to a new quest, I should be leaving a good, uncertain by reason of its own nature, as may be gathered from what has been said, for the sake of a good not uncertain in its nature (for I sought for a fixed good), but only in the possibility of its attainment.

Further reflection convinced me, that if I could really get to the root of the matter, I should be leaving certain evils for a certain good. I thus perceived that I was in a state of great peril, and I compelled myself to seek with all my strength for a remedy, however uncertain it might be; as a sick man struggling with a deadly disease, when he sees that death will surely be upon him unless a remedy be found, is compelled to seek such a remedy with all his strength, inasmuch as his whole hope lies therein. All the objects pursued by the multitude, not only bring no remedy that tends to preserve our being, but even act as hindrances, causing the death not seldom of those who possess them, and always of those who are possessed by them. There are many examples of men who have suffered persecution even to death for the sake of their riches, and of men who in pursuit of wealth have exposed themselves to so many dangers, that they have paid away their life as a penalty for their folly. Examples are no less numerous of men, who have endured the utmost wretchedness for the sake of gaining or preserving their reputation. Lastly, there are innumerable cases of men, who have hastened their death through over-indulgence in sensual pleasure. All these evils seem to have arisen from the fact, that happiness or unhappiness is made wholly to depend on the quality of the object which we love. When a thing is not loved, no quarrels will arise concerning it — no sadness will be felt if it perishes — no envy if it is possessed by another — no fear no hatred, in short no disturbances of the mind. All these arise from the love of what is perishable, such as the objects already mentioned. But love toward a thing eternal and infinite feeds the mind wholly with joy, and is itself unmingled with any sadness, wherefore it is greatly to be desired and sought for with all our strength. Yet it was not at random that I used the words, "If I could go to the root of the matter," for, though what I have urged was perfectly clear to my mind, I could not forthwith lay aside all love of riches, sensual enjoyment, and fame. One thing was evident, namely, that while my mind was employed with these thoughts it turned away from its former objects of desire, and seriously considered the search for a new principle; this state of

things was a great comfort to me, for I perceived that
the evils were not such as to resist all remedies.
Although these intervals were at first rare, and of very
short duration, yet afterward, as the true good became
more and more discernible to me, they became more frequent and more lasting; especially after I had recognized
that the acquisition of wealth, sensual pleasure, or fame,
is only a hindrance, so long as they are sought as ends
not as means; if they be sought as means they will be
under restraint, and, far from being hindrances, will
further not a little the end for which they are sought, as
I will show in due time.

I will here only briefly state what I mean by true
good, and also what is the nature of the highest good.
In order that this may be rightly understood, we must
bear in mind that the terms good and evil are only applied relatively, so that the same thing may be called
both good and bad, according to the relations in view,
in the same way as it may be called perfect or imperfect.
Nothing regarded in its own nature can be called perfect
or imperfect; especially when we are aware that all
things which come to pass, come to pass according to the
eternal order and fixed laws of nature. However, human
weakness cannot attain to this order in its own thoughts,
but meanwhile man conceives a human character much
more stable than his own, and sees that there is no
reason why he should not himself acquire such a character. Thus he is led to seek for means which will bring
him to this pitch of perfection, and calls everything
which will serve as such means a true good. The chief
good is that he should arrive, together with other individuals if possible, at the possession of the aforesaid character. What that character is we shall show in due time,
namely, that it is the knowledge of the union existing
between the mind and the whole of nature. This, then,
is the end for which I strive, to attain to such a character myself, and to endeavor that many should attain to
it with me. In other words, it is part of my happiness
to lend a helping hand, that many others may understand
even as I do, so that their understanding and desire may

entirely agree with my own. In order to bring this about, it is necessary to understand as much of nature as will enable us to attain to the aforesaid character, and also to form a social order such as is most conducive to the attainment of this character by the greatest number with the least difficulty and danger. We must seek the assistance of Moral Philosophy* and the Theory of Education; further, as health is no insignificant means for attaining our end, we must also include the whole science of Medicine, and, as many difficult things are by contrivance rendered easy, and we can in this way gain much time and convenience, the science of Mechanics must in no way be despised. But, before all things, a means must be devised for improving the understanding and purifying it, as far as may be at the outset, so that it may apprehend things without error, and in the best possible way.

Thus it is apparent to every one that I wish to direct all sciences to one end and aim, so that we may attain to the supreme human perfection which we have named; and, therefore, whatsoever in the sciences does not serve to promote our object will have to be rejected as useless. To sum up the matter in a word, all our actions and thoughts must be directed to this one end. Yet, as it is necessary that while we are endeavoring to attain our purpose, and bring the understanding into the right path, we should carry on our life, we are compelled first of all to lay down certain rules of life as provisionally good, to wit, the following:

I. To speak in a manner intelligible to the multitude, and to comply with every general custom that does not hinder the attainment of our purpose. For we can gain from the multitude no small advantages, provided that we strive to accommodate ourselves to its understanding as far as possible: moreover, we shall in this way gain a friendly audience for the reception of the truth.

II. To indulge ourselves with pleasures only in so far as they are necessary for preserving health.

*I do no more here than enumerate the sciences necessary for our purpose; I lay no stress on their order.

III. Lastly, to endeavor to obtain only sufficient money or other commodities to enable us to preserve our life and health, and to follow such general customs as are consistent with our purpose.

Having laid down these preliminary rules, I will betake myself to the first and most important task, namely, the amendment of the understanding, and the rendering it capable of understanding things in the manner necessary for attaining our end.

In order to bring this about, the natural order demands that I should here recapitulate all the modes of perception, which I have hitherto employed for affirming or denying anything with certainty, so that I may choose the best, and at the same time begin to know my own powers and the nature which I wish to perfect.

Reflection shows that all modes of perception or knowledge may be reduced to four:

I. Perception arising from hearsay or from some sign which everyone may name as he pleases.

II. Perception arising from mere experience—that is, from experience not yet classified by the intellect, and only so called because the given event has happened to take place, and we have no contradictory fact to set against it, so that it therefore remains unassailed in our mind.

III. Perception arising when the essence of one thing is inferred from another thing, but not adequately; this comes when from some effect we gather its cause, or when it is inferred from some general proposition that some property is always present.

IV. Lastly, there is the perception arising when a thing is perceived solely through its essence, or through the knowledge of its proximate cause.

All these kinds of perception I will illustrate by examples. By hearsay I know the day of my birth, my parentage, and other matters about which I have never felt any doubt. By mere experience I know that I shall die, for this I can affirm from having seen that others like myself have died, though all did not live for the same period, or die by the same disease. I know by mere experience that oil has the property of feeding fire, and water of extinguishing it. In the same way I know that a dog is a barking animal, man a rational animal, and in fact nearly all the practical knowledge of life.

We deduce one thing from another as follows: when we clearly perceive that we feel a certain body and no other, we thence clearly infer that the mind is united to the body, and that their union is the cause of the given sensation; but we cannot thence absolutely understand the nature of the sensation and the union. Or, after I have become acquainted with the nature of vision, and know that it has the property of making one and the same thing appear smaller when far off than when near, I can infer that the sun is larger than it appears, and can draw other conclusions of the same kind.

Lastly, a thing may be perceived solely through its essence; when, from the fact of knowing something, I know what it is to know that thing, or when, from knowing the essence of the mind, I know that it is united to the body. By the same kind of knowledge we know that two and three make five, or that two lines each parallel to a third, are parallel to one another, etc. The things which I have been able to know by this kind of knowledge are as yet very few.

In order that the whole matter may be put in a clearer light, I will make use of a single illustration as follows: Three numbers are given — it is required to find a fourth, which shall be to the third as the second is to the first. Tradesmen will at once tell us that they know what is required to find the fourth number, for they have not yet forgotten the rule which was given to them arbitrarily without proof by their masters; others construct a universal axiom from their experience with simple numbers, where the fourth number is self-evident, as in the case of 2, 4, 3, 6; here it is evident that if the second number be multiplied by the third, and the product divided by the first, the quotient is 6; when they see that by this process the number is produced which they knew beforehand to be the proportional, they infer that the process always holds good for finding a fourth number proportional. Mathematicians, however, know by the proof of the nineteenth proposition of the seventh book of Euclid, what numbers are proportionals, namely, from the nature and property of proportion it follows that the product of the first and fourth will be equal to the product of the second and third: still they do not see the adequate proportionality of the given numbers or, if they do see it, they see it not by virtue of Euclid's proposition, but intuitively, without going through any process.

In order that from these modes of perception the best may be selected, it is well that we should briefly enumerate the means necessary for attaining our end.

I. To have an exact knowledge of our nature which we desire to perfect, and to know as much as is needful of nature in general.

II. To collect in this way the differences, the agreements, and the oppositions of things.

III. To learn thus exactly how far they can or cannot be modified.

IV. To compare this result with the nature and power of man. We shall thus discern the highest degree of perfection to which man is capable of attaining. We shall then be in a position to see which mode of perception we ought to choose.

As to the first mode, it is evident that from hearsay our knowledge must always be uncertain, and, moreover, can give us no insight into the essence of a thing, as is manifest in our illustration; now one can only arrive at knowledge of a thing through knowledge of its essence, as will hereafter appear. We may, therefore, clearly conclude that the certainty arising from hearsay cannot be scientific in its character. For simple hearsay cannot affect anyone whose understanding does not, so to speak, meet it half way.

The second mode of perception* cannot be said to give us the idea of the proportion of which we are in search. Moreover its results are very uncertain and indefinite, for

* I shall here treat a little more in detail of experience, and shall examine the method adopted by the Empirics, and by recent philosophers.

we shall never discover anything in natural phenomena by its means, except accidental properties, which are never clearly understood, unless the essence of the things in question be known first. Wherefore this mode also must be rejected.

Of the third mode of perception we may say in a manner that it gives us the idea of the thing sought, and that it enables us to draw conclusions without risk of error; yet it is not by itself sufficient to put us in possession of the perfection we aim at.

The fourth mode alone apprehends the adequate essence of a thing without danger of error. This mode, therefore, must be the one which we chiefly employ. How, then, should we avail ourselves of it so as to gain the fourth kind of knowledge with the least delay concerning things previously unknown? I will proceed to explain.

Now that we know what kind of knowledge is necessary for us, we must indicate the way and the method whereby we may gain the said knowledge concerning the things needful to be known. In order to accomplish this, we must first take care not to commit ourselves to a search, going back to infinity—that is, in order to discover the best method for finding out the truth, there is no need of another method to discover such method; nor of a third method for discovering the second, and so on to infinity. By such proceedings, we should never arrive at the knowledge of the truth, or, indeed, at any knowledge at all. The matter stands on the same footing as the making of material tools, which might be argued about in a similar way. For, in order to work iron, a hammer is needed, and the hammer cannot be forthcoming unless it has been made; but, in order to make it, there was need of another hammer and other tools, and so on to infinity. We might thus vainly endeavor to prove that men have no power of working iron. But as men at first made use of the instruments supplied by nature to accomplish very easy pieces of workmanship, laboriously and imperfectly, and then, when these were finished, wrought other things more difficult with less labor and greater perfection; and so gradually mounted from the simplest operations to the making of tools, and from the making of tools to the making of more complex tools, and fresh feats of workmanship, till they arrived at making, with small expenditure of labor, the vast number of complicated mechanisms which they now possess. So, in like manner, the intellect, by its native strength,* makes for itself intellectual instruments, whereby it acquires strength for performing other intellectual operations, and from these operations gets again fresh instruments, or the power of pushing its investigations further, and thus gradually proceeds till it reaches the summit of wisdom.

That this is the path pursued by the understanding may be readily seen, when we understand the nature of the method for finding out the truth, and of the natural instruments so necessary for the construction of more complex instruments, and for the progress of investigation. I thus proceed with my demonstration.

A true idea (for we possess a true idea) is something different from its correlate (*ideatum*); thus a circle is different from the idea of a circle. The idea of a circle is not something having a circumference and a centre, as a circle has; nor is the idea of a body that body itself. Now, as it is something different from its correlate, it is capable of being understood through itself; in other words, the idea, in so far as its actual essence (*essentia formalis*) is concerned, may be the subject of another subjective essence (*essentia objectiva*). And, again, this second subjective essence will, regarded in itself, be something real, and capable of being understood; and so on, indefinitely. For instance, the man Peter is something real; the true idea of Peter is the reality of Peter represented subjectively, and is in itself something real, and quite distinct from the actual Peter. Now, as this true idea of Peter is in itself something real, and has its own individual existence, it will also be capable of being understood — that is, of being the subject of another idea, which will contain by representation (*objective*) all that the idea of Peter contains actually

---

* By native strength, I mean that bestowed on us by external causes, as I shall afterwards explain in my philosophy.

(*formaliter*). And, again, this idea of the idea of Peter has its own individuality, which may become the subject of yet another idea; and so on, indefinitely. This every one may make trial of for himself, by reflecting that he knows what Peter is, and also knows that he knows, and further knows that he knows that he knows, etc. Hence it is plain that, in order to understand the actual Peter, it is not necessary first to understand the idea of Peter, and still less the idea of the idea of Peter. This is the same as saying that, in order to know, there is no need to know that we know, much less to know that we know that we know. This is no more necessary than to know the nature of a circle before knowing the nature of a triangle. But, with these ideas, the contrary is the case: for, in order to know that I know, I must first know. Hence it is clear that certainty is nothing else than the subjective essence of a thing: in other words, the mode in which we perceive an actual reality is certainty. Further, it is also evident that, for the certitude of truth, no further sign is necessary beyond the possession of a true idea: for, as I have shown, it is not necessary to know that we know that we know. Hence, again, it is clear that no one can know the nature of the highest certainty, unless he possesses an adequate idea, or the subjective essence of a thing: for certainty is identical with such subjective essence. Thus, as the truth needs no sign — it being sufficient to possess the subjective essence of things, or, in other words, the ideas of them, in order that all doubts may be removed — it follows that the true method does not consist in seeking for the signs of truth after the acquisition of the idea, but that the true method teaches us the order in which we should seek for truth itself, or the subjective essences of things, or ideas, for all these expressions are synonymous. Again, method must necessarily be concerned with reasoning or understanding — I mean, method is not identical with reasoning in the search for causes, still less is it the comprehension of the causes of things: it is the discernment of a true idea, by distinguishing it from other perceptions and by investigating its nature in order that we may thus know our power of understanding, and may so train our mind that it may, by a given standard, comprehend whatsoever is intelligible, by laying down certain rules as aids, and by avoiding useless mental exertion.

Whence we may gather that method is nothing else than reflective knowledge, or the idea of an idea; and that as there can be no idea of an idea—unless an idea exists previously,—there can be no method without a pre-existent idea. Therefore, that will be a good method which shows us how the mind should be directed, according to the standard of the given true idea.

Again, seeing that the ratio existing between two ideas is the same as the ratio between the actual realities corresponding to those ideas, it follows that the reflective knowledge which has for its object the most perfect being is more excellent than reflective knowledge concerning other objects—in other words, that method will be most perfect which affords the standard of the given idea of the most perfect being whereby we may direct our mind. We thus easily understand how, in proportion as it acquires new ideas, the mind simultaneously acquires fresh instruments for pursuing its inquiries further. For we may gather from what has been said, that a true idea must necessarily first of all exist in us as a natural instrument; and that when this idea is apprehended by the mind, it enables us to understand the difference existing between itself and all other perceptions. In this, one part of the method consists.

Now it is clear that the mind apprehends itself better in proportion as it understands a greater number of natural objects; it follows, therefore, that this portion of the method will be more perfect in proportion as the mind attains to the comprehension of a greater number of objects, and that it will be absolutely perfect when the mind gains a knowledge of the absolutely perfect being or becomes conscious thereof. Again, the more things the mind knows, the better does it understand its own strength and the order of nature; by increased self-knowledge it can direct itself more easily, and lay down rules for its own guidance; and, by increased knowledge of nature, it can more easily avoid what is useless.

And this is the sum total of method, as we have already stated. We may add that the idea in the world of thought is in the same case as its correlate in the world of reality. If, therefore, there be anything in nature which is without connection with any other thing, and if we assign to it a subjective essence, which would in every way correspond to the objective reality, the subjective essence would have no connection with any other ideas — in other words, we could not draw any conclusion with regard to it. On the other hand, those things which are connected with others — as all things that exist in nature — will be understood by the mind, and their subjective essences will maintain the same mutual relations as their objective realities — that is to say, we shall infer from these ideas other ideas, which will in turn be connected with others, and thus our instruments for proceeding with our investigation will increase. This is what we are endeavoring to prove. Further, from what has just been said — namely, that an idea must, in all respects, correspond to its correlate in the world of reality — it is evident that, in order to reproduce in every respect the faithful image of nature, our mind must deduce all its ideas from the idea which represents the origin and source of the whole of nature, so that it may itself become the source of other ideas.

It may, perhaps, provoke astonishment that, after having said that the good method is that which teaches us to direct our mind according to the standard of the given true idea, we should prove our point by reasoning, which would seem to indicate that it is not self-evident. We may, therefore, be questioned as to the validity of our reasoning. If our reasoning be sound, we must take as a starting point a true idea. Now, to be certain that our starting point is really a true idea, we need a proof. This first course of reasoning must be supported by a second, the second by a third, and so on to infinity. To this I make answer that, if by some happy chance anyone had adopted this method in his investigations of nature — that is, if he had acquired new ideas in the proper order, according to the standard of the original true idea, he would never have doubted of the truth of his knowledge, inasmuch as truth, as we have shown, makes itself manifest, and all things would flow, as it were, spontaneously toward him. But as this never, or rarely, happens, I have been forced so to arrange my proceedings, that we may acquire by reflection and forethought what we cannot acquire by chance, and that it may at the same time appear that, for proving the truth, and for valid reasoning, we need no other means than the truth and valid reasoning themselves: for by valid reasoning I have established valid reasoning, and, in like measure, I seek still to establish it. Moreover, this is the order of thinking adopted by men in their inward meditations. The reasons for its rare employment in investigations of nature are to be found in current misconceptions, whereof we shall examine the causes hereafter in our philosophy. Moreover, it demands, as we shall show, a keen and accurate discernment. Lastly, it is hindered by the conditions of human life, which are, as we have already pointed out, extremely changeable. There are also other obstacles, which we will not here inquire into.

If any one asks why I have not at the starting point set forth all the truths of nature in their due order, inasmuch as truth is self-evident, I reply by warning him not to reject as false any paradoxes he may find here, but to take the trouble to reflect on the chain of reasoning by which they are supported; he will then be no longer in doubt that we have attained to the truth. This is why I have begun as above.

If there yet remains some sceptic, who doubts of our primary truth, and of all deductions we make, taking such truth as our standard, he must either be arguing in bad faith, or we must confess that there are men in complete mental blindness either innate or due to misconceptions—that is, to some external influence.

Such persons are not conscious of themselves. If they affirm or doubt anything, they know not that they affirm or doubt; they say that they know nothing, and they say that they are ignorant of the very fact of their knowing nothing. Even this they do not affirm absolutely, they are afraid of confessing that they exist, so long as they know nothing; in fact, they ought to remain dumb, for fear of haply supposing something which should smack of truth. Lastly, with such persons, one should not speak of sciences; for, in what relates to life and conduct, they are compelled by necessity to suppose that they exist, and seek their own advantage, and often affirm and deny, even with an oath. If they deny, grant, or gainsay, they know not that they deny, grant, or gainsay, so that they ought to be regarded as automata, utterly devoid of intelligence.

Let us now return to our proposition. Up to the present we have, first, defined the end to which we desire to direct all our thoughts; secondly, we have determined the mode of perception best adapted to aid us in attaining our perfection; thirdly, we have discovered the way which our mind should take, in order to make a good beginning — namely, that it should use every true idea as a standard in pursuing its inquiries according to fixed rules. Now, in order that it may thus proceed, our method must furnish us, first, with a means of distinguishing a true idea from all other perceptions, and enabling the mind to avoid the latter; secondly, with rules for perceiving unknown things according to the standard of the true idea; thirdly, with an order which enables us to avoid useless labor. When we became acquainted with this method, we saw that, fourthly, it would be perfect when we had attained to the idea of the absolutely perfect Being. This is an observation which should be made at the outset, in order that we may arrive at the knowledge of such a being more quickly.

Let us then make a beginning with the first part of the method, which is, as we have said, to distinguish and separate the true idea from other perceptions, and to keep the mind from confusing with true ideas those which are false, fictitious, and doubtful. I intend to dwell on this point at length, partly to keep a distinction so necessary before the reader's mind, and also because there are some who doubt of true ideas, through not having attended to the distinction between a true perception and all others. Such persons are like men who, while they are awake, doubt not that they are awake, but afterward in a dream, as often happens, thinking that they are surely awake, and then finding that they were in error, become doubtful even of being awake. This state of mind arises through neglect of the distinction between sleeping and waking.

Meanwhile, I give warning that I shall not here give the essence of every perception, and explain it through its proximate cause. Such work lies in the province of philosophy. I shall confine myself to what concerns method — that is, to the character of fictitious, false, and doubtful perception, and the means of freeing ourselves therefrom. Let us then first inquire into the nature of a fictitious idea.

Every perception has for its object either a thing considered as existing, or solely the essence of a thing. Now "fiction" is chiefly occupied with things considered as existing. I will, therefore, consider these first — I mean cases where only the existence of an object is feigned, and the thing thus feigned is understood, or assumed to be understood. For instance, I feign that Peter, whom I know to have gone home, is gone to see me, or something of that kind. With what is such an idea concerned? It is concerned with things possible, and not with things necessary or impossible. I call a thing IMPOSSIBLE, when its existence would imply a contradiction; NECESSARY, when its non-existence would imply a contradiction; POSSIBLE, when neither its existence nor its non-existence imply a contradiction, but when the necessity or impossibility of its nature depends on causes unknown to us, while we feign that it exists. If the necessity or impossibility of its existence depending on external causes were known to us, we could not form any fictitious hypothesis about it; whence it follows that if there be a God or omniscient Being, such an one cannot form fictitious hypotheses. For, as regards ourselves, when I know that I exist, I cannot hypothesize

that I exist or do not exist, any more than I can hypothesize an elephant that can go through the eye of a
needle; nor when I know the nature of God, can I hypothesize that he exists or does not exist. The same
thing must be said of the Chimæra, whereof the nature
implies a contradiction. From these considerations, it is
plain, as I have already stated, that fiction cannot be concerned with eternal truths.

But before proceeding further, I must remark, in passing, that the difference between the essence of one thing
and the essence of another thing is the same as that
which exists between the reality or existence of one thing
and the reality or existence of another; therefore, if we
wished to conceive the existence, for example, of Adam,
simply by means of existence in general, it would be the
same as if, in order to conceive his existence, we went
back to the nature of being, so as to define Adam as a
being. Thus, the more existence is conceived generally,
the more is it conceived confusedly, and the more easily
can it be ascribed to a given object. Contrariwise, the
more it is conceived particularly, the more is it understood clearly, and the less liable is it to be ascribed,
through negligence of Nature's order, to anything save
its proper object. This is worthy of remark.

We now proceed to consider those cases which are
commonly called fictions, though we clearly understand
that the thing is not as we imagine it. For instance,
I know that the earth is round, but nothing prevents my
telling people that it is a hemisphere, and that it is like
a half apple carved in relief on a dish; or, that the sun
moves round the earth, and so on. However, examina-
tion will show us that there is nothing here inconsistent
with what has been said, provided we first admit that
we may have made mistakes, and be now conscious of
them; and, further, that we can hypothesize, or at least
suppose, that others are under the same mistake as ourselves, or can, like us, fall under it. We can, I repeat,
thus hypothesize so long as we see no impossibility.
Thus, when I tell anyone that the earth is not round, etc.,
I merely recall the error which I perhaps made myself,

or which I might have fallen into, and afterward I hypothesize that the person to whom I tell it is still, or may still fall under the same mistake. This I say, I can feign so long as I do not perceive any impossibility or necessity; if I truly understood either one or the other I should not be able to feign, and I should be reduced to saying that I had made the attempt.

It remains for us to consider hypotheses made in problems, which sometimes involve impossibilities. For instance, when we say—let us assume that this burning candle is not burning, or, let us assume that it burns in some imaginary space, or where there are no physical objects. Such assumptions are freely made, though the last is clearly seen to be impossible. But, though this be so, there is no fiction in the case. For, in the first case, I have merely recalled to memory another candle not burning, or conceived the candle before me as without a flame, and then I understand as applying to the latter, leaving its flame out of the question, all that I think of the former. In the second case, I have merely to abstract my thoughts from the objects surrounding the candle, for the mind to devote itself to the contemplation of the candle singly looked at in itself only; I can then draw the conclusion that the candle contains in itself no cause for its own destruction, so that if there were no physical objects the candle, and even the flame, would remain unchangeable, and so on. Thus there is here no fiction, but true and bare assertions.

Let us now pass on to the fictions concerned with essences only, or with some reality or existence simultaneously. Of these we must specially observe that in proportion as the mind's understanding is smaller, and its experience multiplex, so will its power of coining fictions be larger, whereas, as its understanding increases, its capacity for entertaining fictitious ideas becomes less. For instance, in the same way as we are unable, while we are thinking, to feign that we are thinking or not thinking, so, also, when we know the nature of body we cannot imagine an infinite fly; or, when we know the nature of the soul, we cannot imagine it as square, though anything may be expressed verbally. But, as we said above, the less men know of nature the more easily can they coin fictitious ideas, such as trees speaking, men instantly changed into stones, or into fountains, ghosts appearing in mirrors, something issuing from nothing, even gods changed into beasts and men, and infinite other absurdities of the same kind.

Some persons think, perhaps, that fiction is limited by fiction, and not by understanding; in other words, after I have formed some fictitious idea, and have affirmed of my own free will that it exists under a certain form in nature, I am thereby precluded from thinking of it under any other form. For instance, when I have feigned (to repeat their argument) that the nature of body is of a certain kind, and have of my own free will desired to convince myself that it actually exists under this form, I am no longer able to hypothesize that a fly, for example, is infinite; so, when I have hypothesized the essence of the soul, I am not able to think of it as square, etc. But these arguments demand further inquiry. First, their upholders must either grant or deny that we can understand anything. If they grant it, then necessarily the same must be said of understanding as is said of fiction. If they deny it, let us, who know that we do know something, see what they mean. They assert that the soul can be conscious of, and perceive in a variety of ways, not itself nor things which exist, but only things which are neither in itself nor anywhere else, in other words, that the soul can, by its unaided power, create sensations or ideas unconnected with things. In fact, they regard the soul as a sort of god. Further, they assert that we or our soul have such freedom that we can constrain ourselves, or our soul, or even our soul's freedom. For, after it has formed a fictitious idea, and has given its assent thereto, it cannot think or feign it in any other manner, but is constrained by the first fictitious idea to keep all its other thoughts in harmony therewith. Our opponents are thus driven to admit, in support of their fiction, the absurdities which I have just enumerated; and which are not worthy of rational refutation.

While leaving such persons in their error, we will take care to derive from our argument with them a truth serviceable for our purpose, namely, that the mind, in paying attention to a thing hypothetical or false, so as to meditate upon it and understand it, and derive the proper conclusions in due order therefrom, will readily discover its falsity; and if the thing hypothetical be in its nature true, and the mind pays attention to it, so as to understand it, and deduce the truths which are derivable from it, the mind will proceed with an uninterrupted series of apt conclusions; in the same way as it would at once discover (as we showed just now) the absurdity of a false hypothesis, and of the conclusions drawn from it.

We need, therefore, be in no fear of forming hypotheses, so long as we have a clear and distinct perception of what is involved. For, if we were to assert, haply, that men are suddenly turned into beasts, the statement would be extremely general, so general that there would be no conception, that is, no idea or connection of subject and predicate, in our mind. If there were such a conception we should at the same time be aware of the means and the causes whereby the event took place. Moreover, we pay no attention to the nature of the subject and the predicate. Now, if the first idea be not fictitious, and if all the other ideas be deduced therefrom, our hurry to form fictitious ideas will gradually subside. Further, as a fictitious idea cannot be clear and distinct, but is necessarily confused, and as all confusion arises from the fact that the mind has only partial knowledge of a thing either simple or complex, and does not distinguish between the known and the unknown, and, again, that it directs its attention promiscuously to all parts of an object at once without making distinctions, it follows, FIRST, that if the idea be of something very simple, it must necessarily be clear and distinct. For a very simple object cannot be known in part, it must either be known altogether or not at all. SECONDLY, it follows that if a complex object be divided by thought into a number of simple component parts, and if each part be regarded separately, all confusion will disappear. THIRDLY, it follows that fiction cannot be simple, but is made up of the blending of several confused ideas of diverse objects or actions existent in nature, or rather is composed of attention* directed to all such ideas at once, and unaccompanied by any mental assent.

Now a fiction that was simple would be clear and distinct, and therefore true, also a fiction composed only of distinct ideas would be clear and distinct, and therefore true. For instance, when we know the nature of the circle and the square, it is impossible for us to blend together these two figures, and to hypothesize a square circle, any more than a square soul, or things of that kind. Let us shortly come to our conclusion, and again repeat that we need have no fear of confusing with true ideas that which is only a fiction. As for the first sort of fiction of which we have already spoken, when a thing is clearly conceived, we saw that if the existence of that thing is in itself an eternal truth, fiction can have no part in it; but if the existence of the thing conceived be not an eternal truth, we have only to be careful that such existence be compared to the thing's essence, and to consider the order of nature. As for the second sort of fiction, which we stated to be the result of simultaneously directing the attention, without the assent of the intellect, to different confused ideas representing different things and actions existing in nature, we have seen that an absolutely simple thing connot be feigned, but must be understood, and that a complex thing is in the same case if we regard separately the simple parts whereof it is composed; we shall not even be able to hypothesize any untrue action concerning such objects, for we shall be obliged to consider at the same time the causes and the manner of such action.

---

* Observe that fiction regarded in itself, differs only from dreams in that in the latter we do not perceive the external causes which we perceive through the senses while awake. It has hence been inferred that representations occurring in sleep have no connection with objects external to us. We shall presently see that error is the dreaming of a waking man; if it reaches a certain pitch it becomes delirium.

These matters being thus understood, let us pass on to consider the false idea, observing the objects with which it is concerned, and the means of guarding ourselves from falling into false perceptions. Neither of these tasks will present much difficulty, after our inquiry concerning fictitious ideas. The false idea only differs from the fictitious idea in the fact of implying a mental assent—that is as we have already remarked, while the representations are occurring, there are no causes present to us, wherefrom, as in fiction, we can conclude that such representations do not arise from external objects, in fact it is much the same as dreaming with our eyes open, or while awake. Thus a false idea is concerned with (or to speak more correctly), attributable to the existence of a thing whereof the essence is known, or the essence itself, in the same way as a fictitious idea. If attributable to the existence of the thing, it is corrected in the same way as a fictitious idea under similar circumstances. If attributable to the essence, it is likewise corrected in the same way as a fictitious idea. For if the nature of the thing known implies necessary existence, we cannot possibly be in error with regard to its existence; but if the nature of the thing be not an eternal truth, like its essence, but contrariwise, the necessity or impossibility of its existence depends on external causes, then we must follow the same course as we adopted in the case of fiction, for it is corrected in the same manner. As for false ideas concerned with essences, or even with actions, such perceptions are necessarily always confused, being compounded of different confused perceptions of things existing in nature, as, for instance, when men are persuaded that deities are present in woods, in statues, in brute beasts, and the like; that there are bodies which, by their composition alone, give rise to intellect; that corpses reason, walk about and speak; that God is deceived, and so on. But ideas which are clear and distinct can never be false: for ideas of things clearly and distinctly conceived are either very simple themselves, or are compounded from very simple ideas—that is, are deduced therefrom. The impossibility of a very simple idea being

false is evident to every one who understands the nature
of truth or understanding and of falsehood.

As regards that which constitutes the reality of truth,
it is certain that a true idea is distinguished from a false
one, not so much by its extrinsic object as by its intrinsic
nature. If an architect conceives a building properly
constructed, though such a building may never have existed, and may never exist, nevertheless the idea is true;
and the idea remains the same, whether it be put into
execution or not. On the other hand, if any one asserts,
for instance, that Peter exists, without knowing whether
Peter really exists or not, the assertion, as far as its as-
serter is concerned, is false, or not true, even though Peter
actually does exist. The assertion that Peter exists is
true only with regard to him who knows for certain that
Peter does exist. Whence it follows that there is in ideas
something real, whereby the true are distinguished from
the false. This reality must be inquired into, if we are
to find the best standard of truth (we have said that we
ought to determine our thoughts by the given standard
of a true idea, and that method is reflective knowledge),
and to know the properties of our understanding. Neither
must we say that the difference between true and false
arises from the fact that true knowledge consists in knowing things through their primary causes, wherein it is
totally different from false knowledge, as I have just explained it: for thought is said to be true, if it involves
subjectively the essence of any principle which has no
cause, and is known through itself and in itself. Wherefore the reality (*forma*) of true thought must exist in
the thought itself, without reference to other thoughts;
it does not acknowledge the object as its cause, but must
depend on the actual power and nature of the understanding. For, if we suppose that the understanding has
perceived some new entity which has never existed, as
some conceive the understanding of God before He created things (a perception which certainly could not arise
from any object), and has legitimately deduced other
thoughts from the said perception, all such thoughts
would be true, without being determined by any

external object; they would depend solely on the power and nature of the understanding. Thus, that which constitutes the reality of a true thought must be sought in the thought itself and deduced from the nature of the understanding. In order to pursue our investigation, let us confront ourselves with some TRUE idea, whose object we know for certain to be dependent on our power of thinking, and to have nothing corresponding to it in nature. With an idea of this kind before us, we shall, as appears from what has just been said, be more easily able to carry on the research we have in view. For instance, in order to form the conception of a sphere, I invent a cause at my pleasure — namely, a semicircle revolving round its centre, and thus producing a sphere. This is indisputably a true idea; and, although we know that no sphere in nature has ever actually been so formed, the perception remains true, and is the easiest manner of conceiving a sphere. We must observe that this perception asserts the rotation of a semicircle — which assertion would be false, if it were not associated with the conception of a sphere, or of a cause determining a motion of the kind, or absolutely, if the assertion were isolated. The mind would then only tend to the affirmation of the sole motion of a semicircle which is not contained in the conception of a semicircle, and does not arise from the conception of any cause capable of producing such motion.

Thus FALSITY consists only in this, that something is affirmed of a thing, which is not contained in the conception we have formed of that thing, as motion or rest of a semicircle. Whence it follows that simple ideas cannot be other than TRUE — *e. g.*, the simple idea of a semicircle, of motion, of rest, of quantity, etc.

Whatsoever affirmation such ideas contain is equal to the concept formed, and does not extend further. Wherefore we may form as many simple ideas as we please, without any fear of error. It only remains for us to inquire by what power our mind can form true ideas, and how far such power extends. It is certain that such power cannot extend itself infinitely. For when we affirm

somewhat of a thing, which is not contained in the concept we have formed of that thing, such an affirmation
shows a defect of our perception, or that we have formed
fragmentary or mutilated ideas. Thus we have seen that
the motion of a semicircle is false when it is isolated in
the mind, but true when it is associated with the concept
of a sphere, or of some cause determining such a motion.
But if it be the nature of a thinking being, as seems,
prima facie, to be the case, to form true or adequate
thoughts, it is plain that inadequate ideas arise in us
only because we are parts of a thinking being, whose
thoughts—some in their entirety, others in fragments
only—constitute our mind.

But there is another point to be considered, which was
not worth raising in the case of fiction, but which gives
rise to complete deception—namely, that certain things
presented to the imagination also exist in the understanding—in other words, are conceived clearly and distinctly. Hence, so long as we do not separate that
which is distinct from that which is confused, certainty,
or the true idea, becomes mixed with indistinct ideas.
For instance, certain Stoics heard, perhaps, the term
« soul, » and also that the soul is immortal, yet imagined
it only confusedly; they imagined, also, and understood
that very subtle bodies penetrate all others, and are
penetrated by none. By combining these ideas, and
being at the same time certain of the truth of the axiom,
they forthwith became convinced that the mind consists
of very subtle bodies; that these very subtle bodies cannot be divided, etc. But we are freed from mistakes of
this kind, so long as we endeavor to examine all our
perceptions by the standard of the given true idea. We
must take care, as has been said, to separate such perceptions from all those which arise from hearsay or
unclassified experience.

Moreover, such mistakes arise from things being conceived too much in the abstract; for it is sufficiently
self-evident that what I conceive as in its true object I
cannot apply to anything else. Lastly, they arise from a
want of understanding of the primary elements of nature

as a whole; whence we proceed without due order, and confound nature with abstract rules, which, although they be true enough in their sphere, yet, when misapplied, confound themselves, and pervert the order of nature. However, if we proceed with as little abstraction as possible, and begin from primary elements — that is, from the source and origin of nature, as far back as we can reach, — we need not fear any deceptions of this kind. As far as the knowledge of the origin of nature is concerned, there is no danger of our confounding it with abstractions. For when a thing is conceived in the abstract, as are all universal notions, the said universal notions are always more extensive in the mind than the number of individuals forming their contents really existing in nature.

Again, there are many things in nature, the difference between which is so slight as to be hardly perceptible to the understanding; so that it may readily happen that such things are confounded together, if they be conceived abstractedly. But since the first principle of nature cannot (as we shall see hereafter) be conceived abstractedly or universally, and cannot extend further in the understanding than it does in reality, and has no likeness to mutable things, no confusion need be feared in respect to the idea of it, provided (as before shown) that we possess a standard of truth. This is, in fact, a being single and infinite; in other words, it is the sum total of being, beyond which there is no being found.

Thus far we have treated of the false idea. We have now to investigate the doubtful idea — that is, to inquire what can cause us to doubt, and how doubt may be removed. I speak of real doubt existing in the mind, not of such doubt as we see exemplified when a man says that he doubts, though his mind does not really hesitate. The cure of the latter does not fall within the province of method, it belongs rather to inquiries concerning obstinacy and its cure. Real doubt is never produced in the mind by the thing doubted of. In other words, if there were only one idea in the mind, whether that idea were true or false, there would be no doubt of certainty present, only a certain sensation. For an idea is in itself nothing else than a certain sensation; but doubt will arise through another idea, not clear and distinct enough for us to be able to draw any certain conclusion with regard to the matter under consideration; that is, the idea which causes us to doubt is not clear and distinct. To take an example. Supposing that a man has never reflected, taught by experience, or by any other means, that our senses sometimes deceive us, he will never doubt whether the sun be greater or less than it appears. Thus rustics are generally astonished when they hear that the sun is much larger than the earth. But from reflection on the deceitfulness of the senses * doubt arises, and if, after doubting, we acquire a true knowledge of the senses, and how things at a distance are represented through their instrumentality, doubt is again removed. Hence we cannot cast doubt on true ideas by the supposition that there is a deceitful Deity, who leads us astray even in what is most certain. We can only hold such an hypothesis so long as we have no clear and distinct idea — in other words, until we reflect on the knowledge which we have of the first principle of all things, and find that which teaches us that God is not a deceiver, and until we know this with the same certainty as we know from reflecting on the nature of a triangle that its three angles are equal to two right angles. But if we have a knowledge of God equal to that which we have of a triangle, all doubt is removed. In the same way as we can arrive at the said knowledge of a triangle, though not absolutely sure that there is not some arch-deceiver leading us astray, so can we come to a like knowledge of God under the like condition, and when we have attained to it, it is sufficient, as I said before, to remove every doubt which we can possess concerning clear and distinct ideas. Thus, if a man proceeded with our investigations in due order, inquiring first into those things which should first be inquired into, never passing over a link in the chain of association, and with knowledge how to define his questions before seeking to answer them, he

* That is, it is known that the senses sometimes deceive us. But it is only known confusedly, for it is not known how they deceive us.

will never have any ideas save such as are very certain, or, in other words, clear and distinct; for doubt is only a suspension of the spirit concerning some affirmation or negation which it would pronounce upon unhesitatingly if it were not in ignorance of something, without which the knowledge of the matter in hand must needs be imperfect. We may, therefore, conclude that doubt always proceeds from want of due order in investigation.

These are the points I promised to discuss in this first part of my treatise on method.   However, in order not to omit anything which can conduce to the knowledge of the understanding and its faculties, I will add a few words on the subject of memory and forgetfulness.

The point most worthy of attention is, that memory is strengthened both with and without the aid of the understanding.   For the more intelligible a thing is, the more easily it is remembered, and the less intelligible it is, the more easily do we forget it.   For instance, a number of unconnected words is much more difficult to remember than the same number in the form of a narration.   The memory is also strengthened without the aid of the understanding by means of the power wherewith the imagination or the sense called common is affected by some particular physical object.   I say PARTICULAR, for the imagination is only affected by particular objects.   If we read, for instance, a single romantic comedy, we shall remember it very well, so long as we do not read many others of the same kind, for it will reign alone in the memory.   If, however, we read several others of the same kind, we shall think of them altogether, and easily confuse one with another. I say, also PHYSICAL.   For the imagination is only affected by physical objects.   As, then, the memory is strengthened both with and without the aid of the understanding, we may conclude that it is different from the understanding, and that in the matter considered in itself there is neither memory nor forgetfulness.   What, then, is memory?   It is nothing else than the actual sensation of impressions on the brain, accompanied with the thought of a definite duration of the sensation.   This is also shown by reminiscence. For then we think of the sensation, but without the notion of continuous duration; thus the idea of that sensation is not the actual duration of the sensation or actual memory. Whether ideas are or are not subject to corruption will be seen in my philosophy. If this seems too absurd to any one, it will be sufficient for our purpose, if he reflect on the fact that a thing is more easily remembered in proportion to its singularity, as appears from the example of the comedy just cited. Further, a thing is remembered more easily in proportion to its intelligibility; therefore we cannot help remembering that which is extremely singular and sufficiently intelligible.

Thus, then, we have distinguished between a true idea and other perceptions, and shown that ideas fictitious, false, and the rest, originate in the imagination — that is, in certain sensations fortuitous (so to speak) and disconnected, arising not from the power of the mind, but from external causes, according as the body, sleeping or waking, receives various motions.

But one may take any view one likes of the imagination so long as one acknowledges that it is different from the understanding, and that the soul is passive with regard to it. The view taken is immaterial, if we know that the imagination is something indefinite, with regard to which the soul is passive, and that we can by some means or other free ourselves therefrom with the help of the understanding. Let no one then be astonished that before proving the existence of body, and other necessary things, I speak of imagination of body, and of its composition. The view taken is, I repeat, immaterial, so long as we know that imagination is something indefinite, etc. As regards a true idea, we have shown that it is simple or compounded of simple ideas; that it shows how and why something is or has been made; and that its subjective effects in the soul correspond to the actual reality of its object. This conclusion is identical with the saying of the ancients, that true science proceeds from cause to effect; though the ancients, so far as I know, never formed the conception put forward here that the soul acts according to fixed laws; and is, as it were, an immaterial auto-maton.   Hence, as far as is possible at the outset, we have acquired a knowledge of our understanding, and such a standard of a true idea that we need no longer fear con-founding truth with falsehood and fiction.   Neither shall we wonder why we understand some things which in nowise fall within the scope of the imagination, while other things are in the imagination but wholly opposed to the understanding, or others, again, which agree there-with.   We now know that the operations, whereby the effects of imagination are produced, take place under other laws quite different from the laws of the understanding. and that the mind is entirely passive with regard to them. Whence we may also see how easily men may fall into grave errors through not distinguishing accurately between the imagination and the understanding; such as believ-ing that extension must be localized, that it must be finite, that its parts are really distinct one from the other, that it is the primary and single foundation of all things, that it occupies more space at one time than at another, and other similar doctrines, all entirely opposed to truth, as we shall duly show.

Again, since words are a part of the imagination — that is, since we form many conceptions in accordance with confused arrangements of words in the memory, de-pendent on particular bodily conditions — there is no doubt that words may, equally with the imagination, be the cause of many and great errors, unless we keep strictly on our guard.   Moreover, words are formed ac-cording to popular fancy and intelligence, and are, there-fore, signs of things as existing in the imagination, not as existing in the understanding.   This is evident from the fact that to all such things as exist only in the un-derstanding, not in the imagination, negative names are often given, such as incorporeal, infinite, etc.   So, also, many conceptions really affirmative are expressed nega-tively, and *vice versâ*, such as uncreate, independent, infi-nite, immortal, etc., inasmuch as their contraries are much more easily imagined, and, therefore, occurred first to men, and usurped positive names.   Many things we affirm and deny, because the nature of words allows us to do so, though the nature of things does not. While we remain unaware of this fact, we may easily mistake falsehood for truth.

Let us also beware of another great cause of confusion, which prevents the understanding from reflecting on itself. Sometimes, while making no distinction between the imagination and the intellect, we think that what we more readily imagine is clearer to us; and also we think that what we imagine we understand. Thus, we put first that which should be last; the true order of progression is reversed, and no legitimate conclusion is drawn.

Now, in order at length to pass on to the second part of this method, I shall first set forth the object aimed at, and next the means for its attainment. The object aimed at is the acquisition of clear and distinct ideas, such as are produced by the pure intellect, and not by chance physical motions. In order that all ideas may be reduced to unity, we shall endeavor so to associate and arrange them that our mind may, as far as possible, reflect subjectively the reality of nature, both as a whole and as parts.

As for the first point, it is necessary (as we have said) for our purpose that everything should be conceived, either SOLELY THROUGH ITS ESSENCE, or THROUGH ITS PROXIMATE CAUSE. If the thing be self-existent, or as is commonly said, the cause of itself, it must be understood through its essence only; if it be not self-existent, but requires a cause for its existence, it must be understood through its proximate cause. For, in reality, the knowledge of an effect is nothing else than the acquisition of more perfect knowledge of its cause. Therefore, we may never, while we are concerned with inquiries into actual things, draw any conclusions from abstractions; we shall be extremely careful not to confound that which is only in the understanding with that which is in the thing itself. The best basis for drawing a conclusion will be either some particular affirmative essence, or a true and legitimate definition. For the understanding can not descend from universal axioms by themselves to particular things, since axioms are of infinite extent, and do not determine the understanding to contemplate one particular thing more than another. Thus the true method of discovery is to form thoughts from some given definition. This process will be the more fruitful and easy in proportion as the thing given be better defined. Wherefore, the cardinal point of all this second part of method consists in the knowledge of the conditions of good definition, and the means of finding them. I will first treat of the conditions of definition.

A definition, if it is to be called perfect, must explain the inmost essence of a thing, and must take care not to substitute for this any of its properties. In order to illustrate my meaning, without taking an example which would seem to show a desire to expose other people's errors, I will choose the case of something abstract, the definition of which is of little moment. Such is a circle. If a circle be defined as a figure, such that all straight lines drawn from the center to the circumference are equal, every one can see that such a definition does not in the least explain the essence of a circle, but solely one of its properties. Though, as I have said, this is of no importance in the case of figures and other abstractions, it is of great importance in the case of physical beings and realities: for the properties of things are not understood so long as their essences are unknown. If the latter be passed over, there is necessarily a perversion of the succession of ideas which should reflect the succession of nature, and we go far astray from our object.

In order to be free from this fault, the following rules should be observed in definition:

I. If the thing in question be created, the definition must (as we have said) comprehend the proximate cause. For instance, a circle should, according to this rule, be defined as follows: the figure described by any line whereof one end is fixed and the other free. This definition clearly comprehends the proximate cause.

II. A conception or definition of a thing should be such that all the properties of that thing, in so far as it is considered by itself, and not in conjunction with other things, can be deduced from it, as may be seen in the definition given of a circle: for from that it clearly follows that all straight lines drawn from the center to the circumference are equal. That this is a necessary characteristic of a definition is so clear to any one, who reflects on the matter, that there is no need to spend time in proving it, or in showing that, owing to this second condition, every definition should be affirmative. I speak of intellectual affirmation, giving little thought to verbal affirmations which, owing to the poverty of the language, must sometimes, perhaps, be expressed negatively, though the idea contained is affirmative.

The rules for the definition of an uncreated thing are as follows:

I. The exclusion of all idea of cause — that is, the thing must not need explanation by anything outside itself.

II. When the definition of the thing has been given, there must be no room for doubt as to whether the thing exists or not.

III. It must contain, as far as the mind is concerned, no substantives which could be put into an adjectival form; in other words, the object defined must not be explained through abstractions.

IV. Lastly, though this is not absolutely necessary, it should be possible to deduce from the definition all the properties of the thing defined.

All these rules become obvious to any one giving strict attention to the matter.

I have also stated that the best basis for drawing a conclusion is a particular affirmative essence. The more specialized the idea is, the more is it distinct, and therefore clear. Wherefore a knowledge of particular things should be sought for as diligently as possible.

As regards the order of our perceptions, and the manner in which they should be arranged and united, it is necessary that as soon as is possible and rational, we should inquire whether there be any being (and, if so, what being) that is the cause of all things, so that its essence, represented in thought, may be the cause of all our ideas, and then our mind will to the utmost possible extent reflect nature. For it will possess, subjectively, nature's essence, order, and union. Thus we can see that it is before all things necessary for us to deduce all our ideas from physical things — that is, from real entities, proceeding, as far as may be, according to the series of causes, from one real entity to another real entity, never passing to universals and abstractions, either for the purpose of deducing some real entity from them, or deducing them from some real entity. Either of these processes interrupts the true progress of the understanding. But it must be observed that, by the series of causes and real entities, I do not here mean the series of particular and mutable things, but only the series of fixed and eternal things. It would be impossible for human infirmity to follow up the series of particular mutable things, both on account of their multitude, surpassing all calculation, and on account of the infinitely diverse circumstances surrounding one and the same thing, any one of which may be the cause for its existence or non-existence. Indeed, their existence has no connection with their essence, or (as we have said already) is not an eternal truth. Neither is there any need that we should understand their series, for the essences of particular mutable things are not to be gathered from their series or order of existence, which would furnish us with nothing beyond their extrinsic denominations, their relations, or, at most, their circumstances, all of which are very different from their inmost essence. This inmost essence must be sought solely from fixed and eternal things, and from the laws, inscribed (so to speak) in those things as in their true codes, according to which all particular things take place and are arranged; nay, these mutable particular things depend so intimately and essentially (so to phrase it) upon the fixed things, that they cannot either be or be conceived without them.

Whence these fixed and eternal things, though they are themselves particular, will nevertheless, owing to their presence and power everywhere, be to us as universals, or genera of definitions of particular mutable things, and as the proximate causes of all things.

But, though this be so, there seems to be no small difficulty in arriving at the knowledge of these particular
things, for to conceive them all at once would far surpass
the powers of the human understanding. The arrangement whereby one thing is understood before another, as
we have stated, should not be sought from their series of
existence, nor from eternal things. For the latter are all
by nature simultaneous. Other aids are therefore needed
besides those employed for understanding eternal things
and their laws; however, this is not the place to recount
such aids, nor is there any need to do so, until we have
acquired a sufficient knowledge of eternal things and their
infallible laws, and until the nature of our senses has
become plain to us.

Before betaking ourselves to seek knowledge of particular things, it will be seasonable to speak of such aids,
as all tend to teach us the mode of employing our senses,
and to make certain experiments under fixed rules and
arrangement which may suffice to determine the object
of our inquiry, so that we may therefrom infer what laws
of eternal things it has been produced under, and may
gain an insight into its inmost nature, as I will duly
show. Here, to return to my purpose, I will only endeavor to set forth what seems necessary for enabling us
to attain to knowledge of eternal things, and to define
them under the conditions laid down above.

With this end, we must bear in mind what has already
been stated, namely, that when the mind devotes itself to
any thought, so as to examine it and to deduce therefrom in due order all the legitimate conclusions possible,
any falsehood which may lurk in the thought will be
detected; but if the thought be true, the mind will readily
proceed without interruption to deduce truths from it.
This, I say, is necessary for our purpose, for our
thoughts may be brought to a close by the absence of a
foundation. If, therefore, we wish to investigate the first
thing of all, it will be necessary to supply some foundation which may direct our thoughts thither. Further,
since method is reflective knowledge, the foundation
which must direct our thoughts can be nothing else than

the knowledge of that which constitutes the reality of truth, and the knowledge of the understanding, its properties, and powers. When this has been acquired we shall possess a foundation wherefrom we can deduce our thoughts, and a path whereby the intellect, according to its capacity, may attain the knowledge of eternal things, allowance being made for the extent of the intellectual powers.

If, as I stated in the first part, it belongs to the nature of thought to form true ideas, we must here inquire what is meant by the faculties and power of the understanding. The chief part of our method is to understand as well as possible the powers of the intellect, and its nature; we are, therefore, compelled (by the considerations advanced in the second part of the method) necessarily to draw these conclusions from the definition itself of thought and understanding. But, so far, we have not got any rules for finding definitions, and, as we cannot set forth such rules without a previous knowledge of nature, that is without a definition of the understanding and its power, it follows either that the definition of the understanding must be clear in itself, or that we can understand nothing. Nevertheless this definition is not absolutely clear in itself; however, since its properties, like all things that we possess through the understanding, cannot be known clearly and distinctly, unless its nature be known previously, the definition of the understanding makes itself manifest, if we pay attention to its properties, which we know clearly and distinctly. Let us, then, enumerate here the properties of the understanding, let us examine them, and begin by discussing the instruments for research which we find innate in us.

The properties of the understanding which I have chiefly remarked, and which I clearly understand, are the following: —

I. It involves certainty — in other words, it knows that a thing exists in reality as it is reflected subjectively.

II. That it perceives certain things, or forms some ideas absolutely, some ideas from others. Thus it forms the idea of quantity absolutely, without reference to any other thoughts; but ideas of motion it only forms after taking into consideration the idea of quantity.

III. Those ideas which the understanding forms absolutely express infinity; determinate ideas are derived from other ideas. Thus in the idea of quantity, perceived by means of a cause, the quantity is determined, as when a body is perceived to be formed by the motion of a plane, a plane by the motion of a line, or, again, a line by the motion of a point. All these are perceptions which do not serve toward understanding quantity, but only toward determining it. This is proved by the fact that we conceive them as formed as it were by motion, yet this motion is not perceived unless the quantity be perceived also; we can even prolong the motion so as to form an infinite line, which we certainly could not do unless we had an idea of infinite quantity.

IV. The understanding forms positive ideas before forming negative ideas.

V. It perceives things not so much under the condition of duration as under a certain form of eternity, and in an infinite number; or rather in perceiving things it does not consider either their number or duration, whereas, in imagining them, it perceives them in a determinate number, duration, and quantity.

VI. The ideas which we form as clear and distinct, seem so to follow from the sole necessity of our nature, that they appear to depend absolutely on our sole power; with confused ideas the contrary is the case. They are often formed against our will.

VII. The mind can determine in many ways the ideas of things, which the understanding forms from other ideas: thus, for instance, in order to define the plane of an ellipse, it supposes a point adhering to a cord to be moved round two centres, or, again, it conceives an infinity of points, always in the same fixed relation to a given straight line, or a cone cut in an oblique plane, so that the angle of inclination is greater than the angle of the vertex of the cone, or in an infinity of other ways.

VIII. The more ideas express perfection of any object, the more perfect are they themselves; for we do not admire the architect who has planned a chapel so much as the architect who has planned a splendid temple.

I do not stop to consider the rest of what is referred to thought, such as love, joy, etc. They are nothing to our present purpose, and cannot even be conceived unless the understanding be perceived previously. When perception is removed, all these go with it.

False and fictitious ideas have nothing positive about them (as we have abundantly shown) which causes them to be called false or fictitious; they are only considered as such through the defectiveness of knowledge. Therefore, false and fictitious ideas as such can teach us nothing concerning the essence of thought; this must be sought from the positive properties just enumerated; in other words, we must lay down some common basis from which these properties necessarily follow, so that when this is given, the properties are necessarily given also, and when it is removed, they too vanish with it.

.   .   .   .

[The rest of the treatise is wanting.]

THE ETHICS.

PART I. CONCERNING GOD.

DEFINITIONS.

I. BY THAT which is SELF-CAUSED, I mean that of which the essence involves existence, or that of which the nature is only conceivable as existent.

II. A thing is called FINITE AFTER ITS KIND, when it can be limited by another thing of the same nature; for instance, a body is called finite because we always conceive another greater body. So, also, a thought is limited by another thought, but a body is not limited by thought, nor a thought by body.

III. By SUBSTANCE, I mean that which is in itself, and is conceived through itself; in other words, that of which a conception can be formed independently of any other conception.

IV. By ATTRIBUTE, I mean that which the intellect perceives as constituting the essence of substance.

V. By MODE, I mean the modifications * of substance, or that which exists in, and is conceived through, something other than itself.

VI. By GOD, I mean a being absolutely infinite — that is, a substance consisting in infinite attributes, of which each expresses eternal and infinite essentiality.

Explanation.—I say absolutely infinite, not infinite after its kind: for, of a thing infinite only after its kind, infinite attributes may be denied; but that which is absolutely infinite, contains in its essence whatever expresses reality, and involves no negation.

VII. That thing is called free, which exists solely by the necessity of its own nature, and of which the action

* "*Affectiones.*"

39

is determined by itself alone. On the other hand, that thing is necessary, or rather constrained, which is determined by something external to itself to a fixed and definite method of existence or action.

VIII. By ETERNITY, I mean existence itself, in so far as it is conceived necessarily to follow solely from the definition of that which is eternal.

Explanation.— Existence of this kind is conceived as an eternal truth, like the essence of a thing, and, therefore, cannot be explained by means of continuance or time, though continuance may be conceived without a beginning or end.

AXIOMS.

I. Everything which exists, exists either in itself or in something else.

II. That which cannot be conceived through anything else must be conceived through itself.

III. From a given definite cause an effect necessarily follows; and, on the other hand, if no definite cause be granted, it is impossible that an effect can follow.

IV. The knowledge of an effect depends on and involves the knowledge of a cause.

V. Things which have nothing in common cannot be understood, the one by means of the other; the conception of one does not involve the conception of the other.

VI. A true idea must correspond with its ideate or object.

VII. If a thing can be conceived as non-existing, its essence does not involve existence.

PROPOSITIONS.

PROP. I. Substance is by nature prior to its modifications.
Proof.—This is clear from Def. iii. and v.

PROP. II. Two substances, whose attributes are different, have nothing in common.
Proof.— Also evident from Def. iii. For each must exist in itself, and be conceived through itself; in other words, the conception of one does not imply the conception of the other.

PROP. III. Things which have nothing in common cannot be one the cause of the other.

Proof.— If they have nothing in common, it follows that one cannot be apprehended by means of the other (Ax. v.), and, therefore, one cannot be the cause of the other (Ax. iv.). Q. E. D.

PROP. IV. Two or more distinct things are distinguished one from the other either by the difference of the attributes of the substances, or by the difference of their modifications.

Proof.— Everything which exists, exists either in itself or in something else (Ax. i.),— that is (by Def. iii. and v.), nothing is granted in addition to the understanding, except substance and its modifications. Nothing is, therefore, given besides the understanding, by which several things may be distinguished one from the other, except the substances, or, in other words (see Ax. iv.), their attributes and modifications. Q. E. D.

PROP. V. There cannot exist in the universe two or more substances having the same nature or attribute.

Proof.— If several distinct substances be granted, they must be distinguished one from the other, either by the difference of their attributes, or by the difference of their modifications (Prop. iv.). If only by the difference of their attributes, it will be granted that there cannot be more than one with an identical attribute. If by the difference of their modifications — as substance is naturally prior to its modifications (Prop. i.),— it follows that setting the modifications aside, and considering substance in itself, that is truly (Def. iii. and vi.), there cannot be conceived one substance different from another,— that is (by Prop. iv.), there cannot be granted several substances, but one substance only. Q. E. D.

PROP. VI. One substance cannot be produced by another substance.

Proof.—It is impossible that there should be in the universe two substances with an identical attribute, *i. e.*, which have anything common to them both (Prop. ii.), and, therefore (Prop. iii.), one cannot be the cause of another, neither can one be produced by the other. Q. E. D.

Corollary.— Hence it follows that a substance cannot be produced by anything external to itself. For in the universe nothing is granted, save substances and their modifications (as appears from Ax. i. and Def. iii. and v.). Now (by the last Prop.) substance cannot be produced by another substance, therefore it cannot be produced by anything external itself. Q. E. D. This is shown still more readily by the absurdity of the contradictory. For, if substance be produced by an external cause, the knowledge of it would depend on the knowledge of its cause (Ax. iv.), and (by Def. iii.) it would itself not be substance.

Prop. VII. Existence belongs to the nature of substance.

Proof.— Substance cannot be produced by anything external (Corollary, Prop. vi.), it must, therefore, be its own cause — that is, its essence necessarily involves existence, or existence belongs to its nature.

Prop. VIII. Every substance is necessarily infinite.

Proof.— There can be only one substance with an identical attribute, and existence follows from its nature (Prop. vii.); its nature, therefore, involves existence, either as finite or infinite. It does not exist as finite, for (by Def. ii.) it would then be limited by something else of the same kind, which would also necessarily exist (Prop. vii.); and there would be two substances with an identical attribute, which is absurd (Prop. v.). It therefore exists as infinite. Q. E. D.

Note I.— As finite existence involves a partial negation, and infinite existence is the absolute affirmation of the given nature, it follows (solely from Prop. vii.) that every substance is necessarily infinite.

Note II. — No doubt it will be difficult for those who think about things loosely, and have not been accustomed to know them by their primary causes, to comprehend the demonstrations of Prop. vii.: for such persons make no distinction between the modifications of substances and the substances themselves, and are ignorant of the manner in which things are produced; hence they attribute to substances the beginning which they observe in natural objects. Those who are ignorant of true causes, make complete confusion — think that trees might talk just as well as men — that men might be formed from stones as well as from seed; and imagine that any form might be changed into any other. So, also, those who confuse the two natures, divine and human, readily attribute human passions to the deity, especially so long as they do not know how passions originate in the mind. But, if people would consider the nature of substance, they would have no doubt about the truth of Prop. vii. In fact, this proposition would be a universal axiom, and accounted a truism. For, by substance, would be understood that which is in itself, and is conceived through itself — that is, something of which the conception requires not the conception of anything else; whereas modifications exist in something external to themselves, and a conception of them is formed by means of a conception of the thing in which they exist. Therefore, we may have true ideas of non-existent modifications; for, although they may have no ACTUAL existence apart from the conceiving intellect, yet their essence is so involved in something external to themselves that they may through it be conceived. Whereas the only truth substances can have, external to the intellect, must consist in their existence, because they are conceived through themselves. Therefore, for a person to say that he has a clear and distinct — that is, a true — idea of a substance, but that he is not sure whether such substance exists, would be the same as if he said that he had a true idea, but was not sure whether or no it was false (a little consideration will make this plain); or if any one affirmed that substance is created, it would be the same as saying that a false idea was true — in short, the height of absurdity. It must, then, necessarily be admitted that the existence of substance as its essence is an eternal truth. And we can hence conclude by another process of reasoning — that there is but one such substance. I think that this may profitably be done at once; and, in order to proceed regularly with the demonstration, we must premise:

1. The true definition of a thing neither involves nor expresses anything beyond the nature of the thing defined. From this it follows that—

2. No definition implies or expresses a certain number of individuals, inasmuch as it expresses nothing beyond the nature of the thing defined. For instance, the definition of a triangle expresses nothing beyond the actual nature of a triangle: it does not imply any fixed number of triangles.

3. There is necessarily for each individual existent thing a cause why it should exist.

4. This cause of existence must either be contained in the nature and definition of the thing defined, or must be postulated apart from such definition.

It therefore follows that, if a given number of individual things exist in nature, there must be some cause for the existence of exactly that number, neither more nor less. For example, if twenty men exist in the universe (for simplicity's sake, I will suppose them existing simultaneously, and to have had no predecessors), and we want to account for the existence of these twenty men, it will not be enough to show the cause of human existence in general; we must also show why there are exactly twenty men, neither more nor less: for a cause must be assigned for the existence of each individual. Now this cause cannot be contained in the actual nature of man, for the true definition of man does not involve any consideration of the number twenty. Consequently, the cause for the existence of these twenty men, and, consequently, of each of them, must necessarily be sought externally to each individual. Hence we may lay down the absolute rule, that everything which may consist of several individuals must have an external cause. And, as it has been shown already that existence appertains to the nature of substance, existence must necessarily be included in its definition; and from its definition alone existence must be deducible. But from its definition (as we have shown, Notes ii., iii.), we cannot infer the existence of several substances; therefore it follows that there is only one substance of the same nature. Q.E.D.

Prop. IX. The more reality or being a thing has the greater the number of its attributes (Def. iv.).

Prop. X. Each particular attribute of the one substance must be conceived through itself.

Proof.— An attribute is that which the intellect perceives of substance, as constituting its essence (Def. iv.), and, therefore, must be conceived through itself (Def. iii.). Q.E.D.

Note.— It is thus evident that, though two attributes are, in fact, conceived as distinct — that is, one without the help of the other — yet we cannot, therefore, conclude that they constitute two entities, or two different substances. For it is the nature of substance that each of its attributes is conceived through itself, inasmuch as all the attributes it has have always existed simultaneously in it, and none could be produced by any other; but each expresses the reality or being of substance. It is, then, far from an absurdity to ascribe several attributes to one substance: for nothing in nature is more clear than that each and every entity must be conceived under some attribute, and that its reality or being is in proportion to the number of its attributes expressing necessity or eternity and infinity. Consequently it is abundantly clear, that an absolutely infinite being must necessarily be defined as consisting in infinite attributes each of which expresses a certain eternal and infinite essence.

If any one now ask, by what sign shall he be able to distinguish different substances, let him read the following propositions, which show that there is but one substance in the universe, and that it is absolutely infinite, wherefore such a sign would be sought for in vain.

Prop. XI. God, or substance, consisting of infinite attributes, of which each expresses eternal and infinite essentiality, necessarily exists.

Proof.— If this be denied, conceive, if possible, that God does not exist: then his essence does not involve existence. But this (by Prop. vii.) is absurd. Therefore God necessarily exists.

Another proof.— Of everything whatsoever a cause or reason must be assigned, either for its existence, or for its non-existence — *e. g.*, if a triangle exist, a reason or cause must be granted for its existence; if, on the contrary, it does not exist, a cause must also be granted, which prevents it from existing, or annuls its existence. This reason or cause must either be contained in the nature of the thing in question, or be external to it. For instance, the reason for the non-existence of a square circle is indicated in its nature, namely, because it would involve a contradiction. On the other hand, the existence of substance follows also solely from its nature, inasmuch as its nature involves existence. (See Prop. vii.)

But the reason for the existence of a triangle or a circle does not follow from the nature of those figures, but from the order of universal nature in extension. From the latter it must follow, either that a triangle necessarily exists, or that it is impossible that it should exist. So much is self-evident. It follows therefrom that a thing necessarily exists, if no cause or reason be granted which prevents its existence.

If, then, no cause or reason can be given, which prevents the existence of God, or which destroys his existence, we must certainly conclude that he necessarily does exist. If such a reason or cause should be given, it must either be drawn from the very nature of God, or be external to him — that is, drawn from another substance of another nature. For if it were of the same nature, God, by that very fact, would be admitted to exist. But substance of another nature could have nothing in common with God (by Prop. ii.), and therefore would be unable either to cause or to destroy his existence.

As, then, a reason or cause which would annul the divine existence cannot be drawn from anything external to the divine nature, such cause must, perforce, if God does not exist, be drawn from God's own nature, which would involve a contradiction. To make such an affirmation about a being absolutely infinite and supremely perfect, is absurd; therefore, neither in the nature of God, nor externally to his nature, can a cause or reason be assigned which would annul his existence. Therefore, God necessarily exists. Q.E.D.

Another proof.— The potentiality of non-existence is a negation of power, and contrariwise the potentiality of existence is a power, as is obvious. If, then, that which necessarily exists is nothing but finite beings, such finite beings are more powerful than a being absolutely infinite, which is obviously absurd; therefore, either nothing exists, or else a being absolutely infinite necessarily exists also. Now we exist either in ourselves, or in something else which necessarily exists (see Ax. i. and Prop. vii.) Therefore a being absolutely infinite — in other words, God (Def. vi.) — necessarily exists. Q. E. D.

Note.— In this last proof, I have purposely shown God's existence *à posteriori,* so that the proof might be more easily followed, not because, from the same premises, God's existence does not follow *à priori.* For, as the potentiality of existence is a power, it follows that, in proportion as reality increases in the nature of a thing, so also will it increase its strength for existence. Therefore a being absolutely infinite, such as God, has from himself an absolutely infinite power of existence, and hence he does absolutely exist. Perhaps there will be many who will be unable to see the force of this proof, inasmuch as they are accustomed only to consider those things which flow from external causes. Of such things, they see that those which quickly come to pass — that is, quickly come into existence — quickly also disappear; whereas they regard as more difficult of accomplishment — that is, not so easily brought into existence — those things which they conceive as more complicated.

However, to do away with this misconception, I need not here show the measure of truth in the proverb, "What comes quickly, goes quickly," nor discuss whether, from the point of view of universal nature, all things are equally easy, or otherwise: I need only remark, that I am not here speaking of things, which come to pass through causes external to themselves, but only of substances which (by Prop. vi.) cannot be produced by any external cause. Things which are produced by external causes, whether they consist of many parts or few, owe whatsoever perfection or reality they possess solely to the efficacy of their external cause, and there-fore their existence arises solely from the perfection of their external cause, not from their own. Contrariwise, whatsoever perfection is possessed by substance is due to no external cause; wherefore the existence of substance must arise solely from its own nature, which is nothing else but its essence. Thus, the perfection of a thing does not annul its existence, but, on the contrary, asserts it. Imperfection, on the other hand, does annul it; therefore we cannot be more certain of the existence of anything, than of the existence of a being absolutely infinite or perfect — that is, of God. For inasmuch as his essence excludes all imperfection, and involves absolute perfection, all cause for doubt concerning his existence is done away, and the utmost certainty on the question is given. This, I think, will be evident to every moderately attentive reader.

PROP. XII. No attribute of substance can be conceived from which it would follow that substance can be di-vided.

Proof.— The parts into which substance as thus con-ceived would be divided, either will retain the nature of substance, or they will not. If the former, then (by Prop. viii.) each part will necessarily be infinite, and (by Prop. vi.) self-caused, and (by Prop. v.) will perforce consist of a different attribute, so that, in that case, sev-eral substances could be formed out of one substance, which (by Prop. vi.) is absurd. Moreover, the parts (by Prop. ii.) would have nothing in common with their whole, and the whole (by Def. iv. and Prop. x.) could both exist and be conceived without its parts, which everyone will admit to be absurd. If we adopt the sec-ond alternative — namely, that the parts will not retain the nature of substance — then, if the whole substance were divided into equal parts, it would lose the nature of substance, and would cease to exist, which (by Prop. vii.) is absurd.

PROP. XIII. Substance absolutely infinite is indivisible.

Proof.— If it could be divided, the parts into which it was divided would either retain the nature of absolutely infinite substance, or they would not. If the former, we should have several substances of the same nature, which (by Prop. v.) is absurd. If the latter, then (by Prop. vii.) substance absolutely infinite could cease to exist, which (by Prop. xi.) is also absurd.

Corollary.— It follows that no substance, and consequently no extended substance, in so far as it is substance, is divisible.

Note.— The indivisibility of substance may be more easily understood as follows. The nature of substance can only be conceived as infinite, and by a part of substance, nothing else can be understood than finite substance, which (by Prop. viii.) involves a manifest contradiction.

Prop. XIV. Besides God no substance can be granted or conceived.

Proof.— As God is a being absolutely infinite, of whom no attribute that expresses the essence of substance can be denied (by Def. vi.), and he necessarily exists (by Prop. xi.); if any substance besides God were granted it would have to be explained by some attribute of God, and thus two substances with the same attribute would exist, which (by Prop. v.) is absurd; therefore, besides God no substance can be granted, or consequently, be conceived. If it could be conceived, it would necessarily have to be conceived as existent; but this (by the first part of this proof) is absurd. Therefore, besides God no substance can be granted or conceived. Q. E. D.

Corollary I.—Clearly, therefore: 1. God is one, that is (by Def. vi.) only one substance can be granted in the universe, and that substance is absolutely infinite, as we have already indicated (in the note to Prop. x.).

Corollary II.—It follows: 2. That extension and thought are either attributes of God or (by Ax. i.) accidents (*affectiones*) of the attributes of God.

Prop. XV. Whatsoever is, is in God, and without God nothing can be, or be conceived.

Proof.—Besides God, no substance is granted or can be conceived (by Prop. xiv.), that is (by Def. iii.) nothing which is in itself and is conceived through itself. But modes (by Def. v.) can neither be, nor be conceived without substance; wherefore they can only be in the divine nature, and can only through it be conceived. But substances and modes form the sum total of existence (by Ax. i.), therefore, without God nothing can be, or be conceived. Q.E.D.

Note.—Some assert that God, like a man, consists of body and mind, and is susceptible of passions. How far such persons have strayed from the truth is sufficiently evident from what has been said. But these I pass over. For all who have in anywise reflected on the divine nature deny that God has a body. Of this they find excellent proof in the fact that we understand by body a definite quantity, so long, so broad, so deep, bounded by a certain shape, and it is the height of absurdity to predicate such a thing of God, a being absolutely infinite. But meanwhile by the other reasons with which they try to prove their point, they show that they think corporeal or extended substance wholly apart from the divine nature, and say it was created by God. Wherefrom the divine nature can have been created, they are wholly ignorant; thus they clearly show, that they do not know the meaning of their own words. I myself have proved sufficiently clearly, at any rate in my own judgment (Coroll. Prop. vi., and Note 2, Prop. viii.), that no substance can be produced or created by anything other than itself. Further, I showed (in Prop. xiv.), that besides God no substance can be granted or conceived. Hence we drew the conclusion that extended substance is one of the infinite attributes of God. However, in order to explain more fully, I will refute the arguments of my adversaries, which all start from the following points:—

Extended substance, in so far as it is substance, consists, as they think, in parts, wherefore they deny that it can be infinite, or, consequently, that it can appertain to God. This they illustrate with many examples, of which I will take one or two. If extended substance, they say, is infinite, let it be conceived to be divided into two parts: each part will then be either finite or infinite. If

the former, then infinite substance is composed of two
finite parts, which is absurd. If the latter, then one
infinite will be twice as large as another infinite, which
is also absurd.

Further, if an infinite line be measured out in foot
lengths, it will consist of an infinite number of such
parts; it would equally consist of an infinite number of
parts, if each part measured only an inch: therefore, one
infinity would be twelve times as great as the other.

Lastly, if from a single point there be conceived to be
drawn two diverging lines which at first are at a definite
distance apart, but are produced to infinity, it is certain
that the distance between the two lines will be continually increased, until at length it changes from definite to
indefinable. As these absurdities follow, it is said, from
considering quantity as infinite, the conclusion is drawn,
that extended substance must necessarily be finite, and,
consequently, cannot appertain to the nature of God.

The second argument is also drawn from God's supreme
perfection. God, it is said, inasmuch as he is a supremely
perfect being, cannot be passive; but extended substance,
in so far as it is divisible, is passive. It follows, therefore, that extended substance does not appertain to the
essence of God.

Such are the arguments I find on the subject in writers,
who by them try to prove that extended substance is
unworthy of the divine nature, and cannot possibly appertain thereto. However, I think an attentive reader
will see that I have already answered their propositions;
for all their arguments are founded on the hypothesis
that extended substance is composed of parts, and such
a hypothesis I have shown (Prop. xii., and Coroll. Prop.
xiii.) to be absurd. Moreover, any one who reflects will
see that all these absurdities (if absurdities they be,
which I am not now discussing), from which it is sought
to extract the conclusion that extended substance is finite,
do not at all follow from the notion of an infinite quantity,
but merely from the notion that an infinite quantity
is measureable, and composed of finite parts; therefore,
the only fair conclusion to be drawn is that infinite

quantity is not measureable, and cannot be composed of
finite parts. This is exactly what we have already
proved (in Prop. xii.). Wherefore the weapon which
they aimed at us has in reality recoiled upon themselves.
If, from this absurdity of theirs, they persist in drawing
the conclusion that extended substance must be finite, they
will in good sooth be acting like a man who asserts that
circles have the properties of squares, and, finding himself thereby landed in absurdities, proceeds to deny that
circles have any centre, from which all lines drawn to
the circumference are equal. For, taking extended substance, which can only be conceived as infinite, one, and
indivisible (Props. viii., v., xii.) they assert, in order to
prove that it is finite, that it is composed of finite parts,
and that it can be multiplied and divided.

So, also, others, after asserting that a line is composed
of points, can produce many arguments to prove that a
line cannot be infinitely divided. Assuredly it is not less
absurd to assert that extended substance is made up of
bodies or parts, than it would be to assert that a solid
is made up of surfaces, a surface of lines, and a line of
points. This must be admitted by all who know clear
reason to be infallible, and most of all by those who deny
the possibility of a vacuum. For if extended substance
could be so divided that its parts were really separate,
why should not one part admit of being destroyed, the
others remaining joined together as before? And why
should all be so fitted into one another as to leave no
vacuum? Surely in the case of things, which are really
distinct one from the other, one can exist without the
other, and can remain in its original condition. As
then, there does not exist a vacuum in nature (of which
anon), but all parts are bound to come together to prevent it, it follows from this also that the parts cannot
be really distinguished, and that extended substance in
so far as it is substance cannot be divided.

If any one asks me the further question, Why are we
naturally so prone to divide quantity? I answer, that
quantity is conceived by us in two ways; in the abstract
and superficially, as we imagine it; or as substance, as

we conceive it solely by the intellect. If, then, we regard quantity as it is represented in our imagination, which we often and more easily do, we shall find that it is finite, divisible, and compounded of parts; but if we regard it as it is represented in our intellect, and conceive it as substance, which it is very difficult to do, we shall then, as I have sufficiently proved, find that it is infinite, one, and indivisible. This will be plain enough to all, who make a distinction between the intellect and the imagination, especially if it be remembered, that matter is everywhere the same, that its parts are not distinguishable, except in so far as we conceive matter as diversely modified, whence its parts are distinguished, not really, but modally. For instance, water, in so far as it is water, we conceive to be divided, and its parts to be separated one from the other; but not in so far as it is extended substance; from this point of view it is neither separated nor divisible. Further, water, in so far as it is water, is produced and corrupted; but, in so far as it is substance, it is neither produced nor corrupted.

I think I have now answered the second argument; it is, in fact, founded on the same assumption as the first — namely, that matter, in so far as it is substance, is divisible, and composed of parts. Even if it were so, I do not know why it should be considered unworthy of the divine nature, inasmuch as besides God (by Prop. xiv.) no substance can be granted, wherefrom it could receive its modifications. All things, I repeat, are in God, and all things which come to pass, come to pass solely through the laws of the infinite nature of God, and follow (as I will shortly show) from the necessity of his essence. Wherefore it can in nowise be said, that God is passive in respect to anything other than himself, or that extended substance is unworthy of the Divine nature, even if it be supposed divisible, so long as it is granted to be infinite and eternal. But enough of this for the present.

PROP. XVI. From the necessity of the divine nature must follow an infinite number of things in infinite ways—

that is, all things which can fall within the sphere of infinite intellect.

Proof.— This proposition will be clear to everyone, who remembers that from the given definition of any thing the intellect infers several properties, which really necessarily follow therefrom (that is, from the actual essence of the thing defined); and it infers more properties in proportion as the definition of the thing expresses more reality, that is, in proportion as the essence of the thing defined involves more reality. Now, as the divine nature has absolutely infinite attributes (by Def. vi.), of which each expresses infinite essence after its kind, it follows that from the necessity of its nature an infinite number of things (that is, everything which can fall within the sphere of an infinite intellect) must necessarily follow. Q.E.D.

Corollary I.— Hence it follows, that God is the efficient cause of all that can fall within the sphere of an infinite intellect.

Corollary II.— It also follows that God is a cause in himself, and not through an accident of his nature.

Corollary III.— It follows, thirdly, that God is the absolutely first cause.

Prop. XVII. God acts solely by the laws of his own nature, and is not constrained by any one.

Proof.— We have just shown (in Prop. xvi.), that solely from the necessity of the divine nature, or, what is the same thing, solely from the laws of his nature, an infinite number of things absolutely follow in an infinite number of ways; and we proved (in Prop. xv.), that without God nothing can be, nor be conceived; but that all things are in God. Wherefore nothing can exist outside himself, whereby he can be conditioned or constrained to act. Wherefore God acts solely by the laws of his own nature, and is not constrained by any one. Q.E.D.

Corollary I.— It follows: 1. That there can be no cause which, either extrinsically or intrinsically, besides the perfection of his own nature, moves God to act.

Corollary II.— It follows: 2. That God is the sole

free cause. For God alone exists by the sole necessity of his nature (by Prop. xi. and Prop. xiv., Coroll. i.), and acts by the sole necessity of his nature, wherefore God is (by Def. vii.) the sole free cause. Q.E.D.

Note.—Others think that God is a free cause, because he can, as they think, bring it about, that those things which we have said follow from his nature — that is, which are in his power, should not come to pass, or should not be produced by him. But this is the same as if they said, that God could bring it about, that it should not follow from the nature of a triangle, that its three interior angles should not be equal to two right angles; or that from a given cause no effect should follow, which is absurd.

Moreover, I will show below, without the aid of this proposition, that neither intellect nor will appertain to God's nature. I know that there are many who think that they can show, that supreme intellect and free will do appertain to God's nature; for they say they know of nothing more perfect, which they can attribute to God, than that which is the highest perfection in ourselves. Further, although they conceive God as actually supremely intelligent, they yet do not believe, that he can bring into existence everything which he actually understands, for they think that they would thus destroy God's power. If, they contend, God had created everything which is in his intellect, he would not be able to create anything more, and this, they think, would clash with God's omnipotence; therefore, they prefer to assert that God is indifferent to all things, and that he creates nothing except that which he has decided, by some absolute exercise of will, to create. However, I think I have shown sufficiently clearly (by Prop. xvi.), that from God's supreme power, or infinite nature, an infinite number of things — that is, all things have necessarily flowed forth in an infinite number of ways, or always follow from the same necessity; in the same way as from the nature of a triangle it follows from eternity and for eternity, that its three interior angles are equal to two right angles. Wherefore the omnipotence of God has been displayed from all eternity, and will for all eternity remain in the same state of activity. This manner of treating the question attributes to God an omnipotence, in my opinion, far more perfect. For, otherwise, we are compelled to confess that God understands an infinite number of creatable things, which he will never be able to create, for, if he created all that he understands, he would, according to this showing, exhaust his omnipotence, and render himself imperfect. Wherefore, in order to establish that God is perfect, we should be reduced to establishing at the same time, that he cannot bring to pass everything over which his power extends; this seems to be an hypothesis most absurd, and most repugnant to God's omnipotence.

Further (to say a word here concerning the intellect and the will which we attribute to God), if intellect and will appertain to the eternal essence of God, we must take these words in some significations quite different from those they usually bear. For intellect and will, which should constitute the essence of God, would perforce be as far apart as the poles from the human intellect and will, in fact, would have nothing in common with them but the name; there would be about as much correspondence between the two as there is between the Dog, the heavenly constellation, and a dog, an animal that barks. This I will prove as follows: If intellect belongs to the divine nature, it cannot be in nature, as ours is generally thought to be, posterior to, or simultaneous with the things understood, inasmuch as God is prior to all things by reason of his casualty (Prop. xvi. Coroll. i.). On the contrary, the truth and formal essence of things is as it is, because it exists by representation as such in the intellect of God. Wherefore the intellect of God, in so far as it is conceived to constitute God's essence, is, in reality, the cause of things, both of their essence and of their existence. This seems to have been recognized by those who have asserted, that God's intellect, God's will, and God's power, are one and the same. As, therefore, God's intellect is the sole cause of things, namely, both of their essence and existence, it must necessarily differ from them in respect to its essence, and in respect to its existence. For a cause differs from a thing it causes, precisely in the quality which the latter gains from the former.

For example, a man is the cause of another man's existence, but not of his essence (for the latter is an eternal truth), and, therefore, the two men may be entirely similar in essence, but must be different in existence; and hence if the existence of one of them cease, the existence of the other will not necessarily cease also; but if the essence of one could be destroyed, and be made false, the essence of the other would be destroyed also. Wherefore, a thing which is the cause both of the essence and of the existence of a given effect, must differ from such effect both in respect to its essence, and also in respect to its existence. Now the intellect of God is the cause of both the essence and the existence of our intellect; therefore the intellect of God in so far as it is conceived to constitute the divine essence, differs from our intellect both in respect to essence and in respect to existence, nor can it in anywise agree therewith save in name, as we said before. The reasoning would be identical, in the case of the will, as any one can easily see.

PROP. XVIII. God is the indwelling and not the transient cause of all things.

Proof.— All things which are, are in God, and must be conceived through God (by Prop. xv.), therefore (by Prop. xvi., Coroll. i.) God is the cause of those things which are in him. This is our first point. Further, besides God there can be no substance (by Prop. xiv.), that is nothing in itself external to God. This is our second point. God, therefore, is the indwelling and not the transient cause of all things. Q. E. D.

PROP. XIX. God, and all the attributes of God, are eternal.

Proof.— God (by Def. vi.) is substance, which (by Prop. xi.) necessarily exists, that is (by Prop. vii.) existence appertains to its nature, or (what is the same thing) follows from its definition; therefore, God is eternal (by Def. viii.). Further, by the attributes of God we must understand that which (by Def. iv.) expresses the essence of the divine substance — in other words, that which appertains to substance: that, I say, should be involved in the attributes of substance. Now eternity appertains to the nature of substance (as I have already shown in Prop. vii.); therefore, eternity must appertain to each of the attributes, and thus all are eternal. Q.E.D.

Note.— This proposition is also evident from the manner in which (in Prop. xi.) I demonstrated the existence of God; it is evident, I repeat, from that proof, that the existence of God, like his essence, is an eternal truth. Further (in Prop. xix. of my " Principles of the Cartesian Philosophy "), I have proved the eternity of God, in another manner, which I need not here repeat.

PROP. XX. The existence of God and his essence are one and the same.

Proof.— God (by the last Prop.) and all his attributes are eternal, that is (by Def. viii.) each of his attributes expresses existence. Therefore the same attributes of God which explain his eternal essence, explain at the same time his eternal existence — in other words, that which constitutes God's essence constitutes at the same time his existence. Wherefore God's existence and God's essence are one and the same. Q.E.D.

Corollary I.—Hence it follows that God's existence, like his essence, is an eternal truth.

Corollary II.— Secondly, it follows that God, and all the attributes of God, are unchangeable. For if they could be changed in respect to existence, they must also be able to be changed in respect to essence — that is, obviously, be changed from true to false, which is absurd.

PROP. XXI. All things which follow from the absolute nature of any attribute of God must always exist and be infinite, or, in other words, are eternal and infinite through the said attribute.

Proof.— Conceive, if it be possible (supposing the proposition to be denied), that something in some attribute of God can follow from the absolute nature of the said attribute, and that at the same time it is finite, and has a conditioned existence or duration; for instance, the idea of God expressed in the attribute thought. Now thought, in so far as it is supposed to be an attribute of God, is necessarily (by Prop. xi.) in its nature infinite. But, in so far as it possesses the idea of God, it is supposed finite. It cannot, however, be conceived as finite, unless it be limited by thought (by Def. ii.); but it is not limited by thought itself, in so far as it has constituted the idea of God (for so far it is supposed to be finite); therefore, it is limited by thought, in so far as it has not constituted the idea of God, which nevertheless (by Prop. xi.) must necessarily exist.

We have now granted, therefore, thought not constituting the idea of God, and, accordingly, the idea of God does not naturally follow from its nature in so far as it is absolute thought (for it is conceived as constituting, and also as not constituting, the idea of God), which is against our hypothesis. Wherefore, if the idea of God expressed in the attribute thought, or, indeed, anything else in any attribute of God (for we may take any example, as the proof is of universal application) follows from the necessity of the absolute nature of the said attribute, the said thing must necessarily be infinite, which was our first point.

Furthermore, a thing which thus follows from the necessity of the nature of any attribute cannot have a limited duration. For if it can suppose a thing, which follows from the necessity of the nature of some attribute, to exist in some attribute of God, for instance, the idea of God expressed in the attribute thought, and let it be supposed at some time not to have existed, or to be about not to exist.

Now thought being an attribute of God, must necessarily exist unchanged (by Prop. xi., and Prop. xx., Coroll. ii.); and beyond the limits of the duration of the idea of God (supposing the latter at some time not to have existed, or not to be going to exist), thought would perforce have existed without the idea of God, which is contrary to our hypothesis, for we supposed that, thought being given, the idea of God necessarily flowed therefrom. Therefore the idea of God expressed in thought, or anything which necessarily follows from the absolute nature of some attribute of God, cannot have a limited duration, but through the said attribute is eternal, which is our second point. Bear in mind that the same proposition may be affirmed of anything, which in any attribute necessarily follows from God's absolute nature.

Prop. XXII. Whatsoever follows from any attribute of God, in so far as it is modified by a modification, which exists necessarily and as infinite, through the said attribute, must also exist necessarily and as infinite.

Proof.—The proof of this proposition is similar to that of the preceding one.

Prop. XXIII. Every mode, which exists both necessarily and as infinite, must necessarily follow either from the absolute nature of some attribute of God, or from an attribute modified by a modification which exists necessarily, and as infinite.

Proof.—A mode exists in something else, through which it must be conceived (Def. v.), that is (Prop. xv.), it exists solely in God, and solely through God can be conceived. If, therefore, a mode is conceived as necessarily existing and infinite, it must necessarily be inferred or perceived through some attribute of God, in so far as such attribute is conceived as expressing the infinity and necessity of existence, in other words (Def. viii.) eternity; that is, in so far as it is considered absolutely. A mode, therefore, which necessarily exists as infinite, must follow from the absolute nature of some attribute of God, either immediately (Prop. xxi.) or through the means of some modification, which follows from the absolute nature of the said attribute; that is (by Prop. xxii.), which exists necessarily and as infinite.

Prop. XXIV. The essence of things produced by God does not involve existence.

Proof.—This proposition is evident from Def. i. For that of which the nature (considered in itself) involves existence is self-caused, and exists by the sole necessity of its own nature.

Corollary.— Hence it follows that God is not only the cause of things coming into existence, but also of their continuing in existence, that is, in scholastic phraseology, God is cause of the being of things (*essendi rerum*). For whether things exist, or do not exist, whenever we contemplate their essence, we see that it involves neither existence nor duration; consequently, it cannot be the cause of either the one or the other. God must be the sole cause, inasmuch as to him alone does existence appertain. (Prop. xiv. Coroll. i.) Q.E.D.

PROP. XXV. God is the efficient cause not only of the existence of things, but also of their essence.

Proof.— If this be denied, then God is not the cause of the essence of things; and therefore the essence of things can (by Ax. iv.) be conceived without God. This (by Prop. xv.) is absurd. Therefore, God is the cause of the essence of things. Q.E.D.

Note.— This proposition follows more clearly from Prop. xvi. For it is evident thereby that, given the divine nature, the essence of things must be inferred from it, no less than their existence — in a word, God must be called the cause of all things, in the same sense as he is called the cause of himself. This will be made still clearer by the following corollary.

Corollary.— Individual things are nothing but modifications of the attributes of God, or modes by which the attributes of God are expressed in a fixed and definite manner. The proof appears from Prop. xv. and Def. v.

PROP. XXVI. A thing which is conditioned to act in a particular manner, has necessarily been thus conditioned by God; and that which has not been conditioned by God cannot condition itself to act.

Proof.— That by which things are said to be conditioned to act in a particular manner is necessarily something positive (this is obvious); therefore both of its essence and of its existence God by the necessity of his nature is the efficient cause (Props. xxv. and xvi.); this is our first point.

Our second point is plainly to be inferred therefrom. For if a thing, which has not been conditioned by God, could condition itself, the first part of our proof would be false, and this, as we have shown, is absurd.

PROP. XXVII. A thing, which has been conditioned by God to act in a particular way, cannot render itself unconditioned.

Proof.— This proposition is evident from the third axiom.

PROP. XXVIII. Every individual thing, or everything which is finite and has a conditioned existence, cannot exist or be conditioned to act, unless it be conditioned for existence and action by a cause other than itself, which also is finite, and has a conditioned existence; and likewise this cause cannot in its turn exist, or be conditioned to act, unless it be conditioned for existence and action by another cause, which also is finite, and has a conditioned existence, and so on to infinity.

Proof.— Whatsoever is conditioned to exist and act, has been thus conditioned by God (by Prop. xxvi. and Prop. xxiv., Coroll.)

But that which is finite and has a conditioned existence, cannot be produced by the absolute nature of any attribute of God; for whatsoever follows from the absolute nature of any attribute of God is infinite and eternal (by Prop. xxi). It must, therefore, follow from some attribute of God, in so far as the said attribute is considered as in some way modified; for substance and modes make up the sum total of existence (by Ax. i. and Def. iii., v.), while modes are merely modifications of the attributes of God. But from God, or from any of his attributes, in so far as the latter is modified by a modification infinite and eternal, a conditioned thing cannot follow. Wherefore it must follow from, or be conditioned for, existence and action by God or one of his attributes, in so far as the latter are modified by some modification which is finite and has a conditioned existence. This is our first point. Again, this cause or this modification (for the reason by which we established the first part of this proof) must in its turn be conditioned by another cause, which also is finite, and has a conditioned existence, and again, this last by another (for the same reason); and so on (for the same reason) to infinity. Q.E.D.

Note.— As certain things must be produced immediately by God, namely those things which necessarily follow from his absolute nature, through the means of these primary attributes, which, nevertheless, can neither exist nor be conceived without God, it follows:— 1. That God is absolutely the proximate cause of those things immediately produced by him. I say absolutely, not after his kind, as is usually stated. For the effects of God cannot either exist or be conceived without a cause (Prop. xv. and Prop. xxiv., Coroll.). 2. That God cannot properly be styled the remote cause of individual things, except for the sake of distinguishing these from what he immediately produces, or rather from what follows from his absolute nature. For, by a remote cause, we understand a cause which is in no way conjoined to the effect. But all things which are, are in God, and so depend on God, that without him they can neither be nor be conceived.

PROP. XXIX. Nothing in the universe is contingent, but all things are conditioned to exist and operate in a particular manner by the necessity of the divine nature.

Proof.— Whatsoever is, is in God (Prop. xv.). But God cannot be called a thing contingent. For (by Prop. xi.) he exists necessarily, and not contingently. Further, the modes of the divine nature follow therefrom necessarily, and not contingently (Prop. xvi.); and they thus follow, whether we consider the divine nature absolutely or whether we consider it as in any way conditioned to act (Prop. xxvii.). Further, God is not only the cause of these modes, in so far as they simply exist (by Prop. xxiv., Coroll.), but also in so far as they are considered as conditioned for operating in a particular manner (Prop. xxvi.). If they be not conditioned by God (Prop. xxvi.), it is impossible, and not contingent, that they should condition themselves; contrariwise, if they be conditioned by God, it is impossible, and not contingent that they should render themselves unconditioned. Wherefore all things are conditioned by the necessity of the divine nature, not only to exist, but also to exist and operate in a particular manner, and there is nothing that is contingent. Q. E. D.

Note.— Before going any further, I wish here to explain, what we should understand by nature viewed as active (*natura naturans*), and nature viewed as passive (*natura naturata*). I say to explain, or rather call attention to it, for I think that, from what has been said, it is sufficiently clear, that by nature viewed as active we should understand that which is in itself, and is conceived through itself, or those attributes of substance, which express eternal and infinite essence, in other words (Prop. xiv., Coroll. i., and Prop. xvii., Coroll. ii.) God, in so far as he is considered as a free cause.

By nature viewed as passive I understand all that which follows from the necessity of the nature of God, or of any of the attributes of God, that is, all the modes of the attributes of God, in so far as they are considered as things which are in God, and which without God cannot exist or be conceived.

PROP. XXX. Intellect, in function (*actu*) finite, or in function infinite, must comprehend the attributes of God and the modifications of God, and nothing else.

Proof.— A true idea must agree with its object (Ax. vi.); in other words (obviously), that which is contained in the intellect in representation must necessarily be granted in nature. But in nature (by Prop. xiv., Coroll. i.) there is no substance save God, nor any modifications save those (Prop. xv.) which are in God, and cannot without God either be or be conceived. Therefore the intellect, in function finite, or in function infinite, must comprehend the attributes of God and the modifications of God, and nothing else. Q. E. D.

PROP. XXXI. The intellect in function, whether finite or infinite, as will, desire, love, etc., should be referred to passive nature and not to active nature.

Proof.— By the intellect we do not (obviously) mean absolute thought, but only a certain mode of thinking, differing from other modes, such as love, desire, etc., and therefore (Def. v.) requiring to be conceived through absolute thought. It must (by Prop. xv. and Def. vi.), through some attribute of God which expresses the eternal and infinite essence of thought, be so conceived, that without such attribute it could neither be nor be conceived. It must therefore be referred to nature passive rather than to nature active, as must also the other modes of thinking. Q.E.D.

Note.—I do not here, by speaking of intellect in function, admit that there is such a thing as intellect in potentiality: but, wishing to avoid all confusion, I desire to speak only of what is most clearly perceived by us, namely, of the very act of understanding, than which nothing is more clearly perceived. For we cannot perceive anything without adding to our knowledge of the act of understanding.

PROP. XXXII. Will cannot be called a free cause, but only a necessary cause.

Proof.—Will is only a particular mode of thinking, like intellect; therefore (by Prop. xxviii.) no volition can exist, nor be conditioned to act, unless it be conditioned by some cause other than itself, which cause is conditioned by a third cause, and so on to infinity. But if will be supposed infinite, it must also be conditioned to exist and act by God, not by virtue of his being substance absolutely infinite, but by virtue of his possessing an attribute which expresses the infinite and eternal essence of thought (by Prop. xxiii.). Thus, however it be conceived, whether as finite or infinite, it requires a cause by which it should be conditioned to exist and act. Thus (Def. vii.) it cannot be called a free cause, but only a necessary or constrained cause. Q.E.D.

Corollary. I.—Hence it follows, first, that God does not act according to freedom of the will.

Corollary. II.—It follows secondly, that will and intellect stand in the same relation to the nature of God as do motion, and rest, and absolutely all natural phenomena, which must be conditioned by God (Prop. xxix.) to exist and act in a particular manner. For will, like the rest, stands in need of a cause, by which it is conditioned to exist and act in a particular manner. And although, when will or intellect be granted, an infinite number of results may follow, yet God cannot on that account be said to act from freedom of the will, any more than the infinite number of results from motion and rest would justify us in saying that motion and rest act by free will. Wherefore will no more appertains to God than does anything else in nature, but stands in the same relation to him as motion, rest, and the like, which we have shown to follow from the necessity of the divine nature, and to be conditioned by it to exist and act in a particular manner.

PROP. XXXIII. Things could not have been brought into being by God in any manner or in any order different from that which has in fact obtained.

Proof.— All things necessarily follow from the nature of God (Prop. xvi.), and by the nature of God are conditioned to exist and act in a particular way (Prop. xxix). If things, therefore, could have been of a different nature, or have been conditioned to act in a different way, so that the order of nature would have been different, God's nature would also have been able to be different from what it now is; and therefore (by Prop. xi.) that different nature also would have perforce existed, and consequently there would have been able to be two or more Gods. This (by Prop. xiv., Coroll. i.) is absurd. Therefore things could not have been brought into being by God in any other manner, etc. Q.E.D.

Note I.— As I have thus shown, more clearly than the sun at noonday, that there is nothing to justify us in calling things contingent, I wish to explain briefly what meaning we shall attach to the word contingent; but I will first explain the words necessary and impossible.

A thing is called necessary either in respect to its essence or in respect to its cause; for the existence of a thing necessarily follows, either from its essence and definition, or from a given efficient cause. For similar reasons a thing is said to be impossible; namely, inasmuch as its essence or definition involves a contradiction, or because no external cause is granted, which is conditioned to produce such an effect; but a thing can in no respect be called contingent, save in relation to the imperfection of our knowledge.

A thing of which we do not know whether the essence does or does not involve a contradiction, or of which knowing that it does not involve a contradiction, we are still in doubt concerning the existence, because the order of causes escapes us,—such a thing, I say, cannot appear to us either necessary or impossible. Wherefore we call it contingent or possible.

Note II.—It clearly follows from what we have said, that things have been brought into being by God in the highest perfection, inasmuch as they have necessarily followed from a most perfect nature. Nor does this prove any imperfection in God, for it has compelled us to affirm his perfection. From its contrary proposition, we should clearly gather (as I have just shown), that God is not supremely perfect, for if things had been brought into being in any other way, we should have to assign to God a nature different from that, which we are bound to attribute to him from the consideration of an absolutely perfect being.

I do not doubt, that many will scout this idea as absurd, and will refuse to give their minds up to contemplating it, simply because they are accustomed to assign to God a freedom very different from that which we (Def. vii.) have deduced. They assign to him, in short, absolute free will. However, I am also convinced that if such persons reflect on the matter, and duly weigh in their minds our series of propositions, they will reject such freedom as they now attribute to God, not only as nugatory, but also as a great impediment to organized knowledge. There is no need for me to repeat what I said in the note to Prop. xvii. But, for the sake of my opponents, I will show further, that although it be granted that will appertains to the essence of God, it nevertheless follows from his perfection, that things could not have been by him created other than they are, or in a different order; this is easily proved, if we reflect on what our opponents themselves concede, namely, that it depends solely on the decree and will of God, that each thing is what it is. If it were otherwise, God would not be the cause of all things. Further, that all the decrees of God have been ratified from all eternity by God himself. If it were otherwise, God would be convicted of imperfection or change. But in eternity there is no such thing as when, before, or after; hence it follows solely from the perfection of God, that God never can decree, or never could have decreed anything but what is; that God did not exist before his decrees, and would not exist without them. But, it is said, supposing that God had made a different universe, or had ordained other decrees from all eternity concerning nature and her order, we could not therefore conclude any imperfection in God. But persons who say this must admit that God can change his decrees. For if God had ordained any decrees concerning nature and her order, different from those which he has ordained — in other words, if he had willed and conceived something different concerning nature — he would perforce have had a different intellect from that which he has, and also a different will. But if it were allowable to assign to God a different intellect and a different will, without any change in his essence or his perfection, what would there be to prevent him changing the decrees which he has made concerning created things, and nevertheless remaining perfect? For his intellect and will concerning things created and their order are the same, in respect to his essence and perfection, however they be conceived.

Further, all the philosophers whom I have read admit that God's intellect is entirely actual, and not at all potential; as they also admit that God's intellect, and God's will, and God's essence are identical, it follows that, if God had had a different actual intellect and a different will, his essence would also have been different; and thus, as I concluded at first, if things had been brought into being by God in a different way from that which has obtained, God's intellect and will, that is (as is admitted) his essence would perforce have been different, which is absurd.

As these things could not have been brought into being by God in any but the actual way and order which has obtained; and as the truth of this proposition follows from the supreme perfection of God; we can have no sound reason for persuading ourselves to believe that God did not wish to create all the things which were in his intellect, and to create them in the same perfection as he had understood them.

But, it will be said, there is in things no perfection nor imperfection; that which is in them, and which causes them to be called perfect or imperfect, good or bad, depends solely on the will of God. If God had so willed, he might have brought it about that what is now perfection should be extreme imperfection, and *vice versâ.* What is such an assertion, but an open declaration that God, who necessarily understands that which he wishes, might bring it about by his will, that he should understand things differently from the way in which he does understand them? This (as we have just shown) is the height of absurdity. Wherefore, I may turn the argument against its employers, as follows: All things depend on the power of God. In order that things should be different from what they are, God's will would necessarily have to be different. But God's will cannot be different (as we have just most clearly demonstrated) from God's perfection. Therefore neither can things be different. I confess that the theory which subjects all things to the will of an indifferent deity, and asserts that they are all dependent on his fiat, is less far from the truth than the theory of those, who maintain that God acts in all things with a view of promoting what is good. For these latter persons seem to set up something beyond God, which does not depend on God, but which God in acting looks to as an exemplar, or which he aims at as a definite goal. This is only another name for subjecting God to the dominion of destiny, an utter absurdity in respect to God, whom we have shown to be the first and only free cause of the essence of all things and also of their existence. I need, therefore, spend no time in refuting such wild theories.

PROP. XXXIV. God's power is identical with his essence.

Proof. — From the sole necessity of the essence of God it follows that God is the cause of himself (Prop. xi.) and of all things (Prop. xvi. and Coroll.). Wherefore the power of God, by which he and all things are and act, is identical with his essence. Q.E.D.

PROP. XXXV. Whatsoever we conceive to be in the power of God, necessarily exists.

Proof. — Whatsoever is in God's power, must (by the last Prop.) be comprehended in his essence in such a manner, that it necessarily follows therefrom, and therefore necessarily exists. Q.E.D.

PROP. XXXVI. There is no cause from whose nature some effect does not follow.

Proof. — Whatsoever exists expresses God's nature or essence in a given conditioned manner (by Prop. xxv., Coroll.); that is (by Prop. xxxiv.), whatsoever exists, expresses in a given conditioned manner God's power, which is the cause of all things, therefore an effect must (by Prop. xvi.) necessarily follow. Q.E.D.

APPENDIX. — In the foregoing I have explained the nature and properties of God. I have shown that he necessarily exists, that he is one: that he is, and acts solely by the necessity of his own nature; that he is the free cause of all things, and how he is so; that all things are in God, and so depend on him, that without him they could neither exist nor be conceived; lastly, that all things are pre-determined by God, not through his free will or absolute fiat, but from the very nature of God or infinite power. I have further, where occasion offered, taken care to remove the prejudices, which might impede the comprehension of my demonstrations. Yet there still remain misconceptions not a few, which might and may prove very grave hindrances to the understanding of the concatenation of things, as I have explained it above. I have therefore thought it worth while to bring these misconceptions before the bar of reason.

All such opinions spring from the notion commonly,

entertained, that all things in nature act as men themselves act, namely, with an end in view. It is accepted as certain, that God himself directs all things to a definite goal (for it is said that God made all things for man, and man that he might worship him). I will, therefore, consider this opinion, asking first, why it obtains general credence, and why all men are naturally so prone to adopt it? secondly, I will point out its falsity; and, lastly, I will show how it has given rise to prejudices about good and bad, right and wrong, praise and blame, order and confusion, beauty and ugliness, and the like. However, this is not the place to deduce these misconceptions from the nature of the human mind: it will be sufficient here, if I assume as a starting point, what ought to be universally admitted, namely, that all men are born ignorant of the causes of things, that all have the desire to seek for what is useful to them, and that they are conscious of such desire. Herefrom it follows first, that men think themselves free, inasmuch as they are conscious of their volitions and desires, and never even dream, in their ignorance, of the causes which have disposed them to wish and desire. Secondly, that men do all things for an end, namely, for that which is useful to them, and which they seek. Thus it comes to pass that they only look for a knowledge of the final causes of events, and when these are learned, they are content, as having no cause for further doubt. If they cannot learn such causes from external sources, they are compelled to turn to considering themselves, and reflecting what end would have induced them personally to bring about the given event, and thus they necessarily judge other natures by their own. Further, as they find in themselves and outside themselves many means which assist them not a little in their search for what is useful, for instance, eyes for seeing, teeth for chewing, herbs and animals for yielding food, the sun for giving light, the sea for breeding fish, etc., they come to look on the whole of nature as a means for obtaining such conveniences. Now as they are aware, that they found these conveniences and did not make them they think they have cause for believing, that some other being

has made them for their use. As they look upon things
as means, they cannot believe them to be self-created;
but, judging from the means which they are accustomed
to prepare for themselves, they are bound to believe in
some ruler or rulers of the universe endowed with
human freedom, who have arranged and adapted everything for human use. They are bound to estimate the
nature of such rulers (having no information on the
subject) in accordance with their own nature, and therefore they assert that the gods ordained everything for
the use of man, in order to bind man to themselves and
obtain from him the highest honors. Hence also it follows, that everyone thought out for himself, according to
his abilities, a different way of worshipping God, so that
God might love him more than his fellows, and direct
the whole course of nature for the satisfaction of his
blind cupidity and insatiable avarice. Thus the prejudice developed into superstition, and took deep root in
the human mind; and for this reason everyone strove
most zealously to understand and explain the final causes
of things; but in their endeavor to show that nature
does nothing in vain, *i. e.*, nothing which is useless to
man, they only seem to have demonstrated that nature,
the gods, and men are all mad together. Consider, I
pray you, the result: among the many helps of nature
they were bound to find some hindrances, such as storms,
earthquakes, diseases, etc.: so they declared that such
things happen, because the gods are angry at some
wrong done them by men, or at some fault committed
in their worship. Experience day by day protested and
showed by infinite examples, that good and evil fortunes
fall to the lot of pious and impious alike; still they
would not abandon their inveterate prejudice, for it was
more easy for them to class such contradictions among
other unknown things of whose use they were ignorant,
and thus to retain their actual and innate condition of
ignorance, than to destroy the whole fabric of their reasoning and start afresh. They therefore laid down as an
axiom, that God's judgments far transcend human understanding. Such a doctrine might well have sufficed to

conceal the truth from the human race for all eternity, if mathematics had not furnished another standard of verity in considering solely the essence and properties of figures without regard to their final causes. There are other reasons (which I need not mention here) besides mathematics, which might have caused men's minds to be directed to these general prejudices, and have led them to the knowledge of the truth.

I have now sufficiently explained my first point. There is no need to show at length, that nature has no particular goal in view, and that final causes are mere human figments. This, I think, is already evident enough, both from the causes and foundations on which I have shown such prejudice to be based, and also from Prop. xvi., and the Corollary of Prop. xxxii., and, in fact, all those propositions in which I have shown, that everything in nature proceeds from a sort of necessity, and with the utmost perfection. However, I will add a few remarks, in order to overthrow this doctrine of a final cause utterly. That which is really a cause it considers as an effect, and *vice versâ:* it makes that which is by nature first to be last, and that which is highest and most perfect to be most imperfect. Passing over the questions of cause and priority as self-evident, it is plain from Props. xxi., xxii., xxiii. that that effect, is most perfect which is produced immediately by God; the effect which requires for its production several intermediate causes is, in that respect, more imperfect. But if those things which were made immediately by God were made to enable him to attain his end, then the things which come after, for the sake of which the first were made, are necessarily the most excellent of all.

Further, this doctrine does away with the perfection of God: for, if God acts for an object, he necessarily desires something which he lacks. Certainly, theologians and metaphysicians draw a distinction between the object of want and the object of assimilation; still they confess that God made all things for the sake of himself, not for the sake of creation. They are unable to point to anything prior to creation, except God himself, as an object for which God should act, and are therefore driven to admit (as they clearly must), that God lacked those things for whose attainment he created means, and further that he desired them.

We must not omit to notice that the followers of this doctrine, anxious to display their talent in assigning final causes, have imported a new method of argument in proof of their theory—namely, a reduction, not to the impossible, but to ignorance; thus showing that they have no other method of exhibiting their doctrine. For example, if a stone falls from a roof on to some one's head and kills him, they will demonstrate by their new method, that the stone fell in order to kill the man; for, if it had not by God's will fallen with that object, how could so many circumstances (and there are often many concurrent circumstances) have all happened together by chance? Perhaps you will answer that the event is due to the facts that the wind was blowing, and the man was walking that way. "But why," they will insist, "was the wind blowing, and why was the man at that very time walking that way?" If you again answer, that the wind had then sprung up because the sea had begun to be agitated the day before, the weather being previously calm, and that the man had been invited by a friend, they will again insist: "But why was the sea agitated, and why was the man invited at that time?" So they will pursue their questions from cause to cause, till at last you take refuge in the will of God—in other words, the sanctuary of ignorance. So, again, when they survey the frame of the human body, they are amazed; and being ignorant of the causes of so great a work of art conclude that it has been fashioned, not mechanically, but by divine and supernatural skill, and has been so put together that one part shall not hurt another.

Hence any one who seeks for the true causes of miracles, and strives to understand natural phenomena as an intelligent being, and not to gaze at them like a fool, is set down and denounced as an impious heretic by those, whom the masses adore as the interpreters of nature and the gods. Such persons know that, with the removal of ignorance, the wonder which forms their only available means for proving and preserving their authority would vanish also. But I now quit this subject, and pass on to my third point.

After men persuaded themselves, that everything which is created is created for their sake, they were bound to consider as the chief quality in everything that which is most useful to themselves, and to account those things the best of all which have the most beneficial effect on mankind. Further, they were bound to form abstract notions for the explanation of the nature of things, such as GOODNESS, BADNESS, ORDER, CONFUSION, WARMTH, COLD, BEAUTY, DEFORMITY, and so on; and from the belief that they are free agents arose the further notions PRAISE and BLAME, SIN and MERIT.

I will speak of these latter hereafter, when I treat of human nature; the former I will briefly explain here.

Everything which conduces to health and the worship of God they have called GOOD, everything which hinders these objects they have styled BAD; and inasmuch as those who do not understand the nature of things do not verify phenomena in any way, but merely imagine them after a fashion, and mistake their imagination for understanding, such persons firmly believe that there is an ORDER in things, being really ignorant both of things and their own nature. When phenomena are of such a kind, that the impression they make on our senses requires little effort of imagination, and can consequently be easily remembered, we say that they are WELL-ORDERED; if the contrary, that they are ILL-ORDERED or CONFUSED. Further, as things which are easily imagined are more pleasing to us, men prefer order to confusion — as though there were any order in nature, except in relation to our imagination — and say that God has created all things in order; thus, without knowing it, attributing imagination to God, unless, indeed, they would have it that God foresaw human imagination, and arranged everything, so that it should be most easily imagined. If this be their theory they would not, perhaps, be daunted by the fact

that we find an infinite number of phenomena, far surpassing our imagination, and very many others which
confound its weakness. But enough has been said on
this subject. The other abstract notions are nothing but
modes of imagining, in which the imagination is differently affected, though they are considered by the ignorant
as the chief attributes of things, inasmuch as they believe
that everything was created for the sake of themselves;
and, according as they are affected by it, style it good
or bad, healthy or rotten and corrupt. For instance, if
the motion whose objects we see communicate to our
nerves be conducive to health, the objects causing it are
styled BEAUTIFUL; if a contrary motion be excited, they
are styled UGLY.

Things which are perceived through our sense of smell
are styled fragrant or fetid; if through our taste, sweet
or bitter, full-flavored or insipid, if through our touch,
hard or soft, rough or smooth, etc.

Whatsoever affects our ears is said to give rise to noise,
sound, or harmony. In this last case, there are men lu-
natic enough to believe that even God himself takes
pleasure in harmony; and philosophers are not lacking
who have persuaded themselves, that the motion of the
heavenly bodies gives rise to harmony — all of which instances sufficiently show that everyone judges of things
according to the state of his brain, or rather mistakes for
things the forms of his imagination. We need no longer
wonder that there have arisen all the controversies we
have witnessed and finally scepticism: for, although human bodies in many respects agree, yet in very many
others they differ; so that what seems good to one
seems bad to another; what seems well ordered to one
seems confused to another; what is pleasing to one dis-
pleases another, and so on. I need not further enumerate, because this is not the place to treat the subject at
length, and also because the fact is sufficiently well
known. It is commonly said: "So many men, so many
minds; everyone is wise in his own way; brains differ as
completely as palates." All of which proverbs show, that
men judge of things according to their mental disposi-

tion, and rather imagine than understand: for, if they understood phenomena, they would, as mathematics attest, be convinced, if not attracted, by what I have urged.

We have now perceived, that all the explanations commonly given of nature are mere modes of imagining, and do not indicate the true nature of anything, but only the constitution of the imagination; and, although they have names, as though they were entities, existing externally to the imagination, I call them entities imaginary rather than real; and, therefore, all arguments against us drawn from such abstractions are easily rebutted.

Many argue in this way. If all things follow from a necessity of the absolutely perfect nature of God, why are there so many imperfections in nature? such, for instance, as things corrupt to the point of putridity, loathsome deformity, confusion, evil, sin, etc. But these reasoners are, as I have said, easily confuted, for the perfection of things is to be reckoned only from their own nature and power; things are not more or less perfect, according as they delight or offend human senses, or according as they are serviceable or repugnant to mankind. To those who ask why God did not so create all men, that they should be governed only by reason, I give no answer but this: because matter was not lacking to him for the creation of every degree of perfection from highest to lowest; or, more strictly, because the laws of his nature are so vast, as to suffice for the production of everything conceivable by an infinite intelligence, as I have shown in Prop. xvi.

Such are the misconceptions I have undertaken to note; if there are any more of the same sort, everyone may easily dissipate them for himself with the aid of a little reflection.

PART II.

OF THE NATURE AND ORIGIN OF THE MIND.

PREFACE.

I NOW pass on to explaining the results, which must necessarily follow from the essence of God, or of the eternal and infinite being; not, indeed, all of them (for we proved in Part. i., Prop. xvi., that an infinite number must follow in an infinite number of ways), but only those which are able to lead us, as it were by the hand, to the knowledge of the human mind and its highest blessedness.

DEFINITIONS.

I. By BODY I mean a mode which expresses in a certain determinate manner the essence of God, in so far as he is considered as an extended thing. (See Part i., Prop. xxv. Coroll.).

II. I consider as belonging to the essence of a thing that, which being given, the thing is necessarily given also, and, which being removed, the thing is necessarily removed also; in other words, that without which the thing, and which itself without the thing, can neither be nor be conceived.

III. By IDEA, I mean the mental conception which is formed by the mind as a thinking thing.

Explanation.— I say CONCEPTION rather than perception, because the word perception seems to imply that the mind is passive in respect to the object; whereas conception seems to express an activity of the mind.

IV. By AN ADEQUATE IDEA, I mean an idea which, in so far as it is considered in itself, without relation to the object, has all the properties or intrinsic marks of a true idea.

78

Explanation.— I say INTRINSIC, in order to exclude that mark which is extrinsic, namely, the agreement between the idea and its object (*ideatum*).

V. DURATION is the indefinite continuance of existing.

Explanation.— I say INDEFINITE, because it cannot be determined through the existence itself of the existing thing, or by its efficient cause, which necessarily gives the existence of the thing, but does not take it away.

VI. REALITY and PERFECTION I use as synonymous terms.

VII. By PARTICULAR THINGS, I mean things which are finite and have a conditioned existence; but if several individual things concur in one action, so as to be all simultaneously the effect of one cause, I consider them all so far, as one particular thing.

AXIOMS.

I. The essence of man does not involve necessary existence, that is, it may, in the order of nature, come to pass that this or that man does or does not exist.

II. Man thinks.

III. Modes of thinking, such as love, desire, or any other of the passions, do not take place, unless there be in the same individual an idea of the thing loved, desired, etc. But the idea can exist without the presence of any other mode of thinking.

IV. We perceive that a certain body is affected in many ways.

V. We feel and perceive no particular things, save bodies and modes of thought.

N. B. The postulates are given after the conclusion of Prop. xiii.

PROPOSITIONS.

PROP. I. Thought is an attribute of God, or God is a thinking thing.

Proof.— Particular thoughts, or this or that thought, are modes which, in a certain conditioned manner, express the nature of God (Part i., Prop. xxv., Coroll.). God therefore possesses the attribute (Part i., Def. v.) of which the concept is involved in all particular thoughts, which latter are conceived thereby. Thought, therefore, is one of the infinite attributes of God, which express God's eternal and infinite essence (Part i., Def. vi.). In other words, God is a thinking thing. Q.E.D.

Note.— This proposition is also evident from the fact, that we are able to conceive an infinite thinking being. For, in proportion as a thinking being is conceived as thinking more thoughts, so it is conceived as containing more reality or perfection. Therefore a being which can think an infinite number of things in an infinite number of ways, is, necessarily, in respect of thinking, infinite. As, therefore, from the consideration of thought alone we conceive an infinite being, thought is necessarily (Part i., Def. iv. and vi.) one of the infinite attributes of God, as we were desirous of showing.

Prop. II. Extension is an attribute of God, or God is an extended thing.

Proof.— The proof of this proposition is similar to that of the last.

Prop. III. In God there is necessarily the idea not only of his essence, but also of all things which necessarily follow from his essence.

Proof.— God (by the first Prop. of this Part) can think an infinite number of things in infinite ways, or (what is the same thing, by Prop. xvi., Part i.) can form the idea of his essence, and of all things which necessarily follow therefrom. Now all that is in the power of God necessarily is. (Part i., Prop. xxxv.) Therefore, such an idea as we are considering necessarily is, and in God alone. Q.E.D. (Part i., Prop. xv.)

Note.— The multitude understand by the power of God the free will of God, and the right over all things that exist, which latter are accordingly generally considered as contingent. For it is said that God has the power to destroy all things, and to reduce them to nothing. Further, the power of God is very often likened to the power of kings. But this doctrine we have refuted (Part i., Prop. xxxii., Corolls. i. and ii.), and we have shown (Part i., Prop. xvi.) that God acts by the same necessity, as that by which he understands himself; in other words, as it follows from the necessity of the divine nature (as all admit), that God understands himself, so also does it follow by the same necessity, that God performs infinite acts in infinite ways. We further showed (Part i., Prop. xxxiv.) that God's power is identical with God's essence in action; therefore it is as impossible for us to conceive God as not acting as to conceive him as non-existent. If we might pursue the subject further, I could point out, that the power which is commonly attributed to God is not only human (as showing that God is conceived by the multitude as a man, or in the likeness of a man) but involves a negation of power. However, I am unwilling to go over the same ground so often. I would only beg the reader again and again, to turn over frequently in his mind what I have said in Part i. from Prop. xvi. to the end. No one will be able to follow my meaning, unless he is scrupulously careful not to confound the power of God with the human power and right of kings.

PROP. IV. The idea of God, from which an infinite number of things follow in infinite ways, can only be one.

Proof.— Infinite intellect comprehends nothing save the attributes of God and his modifications (Part i., Prop. xxx.). Now God is one (Part i., Prop xiv., Coroll.). Therefore the idea of God, wherefrom an infinite number of things follow in infinite ways, can only be one. Q.E.D.

PROP. V. The actual being of ideas owns God as its cause, only in so far as he is considered as a thinking thing, not in so far as he is unfolded in any other attribute; that is, the ideas both of the attributes of God and of particular things do not own as their efficient cause their objects (*ideata*) or the things perceived, but God himself in so far as he is a thinking thing.

Proof.— This proposition is evident from Prop. iii. of this Part. We there drew the conclusion, that God can form the idea of his essence, and of all things which follow necessarily therefrom, solely because he is a thinking thing, and not because he is the object of his own idea. Wherefore the actual being of ideas owns for cause God, in so far as he is a thinking thing. It may be differently proved as follows: the actual being of ideas is (obviously) a mode of thought, that is (Part i., Prop. xxv., Coroll.) a mode which expresses in a certain manner the nature of God, in so far as he is a thinking thing, and therefore (Part i., Prop. x.) involves the conception of no other attribute of God, and consequently (by Part i., Ax. iv.) is not the effect of any attribute save thought. Therefore the actual being of ideas owns God as its cause, in so far as he is considered as a thinking thing, etc. Q.E.D.

PROP. VI. The modes of any given attribute are caused by God, in so far as he is considered through the attribute of which they are modes, and not in so far as he is considered through any other attribute.

Proof.—Each attribute is conceived through itself, without any other (Part i., Prop. x.); wherefore the modes of each attribute involve the conception of that attribute, but not of any other. Thus (Part i., Ax. iv.) they are caused by God, only in so far as he is considered through the attribute whose modes they are, and not in so far as he is considered through any other. Q.E.D.

Corollary.—Hence the actual being of things, which are not modes of thought, does not follow from the divine nature, because that nature has prior knowledge of the things. Things represented in ideas follow, and are derived from their particular attribute, in the same manner, and with the same necessity as ideas follow (according to what we have shown) from the attribute of thought.

PROP. VII. The order and connection of ideas is the same as the order and connection of things.

Proof.—This proposition is evident from Part i., Ax. iv. For the idea of everything that is caused depends on a knowledge of the cause, whereof it is an effect.

Corollary.—Hence God's power of thinking is equal to his realized power of action—that is, whatsoever follows from the infinite nature of God in the world of extension (*formaliter*), follows without exception in the same order and connection from the idea of God in the world of thought (*objective*).

Note.— Before going any further, I wish to recall to mind what has been pointed out above — namely, that whatsoever can be perceived by the infinite intellect as constituting the essence of substance, belongs altogether only to one substance: consequently, substance thinking and substance extended are one and the same substance, comprehended now through one attribute, now through the other. So, also, a mode of extension and the idea of that mode are one and the same thing, though expressed in two ways. This truth seems to have been dimly recognized by those Jews who maintained that God, God's intellect, and the things understood by God are identical. For instance, a circle existing in nature, and the idea of a circle existing, which is also in God, are one and the same thing displayed through different attributes. Thus, whether we conceive nature under the attribute of extension, or under the attribute of thought, or under any other attribute, we shall find the same order, or one and the same chain of causes — that is, the same things following in either case.

I said that God is the cause of an idea — for instance, of the idea of a circle — in so far as he is a thinking thing; and of a circle, in so far as he is an extended thing, simply because the actual being of the idea of a circle can only be perceived as a proximate cause through another mode of thinking, and that again through another, and so on to infinity; so that, so long as we consider things as modes of thinking, we must explain the order of the whole of nature, or the whole chain of causes, through the attribute of thought only. And, in so far as we consider things as modes of extension, we must explain the order of the whole nature through the attribute of extension only; and so on, in the case of other attributes. Wherefore of things as they are in themselves God is really the cause, inasmuch as he consists of infinite attributes. I cannot for the present explain my meaning more clearly.

PROP. VIII. The ideas of particular things, or of modes, that do not exist, must be comprehended in the infinite idea of God, in the same way as the formal essences of particular things or modes are contained in the attributes of God.

Proof. — This proposition is evident from the last; it is understood more clearly from the preceding note.

Corollary. — Hence, so long as · particular things do not exist, except in so far as they are comprehended in the attributes of God, their representations in thought or ideas do not exist, except in so far as the infinite idea of God exists; and when particular things are said to exist, not only in so far as they are involved in the attributes of God, but also in so far as they are said to continue, their ideas will also involve existence, through which they are said to continue.

Note. — If anyone desires an example to throw more light on this question, I shall, I fear, not be able to give him any, which adequately explains the thing of which I here speak, inasmuch as it is unique, however, I will endeavor to illustrate it as far as possible. The nature of a circle is such that if any number of straight lines intersect within it, the rectangles formed by their segments will be equal to one another; thus, infinite equal rectangles are contained in a circle. Yet none of these rectangles can be said to exist, except in so far as the circle exists; nor can the idea of any of these rectangles be said to exist, except in so far as they are comprehended in the idea of the circle. Let us grant that, from this infinite number of rectangles, two only exist. The ideas of these two not only exist, in so far as they are contained in the idea of the circle, but also as they involve the existence of those rectangles; wherefore they are distinguished from the remaining ideas of the remaining rectangles.

Prop. IX. The idea of an individual thing actually existing is caused by God, not in so far as he is infinite, but in so far as he is considered as effected by another idea of a thing actually existing, of which he is the cause, in so far as he is affected by a third idea, and so on to infinity.

Proof. — The idea of an individual thing actually exist-

ing is an individual mode of thinking, and is distinct
from other modes (by the Corollary and Note to Prop.
viii. of this part); thus (by Prop. vi. of this part) it is
caused by God, in so far only as he is a thinking thing.
But not (by Prop. xxviii. of Part i.) in so far as he is a
thing thinking absolutely, only in so far as he is considered as affected by another mode of thinking; and he
is the cause of this latter, as being affected by a third,
and so on to infinity.   Now, the order and connection of
ideas is (by Prop. vii. of this book) the same as the order
and connection of causes.   Therefore of a given individual idea another individual idea, or God, in so far as
he is considered as modified by that idea, is the cause;
and of this second idea God is the cause in so far as he
is affected by another idea and so on to infinity.   Q. E. D.

Corollary.— Whatsoever takes place in the individual object of any idea, the knowledge thereof is in God, in so
far only as he has the idea of the object.

Proof.— Whatsoever takes place in the object of any
idea, its idea is in God (by Prop. iii. of this part), not
in so far as he is infinite, but in so far as he is considered as affected by another idea of an individual thing
(by the last Prop.); but (by Prop. vii. of this part) the order
and connection of ideas is the same as the order and
connection of things.   The knowledge, therefore, of that
which takes place in any individual object will be in God,
in so far only as he has the idea of that object.   Q. E. D.

PROP. X. — The being or substance does not appertain
to the essence of man — in other words, substance does
not constitute the actual being* of man.

Proof.— The being of substance involves necessary existence (Part i., Prop. vii.). If, therefore, the being of substance appertains to the essence of man, substance being
granted, man would necessarily be granted also (II. Def.
ii), and, consequently, man would necessarily exist, which
is absurd (II. Ax. i.).   Therefore, etc.   Q. E. D.

Note.— This proposition may also be proved from I. v.,
in which it is shown that there cannot be two substances
of the same nature; for as there may be many men, the

* « Forma. »

being of substance is not that which constitutes the actual being of man. Again, the proposition is evident from the other properties of substance — namely, that substance is in its nature infinite, immutable, indivisible, etc., as anyone may see for himself.

Corollary. — Hence it follows, that the essence of man is constituted by certain modifications of the attributes of God. For (by the last Prop.) the being of substance does not belong to the essence of man. That essence therefore (by i. 15) is something which is in God, and which without God can neither be nor be conceived, whether it be a modification (i. 25 Coroll.), or a mode which expresses God's nature in a certain conditioned manner.

Note. — Everyone must surely admit, that nothing can be or be conceived without God. All men agree that God is the one and only cause of all things, both of their essence and of their existence; that is, God is not only the cause of things in respect to their being made (*secundum fieri*), but also in respect to their being (*secundum esse*).

At the same time many assert, that that, without which a thing cannot be nor be conceived, belongs to the essence of that thing; wherefore they believe that either the nature of God appertains to the essence of created things, or else that created things can be or be conceived without God; or else, as is more probably the case, they hold inconsistent doctrines. I think the cause for such confusion is mainly, that they do not keep to the proper order of philosophic thinking. The nature of God, which should be reflected on first, inasmuch as it is prior both in the order of knowledge and the order of nature, they have taken to be last in the order of knowledge, and have put into the first place what they call the objects of sensation; hence, while they are considering natural phenomena, they give no attention at all to the divine nature, and, when afterward they apply their mind to the study of the divine nature, they are quite unable to bear in mind the first hypotheses, with which they have overlaid the knowledge of natural phenomena, inasmuch as such hypotheses are no help toward understanding the Divine nature. So that it is hardly to be wondered at, that these persons contradict themselves freely.

However, I pass over this point. My intention here was only to give a reason for not saying, that that, without which a thing cannot be or be conceived, belongs to the essence of that thing: individual things cannot be or be conceived without God, yet God does not appertain to their essence. I said that "I considered as belonging to the essence of a thing that, which being given, the thing is necessarily given also, and which being removed, the thing is necessarily removed also; or that without which the thing, and which itself without the thing can neither be nor be conceived." (II. Def. ii.)

PPOP. XI. The first element which constitutes the actual being of the human mind, is the idea of some particular thing actually existing.

Proof.—The essence of man (by the Coroll. of the last Prop.) is constituted by certain modes of the attributes of God, namely (by II. Ax. ii.), by the modes of thinking, of all which (by II. Ax. iii.) the idea is prior in nature, and, when the idea is given, the other modes (namely, those of which the idea is prior in nature) must be in the same individual (by the same Axiom). Therefore an idea is the first element constituting the human mind. But not the idea of a non-existent thing, for then (II viii. Coroll.) the idea itself cannot be said to exist; it must therefore be the idea of something actually existing. But not of an infinite thing. For an infinite thing (I. xxi., xxii.) must always necessarily exist; this would (by II. Ax. i.) involve an absurdity. Therefore the first element, which constitutes the actual being of the human mind, is the idea of something actually existing. Q.E.D.

Corollary.— Hence it follows, that the human mind is part of the infinite intellect of God; thus when we say, that the human mind perceives this or that, we make the assertion, that God has this or that idea, not in so far as he is infinite, but in so far as he is displayed through the nature of the human mind, or in so far as he constitutes the essence of the human mind; and when we say that God has this or that idea, not only in so far as he constitutes the essence of the human mind, but also in so far as he, simultaneously with the human mind, has the further idea of another thing, we assert that the human mind perceives a thing in part or inadequately.

Note.— Here, I doubt not, readers will come to a stand, and will call to mind many things which will cause them to hesitate; I therefore beg them to accompany me slowly, step by step, and not to pronounce on my statements, till they have read to the end.

PROP. XII. Whatsoever comes to pass in the object of the idea, which constitutes the human mind, must be perceived by the human mind, or there will necessarily be an idea in the human mind of the said occurrence. That is, if the object of the idea constituting the human mind be a body, nothing can take place in that body without being perceived by the mind.

Proof.—Whatsoever comes to pass in the object of any idea, the knowledge thereof is necessarily in God (II. ix. Coroll.), in so far as he is considered as affected by the idea of the said object, that is (II. xi.), in so far as he constitutes the mind of anything. Therefore, whatsoever takes place in the object constituting the idea of the human mind, the knowledge thereof is necessarily in God, in so far as he constitutes the nature of the human mind; that is (by II. xi. Coroll.) the knowledge of the said thing will necessarily be in the mind, in other words the mind perceives it.

Note.— This proposition is also evident, and is more clearly to be understood from II. vii., which see.

PROP. XIII. The object of the idea constituting the human mind is the body, in other words a certain mode of extension which actually exists, and nothing else.

Proof.— If indeed the body were not the object of the human mind, the ideas of the modifications of the body would not be in God (II. ix. Coroll.) in virtue of his constituting our mind, but in virtue of his constituting the mind of something else; that is (II. xi. Coroll.), the ideas of the modifications of the body would not be in our mind; now (by II. Ax. iv.) we do possess the ideas of the modifications of the body. Therefore the object of the idea constituting the human mind is the body, and the body as it actually exists (II. xi.). Further, if there were any other object of the idea constituting the mind besides body, then, as nothing can exist from which some effect does not follow (I. xxxvi.) there would necessarily have to be in our mind an idea, which would be the effect of that other object (II. xi.); but (II. Ax. v.) there is no such idea. Wherefore the object of our mind is the body as it exists, and nothing else. Q. E. D.

Note.—We thus comprehend, not only that the human mind is united to the body, but also the nature of the union between mind and body. However no one will be able to grasp this adequately or distinctly, unless he first has adequate knowledge of the nature of our body. The propositions we have advanced hitherto have been entirely general, applying not more to men than to other individual things, all of which, though in different degrees, are animated.* For of everything there is necessarily an idea in God, of which God is the cause, in the same way as there is an idea of the human body; thus whatever we have asserted of the idea of the human body must necessarily also be asserted of the idea of everything else. Still, on the other hand, we cannot deny that ideas, like objects, differ one from the other, one being more excellent than another and containing more reality, just as the object of one idea is more excellent than the object of another idea, and contains more reality.

Wherefore, in order to determine, wherein the human mind differs from other things, and wherein it surpasses them, it is necessary for us to know the nature of its object, that is, of the human body. What this nature is, I am not able here to explain, nor is it necessary for the proof of what I advance, that I should do so. I will only say generally, that in proportion as any given body is more fitted

* "Animata."

than others for doing many actions or receiving many impressions at once, so also is the mind, of which it is the object, more fitted than others for forming many simultaneous perceptions; and the more the actions of one body depend on itself alone, and the fewer other bodies concur with it in action, the more fitted is the mind of which it is the object for distinct comprehension. We may thus recognize the superiority of one mind over others, and may further see the cause, why we have only a very confused knowledge of our body, and also many kindred questions, which I will, in the following propositions, deduce from what has been advanced. Wherefore I have thought it worth while to explain and prove more strictly my present statements. In order to do so, I must premise a few propositions concerning the nature of bodies.

Axiom I. All bodies are either in motion or at rest.

Axiom II. Every body is moved sometimes more slowly, sometimes more quickly.

Lemma I. Bodies are distinguished from one another in respect of motion and rest, quickness and slowness, and not in respect of substance.

Proof.—The first part of this proposition is, I take it, self-evident. That bodies are not distinguished in respect of substance, is plain both from I. v. and I. viii. It is brought out still more clearly from I. xv., note.

Lemma II. All bodies agree in certain respects.

Proof.—All bodies agree in the fact, that they involve the conception of one and the same attribute (II., Def. i.). Further, in the fact that they may be moved less or more quickly, and may be absolutely in motion or at rest.

Lemma III. A body in motion or at rest must be determined to motion or rest by another body, which other body has been determined to motion or rest by a third body, and that third again by a fourth, and so on to infinity.

Proof.—Bodies are individual things (II., Def. i.) which (Lemma I.) are distinguished one from the other in respect to motion and rest; thus (I. xxviii.) each must necessarily be determined to motion or rest by another individual thing, namely (II. vi.), by another body, which other body is also (Ax. i.), in motion or at rest. And this body again can only have been set in motion or caused to rest by being determined by a third body to motion or rest. This third body again by a fourth, and so on to infinity. Q. E. D.

Corollary.—Hence it follows, that a body in motion keeps in motion, until it is determined to a state of rest by some other body; and a body at rest remains so, until it is determined to a state of motion by some other body. This is indeed self-evident. For when I suppose, for instance, that a given body, A, is at rest, and do not take into consideration other bodies in motion, I cannot affirm anything concerning the body A, except that it is at rest. If it afterward comes to pass that A is in motion, this cannot have resulted from its having been at rest, for no other consequence could have been involved than its remaining at rest. If, on the other hand, A be given in motion, we shall, so long as we only consider A, be unable to affirm anything concerning it, except that it is in motion. If A is subsequently found to be at rest, this rest cannot be the result of A's previous motion, for such motion can only have led to continued motion; the state of rest therefore must have resulted from something, which was not in A, namely, from an external cause determining A to a state of rest.

Axiom I. All modes, wherein one body is affected by another body, follow simultaneously from the nature of the body affected and the body affecting; so that one and the same body may be moved in different modes, according to the difference in the nature of the bodies moving it; on the other hand, different bodies may be moved in different modes by one and the same body.

Axiom II. When a body in motion impinges on another body at rest, which it is unable to move, it recoils in order to continue its motion, and the angle made by the line of motion in the recoil and the plane of the body at rest, whereon the moving body has impinged, will be equal to the angle formed by the line of motion of incidence and the same plane.

So far we have been speaking only of the most simple bodies, which are only distinguished one from the other by motion and rest, quickness and slowness. We now pass on to compound bodies.

Definition.—When any given bodies of the same or different magnitude are compelled by other bodies to remain in contact, or if they be moved at the same or different rates of speed, so that their mutual movements should preserve among themselves a certain fixed relation, we say that such bodies are in union, and that together they compose one body or individual, which is distinguished from other bodies by this fact of union.

AXIOM III. In proportion as the parts of an individual, or a compound body, are in contact over a greater or less superficies, they will with greater or less difficulty admit of being moved from their position; consequently the individual will, with greater or less difficulty, be brought to assume another form. Those bodies whose parts are in contact over large superficies, are called HARD; those, whose parts are in contact over small superficies, are called SOFT; those, whose parts are in motion among one another, are called FLUID.

LEMMA IV. If from a body or individual, compounded of several bodies, certain bodies be separated, and if at the same time, an equal number of other bodies of the same nature take their place, the individual will preserve its nature as before, without any change in its actuality (*forma*).

Proof. — Bodies (Lemma i.) are not distinguished in respect of substance: that which constitutes the actuality (*formam*) of an individual consists (by the last Def.) in a union of bodies; but this union, although there is a continual change of bodies, will (by our hypothesis) be maintained; the individual, therefore, will retain its nature as before, both in respect of substance and in respect of mode. Q.E.D.

LEMMA V. If the parts composing an individual become greater or less, but in such proportion, that they all preserve the same mutual relations of motion and rest, the individual will still preserve its original nature, and its actuality will not be changed.

Proof.—The same as for the last Lemma.

LEMMA VI. If certain bodies composing an individual be compelled to change the motion, which they have in one direction, for motion in another direction, but in such a manner, that they be able to continue their motions and their mutual communication in the same relations as before, the individual will retain its own nature without any change of its actuality.

Proof.—This proposition is self-evident, for the individual is supposed to retain all that, which, in its definition, we spoke of as its actual being.

LEMMA VII. Furthermore, the individual thus composed preserves its nature whether it be, as a whole, in motion or at rest, whether it be moved in this or that direction; so long as each part retains its motion, and preserves its communication with other parts as before.

Proof.—This proposition is evident from the definition of an individual prefixed to Lemma iv.

Note.—We thus see, how a composite individual may be affected in many different ways, and preserve its nature notwithstanding. Thus far we have conceived an individual as composed of bodies only distinguished one from the other in respect of motion and rest, speed and slowness; that is, of bodies of the most simple character. If, however, we now conceive another individual composed of several individuals of diverse natures, we shall find that the number of ways in which it can be affected, without losing its nature, will be greatly multiplied. Each of its parts would consist of several bodies, and therefore (by Lemma vi.) each part would admit, without change to its nature, of quicker or slower motion, and would consequently be able to transmit its motions more quickly or more slowly to the remaining parts. If we further conceive a third kind of individuals composed of individuals of this second kind, we shall find that they may be affected in a still greater number of ways without changing their actuality. We may easily proceed thus to infinity, and conceive the whole of nature as one individual, whose parts, that is, all bodies, vary in infinite ways, without any change in the individual as a whole. I should feel bound to explain and demonstrate this point at more length, if I were writing a special treatise on body. But I have already said that such is not my object, I have only touched on the question, because it enables me to prove easily that which I have in view.

POSTULATES.

I. The human body is composed of a number of individual parts, of diverse nature, each one of which is in itself extremely complex.

II. Of the individual parts composing the human body some are fluid, some soft, some hard.

III. The individual parts composing the human body, and consequently the human body itself, are affected in a variety of ways by external bodies.

IV. The human body stands in need for its preservation of a number of other bodies, by which it is continually, so to speak, regenerated.

V. When the fluid part of the human body is determined by an external body to impinge often on another soft part, it changes the surface of the latter, and, as it were, leaves the impression thereupon of the external body which impels it.

VI. The human body can move external bodies, and arrange them in a variety of ways.

PROP. XIV. The human mind is capable of perceiving a great number of things, and is so in proportion as its body is capable of receiving a great number of impressions.

Proof.—The human body (by Post. iii. and vi.) is affected in very many ways by external bodies, and is capable in very many ways of affecting external bodies. But (II. xii.) the human mind must perceive all that takes place in the human body; the human mind is, therefore, capable of perceiving a great number of things, and is so in proportion, etc. Q.E.D.

PROP. XV. The idea, which constitutes the actual being of the human mind, is not simple, but compounded of a great number of ideas.

Proof.— The idea constituting the actual being of the human mind is the idea of the body (II. xiii.), which (Post. i.) is composed of a great number of complex individual parts. But there is necessarily in God the idea of each individual part whereof the body is composed (II. viii., Coroll.); therefore (II. vii.), the idea of the human body is composed of these numerous ideas of its component parts. Q. E. D.

PROP. XVI. The idea of every mode, in which the human body is affected by external bodies, must involve the nature of the human body, and also the nature of the external body.

Proof.— All the modes, in which any given body is affected, follow from the nature of the body affected, and also from the nature of the affecting body (by Ax. i., after the Coroll. of Lemma iii.), wherefore their idea also necessarily (by I. Ax. iv.) involves the nature of both bodies; therefore, the idea of every mode, in which the human body is affected by external bodies, involves the nature of the human body and of the external body. Q. E. D.

Corollary I.— Hence it follows, first, that the human mind perceives the nature of a variety of bodies, together with the nature of its own.

Corollary II.— It follows, secondly, that the ideas, which we have of external bodies, indicate rather the constitution of our own body than the nature of external bodies. I have amply illustrated this in the Appendix to Part I.

PROP. XVII. If the human body is affected in a manner which involves the nature of any external body, the human mind will regard the said external body as actually existing, or as present to itself, until the human body be affected in such a way, as to exclude the existence or the presence of the said external body.

Proof.— This proposition is self-evident, for so long as the human body continues to be thus affected, so long will the human mind (II. xii.) regard this modification of the body — that is (by the last Prop.), it will have the idea of the mode as actually existing, and this idea involves the nature of the external body. In other words, it will have the idea which does not exclude, but postulates the existence or presence of, the nature of the external body; therefore the mind (by II. xvi., Coroll. i.) will regard the external body as actually existing, until it is affected, etc. Q.E.D.

Corollary.—The mind is able to regard as present external bodies, by which the human body has once been affected, even though they be no longer in existence or present.

Proof.—When external bodies determine the fluid parts of the human body, so that they often impinge on the softer parts, they change the surface of the last named (Post. v.); hence (Ax. ii., after Coroll. of Lemma iii.) they are refracted therefrom in a different manner from that which they followed before such change; and, further, when afterward they impinge on the new surfaces by their own spontaneous movement, they will be refracted in the same manner, as though they had been impelled toward those surfaces by external bodies; consequently, they will, while they continue to be thus refracted, affect the human body in the same manner, whereof the mind (II. xii.) will again take cognizance— that is (II. xvii.), the mind will again regard the external body as present, and will do so, as often as the fluid parts of the human body impinge on the aforesaid surfaces by their own spontaneous motion. Wherefore, although the external bodies, by which the human body has once been affected, be no longer in existence, the mind will nevertheless regard them as present, as often as this action of the body is repeated. Q.E.D.

Note.—We thus see how it comes about, as is often the case, that we regard as present things which are not. It is possible that the same result may be brought about by other causes; but I think it suffices for me here to have indicated one possible explanation, just as well as if I had pointed out the true cause. Indeed, I do not think I am very far from the truth, for all my assumptions are based on postulates, which rest, almost without exception, on experience, that cannot be controverted by those who have shown, as we have, that the human body, as we feel it, exists (Coroll. after II. xiii). Furthermore (II. vii., Coroll., II. xvi., Coroll. ii.), we clearly understand what is the difference between the idea, say, of Peter, which constitutes the essence of Peter's mind, and the idea of the said Peter, which is in another man, say, Paul. The former directly answers to the essence of Peter's own body, and only implies existence so long as Peter exists; the latter indicates rather the disposition of Paul's body than the nature of Peter, and, therefore, while this disposition of Paul's body lasts, Paul's mind will regard Peter as present to itself, even though he no longer exists. Further, to retain the usual phraseology, the modifications of the human body, of which the ideas represent external bodies as present to us, we will call the images of things, though they do not recall the figure of things. When the mind regards bodies in this fashion, we say that it imagines. I will here draw attention to the fact, in order to indicate where error lies, that the imaginations of the mind, looked at in themselves, do not contain error. The mind does not err in the mere act of imagining, but only in so far as it is regarded as being without the idea, which excludes the existence of such things as it imagines to be present to it. If the mind, while imagining non-existent things as present to it, is at the same time conscious that they do not really exist, this power of imagination must be set down to the efficacy of its nature, and not to a fault, especially if this faculty of imagination depend solely on its own nature — that is (I. Def. vii.), if this faculty of imagination be free.

PROP. XVIII. If the human body has once been affected by two or more bodies at the same time, when the mind afterward imagines any of them, it will straightway remember the others also.

Proof.—The mind (II. xvii. Coroll.) imagines any given body, because the human body is affected and disposed by the impressions from an external body, in the same manner as it is affected when certain of its parts are acted on by the said external body; but (by our hypothesis) the body was then so disposed, that the mind imagined two bodies at once; therefore, it will also in the second case imagine two bodies at once, and the mind, when it imagines one, will straightway remember the other. Q.E.D.

Note.—We now clearly see what MEMORY is. It is simply a certain association of ideas involving the nature of things outside the human body, which association arises in the mind according to the order and association of the modifications (*affectiones*) of the human body. I say, first, it is an association of those ideas only, which involve the nature of things outside the human body: not of ideas which answer to the nature of the said things: ideas of the modifications of the human body are, strictly speaking (II. xvi.), those which involve the nature both of the human body and of external bodies. I say, secondly, that this association arises according to the order and association of the modifications of the human body, in order to distinguish it from that association of ideas, which arises from the order of the intellect, whereby the mind perceives things through their primary causes, and which is in all men the same. And hence we can further clearly understand, why the mind from the thought of one thing, should straightway arrive at the thought of another thing, which has no similarity with the first; for instance, from the thought of the word *pomum* (an apple), a Roman would straightway arrive at the thought of the fruit apple, which has no similitude with the articulate sound in question, nor anything in common with it, except that the body of the man has often been affected by these two things; that is, that the man has often heard the word *pomum*, while he was looking at the fruit; similarly every man will go on from one thought to another, according as his habit has ordered the images of things in his body. For a soldier, for instance, when he sees the tracks of a horse in sand, will at once pass from the thought of a horse to the thought of a horseman, and thence to the thought of war, etc.; while a countryman will proceed from the thought of a horse to the thought of a plow, a field, etc. Thus every man will follow this or that train of thought, according as he has been in the habit of conjoining and associating the mental images of things in this or that manner.

PROP. XIX.   The human mind has no knowledge of the body, and does not know it to exist, save through the ideas of the modifications whereby the body is affected.

Proof.— The human mind is the very idea or knowledge of the human body (II. xiii.), which (II. ix.) is in God, in so far as he is regarded as affected by another idea of a particular thing actually existing: or, inasmuch as (Post. iv.) the human body stands in need of very many bodies whereby it is, as it were, continually regenerated; and the order and connection of ideas is the same as the order and connection of causes (II. vii.); this idea will therefore be in God, in so far as he is regarded as affected by the ideas of very many particular things. Thus God has the idea of the human body, or knows the human body, in so far as he is affected by very many other ideas, and not in so far as he constitutes the nature of the human mind; that is (by II. xi. Coroll.), the human mind does not know the human body.   But the ideas of the modifications of body are in God, in so far as he constitutes the nature of the human mind, or the human mind perceives those modifications (II. xii.), and consequently (II. xvi.) the human body itself, and as actually existing; therefore the mind perceives thus far only the human body.   Q.E.D.

PROP. XX. The idea or knowledge of the human mind is also in God, following in God in the same manner, and being referred to God in the same manner, as the idea or knowledge of the human body.

Proof.— Thought is an attribute of God (II. i.); therefore (II. iii.) there must necessarily be in God the idea both of thought itself and of all its modifications, consequently also of the human mind (II. xi.).   Further, this idea or knowledge of the mind does not follow from God, in so far as he is infinite, but in so far as he is affected by another idea of an individual thing (II. ix.).   But (II. vii.) the order and connection of ideas is the same as the order and connection of causes; therefore this idea or knowledge of the mind is in God and is referred to God, in the same manner as the idea or knowledge of the body.   Q.E.D.

PROP. XXI. This idea of the mind is united to the mind in the same way as the mind is united to the body.

Proof.— That the mind is united to the body we have shown from the fact, that the body is the object of the mind (II. xii. and xiii.); and so for the same reason the idea of the mind must be united with its object, that is, with the mind in the same manner as the mind is united to the body. Q.E.D.

Note.—This proposition is comprehended much more clearly from what we said in the note to II. vii. We there showed that the idea of body and body, that is, mind and body (II. xiii.), are one and the same individual conceived now under the attribute of thought, now under the attribute of extension; wherefore the idea of the mind and the mind itself are one and the same thing, which is conceived under one and the same attribute, namely, thought. The idea of the mind, I repeat, and the mind itself are in God by the same necessity and follow from him from the same power of thinking. Strictly speaking, the idea of the mind, that is, the idea of an idea, is nothing but the distinctive quality (*forma*) of the idea in so far as it is conceived as a mode of thought without reference to the object; if a man knows anything, he, by that very fact, knows that he knows it, and at the same time knows that he knows that he knows it, and so on to infinity. But I will treat of this hereafter.

PROP. XXII. The human mind perceives not only the modifications of the body, but also the ideas of such modifications.

Proof.— The ideas of the ideas of modifications follow in God in the same manner, and are referred to God in the same manner, as the ideas of the said modifications. This is proved in the same way as II. xx. But the ideas of the modifications of the body are in the human mind (II. xii.), that is, in God, in so far as he constitutes the essence of the human mind; therefore the ideas of these ideas will be in God, in so far as he has the knowledge or idea of the human mind, that is (II. xxi.), they will be in the human mind itself, which therefore perceives not only the modifications of the body, but also the ideas of such modifications.   Q.E.D.

PROP. XXIII. The mind does not know itself, except in so far as it perceives the ideas of the modifications of the body.

Proof.— The idea or knowledge of the mind (II. xx.) follows in God in the same manner, and is referred to God in the same manner, as the idea or knowledge of the body.   But since (II. xix.) the human' mind does not know the human body itself, that is (II. xi. Coroll.) since the knowledge of the human body is not referred to God, in so far as he constitutes the nature of the human mind; therefore, neither is the knowledge of the mind referred to God, in so far as he constitutes the essence of the human mind; therefore (by the same Coroll. II. xi.), the human mind thus far has no knowledge of itself.   Further the ideas of the modifications, whereby the body is affected, involve the nature of the human body itself (II. xvi.), that is (II. xiii.), they agree with the nature of the mind; wherefore the knowledge of these ideas necessarily involves knowledge of the mind; but (by the last Prop.) the knowledge of these ideas is in the human mind itself; wherefore the human mind thus far only has knowledge of itself.   Q.E.D.

PROP. XXIV. The human mind does not involve an adequate knowledge of the parts composing the human body.

Proof.— The parts composing the human body do not belong to the essence of that body, except in so far as they communicate their motions to one another in a certain' fixed relation (Def. after Lemma iii), not in so far as they can be regarded as individuals without relation to the human body.   The parts of the human body are highly complex individuals (Post. i.), whose parts (Lemma iv.) can be separated from the human body without in any way destroying the nature and distinctive quality of the latter, and they can communicate their motions (Ax. i., after Lemma iii.) to other bodies in another relation; therefore (II. iii.) the idea or knowledge of each part will be in God, inasmuch (II. ix.) as he is regarded as affected by another idea of a particular thing, which par-

ticular thing is prior in the order of nature to the aforesaid part (II. vii.). We may affirm the same thing of
each part of each individual composing the human body;
therefore, the knowledge of each part composing the human body is in God, in so far as he is affected by very
many ideas of things, and not in so far as he has the
idea of the human body only, in other words, the idea
which constitutes the nature of the human mind (II. xiii.);
therefore (II. xi. Coroll.) the human mind does not involve an adequate knowledge of the human body. Q.E.D.

PROP. XXV. The idea of each modification of the human body does not involve an adequate knowledge of
the external body.

Proof.—We have shown that the idea of a modification
of the human body involves the nature of an external
body, in so far as that external body conditions the
human body in a given manner. But, in so far as the
external body is an individual, which has no reference to
the human body, the knowledge or idea thereof is in God
(II. ix.), in so far as God is regarded as affected by the
idea of a further thing, which (II. vii.) is naturally prior
to the said external body. Wherefore an adequate knowledge of the external body is not in God, in so far as he
has the idea of the modification of the human body; in
other words, the idea of the modification of the human
body does not involve an adequate knowledge of the
external body. Q.E.D.

PROP. XXVI. The human mind does not perceive any
external body as actually existing, except through the
ideas of the modifications of its own body.

Proof.— If the human body is in no way affected by a
given external body, then (II. vii.) neither is the idea of
the human body, in other words, the human mind, affected
in any way by the idea of the existence of the said external body, nor does it in any manner perceive its existence. But, in so far as the human body is affected in any
way by a given external body, thus far (II. xvi. and
Coroll.) it perceives that external body. Q.E.D.

Corollary.— In so far as the human mind imagines an
external body, it has not an adequate knowledge thereof.

Proof.— When the human mind regards external bodies through the ideas of the modifications of its own body, we say that it imagines (see II. xvii. note); now the mind can only imagine external bodies as actually existing. Therefore (by II. xxv.), in so far as the mind imagines external bodies, it has not an adequate knowledge of them.   Q.E.D.

Prop. XXVII. The idea of each modification of the human body does not involve an adequate knowledge of the human body itself.

Proof.— Every idea of the modification of the human body involves the nature of the human body, in so far as the human body is regarded as affected in a given manner (II. xvi.).   But, inasmuch as the human body is an individual which may be affected in many other ways, the idea of the said modification, etc.   Q.E.D.

Prop. XXVIII. The ideas of the modifications of the human body, in so far as they have reference only to the human mind, are not clear and distinct, but confused.

Proof.— The ideas of the modifications of the human body involve the nature both of the human body and of external bodies (II. xvi.); they must involve the nature not only of the human body but also of its parts; for the modifications are modes (Post. iii.), whereby the parts of the human body, and, consequently, the human body as a whole are affected.   But (by II. xxiv., xxv.) the adequate knowledge of external bodies, as also of the parts composing the human body, is not in God, in so far as he is regarded as affected by the human mind, but in so far as he is regarded as affected by other ideas.   These ideas of modifications, in so far as they are referred to the human mind alone, are as consequences without premises, in other words, confused ideas.   Q.E.D.

Note.— The idea which constitutes the nature of the human mind is, in the same manner, proved not to be, when considered in itself alone, clear and distinct; as also is the case with the idea of the human mind, and the ideas of the ideas of the modifications of the human body, in so far as they are referred to the mind only, as everyone may easily see.

PROP. XXIX. The idea of the idea of each modification of the human body does not involve an adequate knowledge of the human mind.

Proof.— The idea of a modification of the human body (II. xxvii.) does not involve an adequate knowledge of the said body, in other words, does not adequately express its nature; that is (II. xiii.) it does not agree with the nature of the mind adequately; therefore (I. Ax. vi.), the idea of this idea does not adequately express the nature of the human mind, or does not involve an adequate knowledge thereof.

Corollary.— Hence it follows that the human mind, when it perceives things after the common order of nature, has not an adequate but only a confused and fragmentary knowledge of itself, of its own body, and of external bodies. For the mind does not know itself, except in so far as it perceives the ideas of the modifications of body (II. xxiii.). It only perceives its own body (II. xix.) through the ideas of the modifications, and only perceives external bodies through the same means; thus, in so far as it has such ideas of modification, it has not an adequate knowledge of itself (II. xxix.), nor of its own body (II. xxvii.), nor of external bodies (II. xxv.), but only a fragmentary and confused knowledge thereof (II. xxviii. and note). Q. E. D.

Note.—I say expressly, that the mind has not an adequate but only a confused knowledge of itself, its own body, and of external bodies, whenever it perceives things after the common order of nature; that is, whenever it is determined from without, namely, by the fortuitous play of circumstance, to regard this or that; not at such times as it is determined from within, that is, by the fact of regarding several things at once, to understand their points of agreement, difference, and contrast. Whenever it is determined in anywise from within, it regards things clearly and distinctly, as I will show below.

PROP. XXX. We can only have a very inadequate knowledge of the duration of our body.

Proof.— The duration of our body does not depend on its essence (II. Ax. i.), nor on the absolute nature of

God (I. xxi.).   But (I. xxviii.) it is conditioned to exist
and operate by causes, which in their turn are conditioned
to exist and operate in a fixed and definite relation by
other causes, these last again being conditioned by others,
and so on to infinity.   The duration of our body therefore depends on the common order of nature, or the constitution of things.   Now, however a thing may be
constituted, the adequate knowledge of that thing is in
God, in so far as he has the ideas of all things, and not
in so far as he has the idea of the human body only.
(II. ix. Coroll.)   Wherefore the knowledge of the duration
of our body is in God very inadequate, in so far as he is
only regarded as constituting the nature of the human
mind; that is (II. xi. Coroll.), this knowledge is very
inadequate in our mind.   Q. E. D.

PROP. XXXI. We can only have a very inadequate knowledge of the duration of particular things external to ourselves.

Proof.—Every particular thing, like the human body,
must be conditioned by another particular thing to exist
and operate in a fixed and definite relation; this other
particular thing must likewise be conditioned by a third,
and so on to infinity.   (I. xxviii.)   As we have shown in
the foregoing proposition, from this common property of
particular things, we have only a very inadequate knowledge of the duration of our body; we must draw a similar
conclusion with regard to the duration of particular things,
namely, that we can only have a very inadequate knowledge of the duration thereof.   Q. E. D.

Corollary.— Hence it follows that all particular things
are contingent and perishable.   For we can have no
adequate idea of their duration (by the last Prop.), and
this is what we must understand by the contingency
and perishableness of things.   (I. xxxiii., Note i.)   For
(I. xxix.), except in this sense, nothing is contingent.

PROP. XXXII. All ideas, in so far as they are referred to God, are true.

Proof.—All ideas which are in God agree in every respect with their objects (II. vii. Coroll.), therefore (I.
Ax. vi.) they are all true.   Q. E. D.

PROP. XXXIII. There is nothing positive in ideas, which causes them to be called false.

Proof.—If this be denied, conceive, if possible, a positive mode of thinking, which should constitute the distinctive quality of falsehood. Such a mode of thinking cannot be in God (II. xxxii.); external to God it cannot be or be conceived (I. xv.). Therefore there is nothing positive in ideas which causes them to be called false. Q.E.D.

PROP. XXXIV. Every idea, which in us is absolute or adequate and perfect, is true.

Proof.—When we say that an idea in us is adequate and perfect, we say, in other words (II. xi. Coroll.), that the idea is adequate and perfect in God, in so far as he constitutes the essence of our minds; consequently (II. xxxii.), we say that such an idea is true. Q.E.D.

PROP. XXXV. Falsity consists in the privation of knowledge, which inadequate, fragmentary, or confused ideas involve.

Proof.—There is nothing positive in ideas, which causes them to be called false (II. xxxiii); but falsity cannot consist in simple privation (for minds, not bodies, are said to err and to be mistaken), neither can it consist in absolute ignorance, for ignorance and error are not identical; wherefore it consists in the privation of knowledge, which inadequate, fragmentary, or confused ideas involve. Q.E.D.

Note.—In the note to II. xvii. I explained how error consists in the privation of knowledge, but in order to throw more light on the subject I will give an example. For instance, men are mistaken in thinking themselves free; their opinion is made up of consciousness of their own actions, and ignorance of the causes by which they are conditioned. Their idea of freedom, therefore, is simply their ignorance of any cause for their actions. As for their saying that human actions depend on the will, this is a mere phrase without any idea to correspond thereto. What the will is, and how it moves the body, they none of them know; those who boast of such knowledge, and feign dwellings and habitations for the soul, are wont to provoke either laughter or disgust. So, again, when we look at the sun, we imagine that it is distant from us about two hundred feet; this error does not lie solely in this fancy, but in the fact that, while we thus imagine, we do not know the sun's true distance or the cause of the fancy. For although we afterward learn, that the sun is distant from us more than six hundred of the earth's diameters, we none the less shall fancy it to be near; for we do not imagine the sun as near us, because we are ignorant of its true distance, but because the modification of our body involves the essence of the sun, in so far as our said body is affected thereby.

PROP. XXXVI. Inadequate and confused ideas follow by the same necessity, as adequate or clear and distinct ideas.

Proof.—All ideas are in God (I. xv.), and in so far as they are referred to God are true (II. xxxii.) and (II. vii. Coroll.) adequate; therefore there are no ideas confused or inadequate, except in respect to a particular mind (cf. II. xxiv. and xxviii.); therefore all ideas, whether adequate or inadequate, follow by the same necessity (II. vi.). Q.E.D.

PROP. XXXVII. That which is common to all (cf. Lemma II. above), and which is equally in a part and in the whole, does not constitute the essence of any particular thing.

Proof.—If this be denied, conceive, if possible, that it constitutes the essence of some particular thing; for instance, the essence of B. Then (II. Def. ii.) it cannot without B either exist or be conceived; but this is against our hypothesis. Therefore it does not appertain to B's essence nor does it constitute the essence of any particular thing. Q.E.D.

PROP. XXXVIII. Those things, which are common to all, and which are equally in a part and in the whole, cannot be conceived except adequately.

Proof.—Let A be something which is common to all bodies, and which is equally present in the part of any given body and in the whole. I say A cannot be conceived except adequately. For the idea thereof in God will necessarily therefore be adequate (II. vii. Coroll.)

both in so far as God has the idea of the human body, and also in so far as he has the idea of the modifications of the human body (II. xvi., xxv., xxvii.), involve in part the nature of the human body and the nature of external bodies; that is (II. xii., xiii.), the idea in God will necessarily be adequate, both in so far as he constitutes the human mind, and in so far as he has the ideas, which are in the human mind. Therefore the mind (II. xi. Coroll.) necessarily perceives A adequately, and has this adequate perception, both in so far as it perceives itself and in so far as it perceives its own or any external body, nor can A be conceived in any other manner. Q.E.D.

Corollary. — Hence it follows that there are certain ideas or notions common to all men; for (by Lemma ii.) all bodies agree in certain respects, which (by the foregoing Prop.) must be adequately or clearly and distinctly perceived by all.

PROP. XXXIX. That, which is common to and a property of the human body and such other bodies as are wont to affect the human body, and which is present equally in each part of either, or in the whole, will be represented by an adequate idea in the mind.

Proof. — If A be that, which is common to and a property of the human body and external bodies, and equally present in the human body and in the said external bodies, in each part of each external body and in the whole there will be an adequate idea of A in God (II. vii. Coroll.) both in so far as he has the idea of the human body, and in so far as he has the ideas of the given external bodies. Let it now be granted, that the human body is affected by an external body through that, which it has in common therewith, namely, A; the idea of this modification will involve the property A (II. xvi.), and therefore (II. vii. Coroll.) the idea of this modification, in so far as it involves the property A, will be adequate in God, in so far as God is affected by the idea of the human body; that is (II. xiii.), in so far as he constitutes the nature of the human mind; therefore (II. xi. Coroll.) this idea is also adequate in the human mind. Q.E.D.

Corollary.— Hence it follows that the mind is fitted to perceive adequately more things, in proportion as its body has more in common with other bodies.

PROP. XL. Whatsoever ideas in the mind follow from ideas which are therein adequate, are also themselves adequate.

Proof.— This proposition is self-evident. For when we say that an idea in the human mind follows from ideas which are therein adequate, we say, in other words (II. xi. Coroll.) that an idea is in the divine intellect, whereof God is the cause, not in so far as he is infinite, nor in so far as he is affected by the ideas of very many particular things, but only in so far as he constitutes the essence of the human mind.

Note I.— I have thus set forth the cause of those notions, which are common to all men, and which form the basis of our ratiocination. But there are other causes of certain axioms or notions, which it would be to the purpose to set forth by this method of ours; for it would thus appear what notions are more useful than others, and what notions have scarcely any use at all. Furthermore, we should see what notions are common to all men, and what notions are only clear and distinct to those who are unshackeled by prejudice, and we should detect those which are ill-founded. Again we should discern whence the notions called SECONDARY derived their origin, and consequently the axioms on which they are founded, and other points of interest connected with these questions. But I have decided to pass over the subject here, partly because I have set it aside for another treatise, partly because I am afraid of wearying the reader by too great prolixity. Nevertheless, in order not to omit anything necessary to be known, I will briefly set down the causes, whence are derived the terms styled TRANSCENDENTAL, such as Being, Thing, Something. These terms arose from the fact, that the human body, being limited, is only capable of distinctly forming a certain number of images (what an image is I explained in II. xvii. note) within itself at the same time; if this number be exceeded the images will begin to be confused; if this number

of images which the body is capable of forming
distinctly within itself, be largely exceeded, all will become entirely confused one with another. This being
so, it is evident (from II. Prop. xvii. Coroll. and xviii.)
that the human mind can distinctly imagine as many
things simultaneously, as its body can form images simultaneously. When the images become quite confused in
the body, the mind also imagines all bodies confusedly
without any distinction, and will comprehend them, as it
were, under one attribute, namely, under the attribute
of Being, Thing, etc. The same conclusion can be drawn
from the fact that images are not always equally vivid,
and from other analogous causes, which there is no need
to explain here; for the purpose which we have in view
it is sufficient for us to consider one only. All may be
reduced to this, that these terms represent ideas in the
highest degree confused. From similar causes arise those
notions, which we call GENERAL, such as man, horse, dog,
etc. They arise, to wit, from the fact that so many images, for instance, of men, are formed simultaneously in
the human mind, that the powers of imagination break
down, not indeed utterly, but to the extent of the mind
losing count of small differences between individuals
(e. g., color, size, etc.) and their definite number, and
only distinctly imagining that, in which all the individuals,
in so far as the body is affected by them, agree; for that
is the point, in which each of the said individuals chiefly
affected the body; this the mind expresses by the name
man, and this it predicates of an infinite number of particular individuals. For, as we have said, it is unable to
imagine the definite number of individuals. We must,
however, bear in mind, that these general notions are
not formed by all men in the same way, but vary in each
individual according as the point varies, whereby the body
has been most often affected and which the mind most
easily imagines or remembers. For instance, those who
have most often regarded with admiration the stature of
man, will by the name of man understand an animal of
erect stature; those who have been accustomed to regard
some other attribute, will form a different general image

of man, for instance, that man is a laughing animal, a two-footed animal without feathers, a rational animal, and thus, in other cases, everyone will form general images of things according to the habit of his body.

It is thus not to be wondered at, that among philosophers, who seek to explain things in nature merely by the images formed of them, so many controversies should have arisen.

Note II.—From all that has been said above it is clear, that we, in many cases, perceive and form our general notions: (1.) From particular things represented to our intellect fragmentarily, confusedly, and without order through our senses (II. xxix. Coroll.). I have settled to call such perceptions by the name of knowledge from the mere suggestions of experience. (2.) From symbols, *e.g.*, from the fact of having read or heard certain words we remember things and form certain ideas concerning them, similar to those through which ·we imagine things (II. xviii. note). I shall call both these ways of regarding things KNOWLEDGE OF THE FIRST KIND, OPINION, or IMAGINATION. (3.) From the fact that we have notions common to all men, and adequate ideas of the properties of things (II. xxxviii. Coroll. xxxix. and Coroll. and xl.); this I call REASON and KNOWLEDGE OF THE SECOND KIND. Besides these two kinds of knowledge, there is, as I will hereafter show, a third kind of knowledge, which we will call intuition. This kind of knowledge proceeds from an adequate idea of the absolute essence of certain attributes of God to the adequate knowledge of the essence of things. I will illustrate all three kinds of knowledge by a single example. Three numbers are given for finding a fourth, which shall be to the third as the second is to the first. Tradesmen without hesitation multiply the second by the third, and divide the product by the first; either because they have not forgotten the rule which they received from a master without any proof, or because they have often made trial of it with simple numbers, or by virtue of the proof of the nineteenth proposition of the seventh book of Euclid, namely, in virtue of the general property of proportionals.

But with very simple numbers there is no need of this. For instance, one, two, three, being given, everyone can see that the fourth proportional is six; and this is much clearer, because we infer the fourth number from an intuitive grasping of the ratio, which the first bears to the second.

PROP. XLI. Knowledge of the first kind is the only source of falsity, knowledge of the second and third kinds is necessarily true.

Proof.— To knowledge of the first kind we have (in the foregoing note) assigned all those ideas, which are inadequate and confused; therefore this kind of knowledge is the only source of falsity (II. xxxv.). Furthermore, we assigned to the second and third kinds of knowledge those ideas which are adequate; therefore these kinds are necessarily true (II. xxxiv.). Q. E. D.

PROP. XLII. Knowledge of the second and third kinds, not knowledge of the first kind, teaches us to distinguish the true from the false.

Proof.— This proposition is self-evident. He, who knows how to distinguish between true and false, must have an adequate idea of true and false. That is (II. xl., note ii.), he must know the true and the false by the second or third kind of knowledge.

PROP. XLIII. He, who has a true idea, simultaneously knows that he has a true idea, and cannot doubt of the truth of the thing perceived.

Proof.— A true idea in us is an idea which is adequate in God, in so far as he is displayed through the nature of the human mind (II. xi. Coroll.). Let us suppose that there is in God, in so far as he is displayed through the human mind, an adequate idea, A. The idea of this idea must also necessarily be in God, and be referred to him in the same way as the idea A (by II. xx., whereof the proof is of universal application). But the idea A is supposed to be referred to God, in so far as he is displayed through the human mind; therefore the idea of the idea A must be referred to God in the same manner; that is (by II. xi. Coroll.), the adequate idea of the idea A will be in the mind, which has the adequate idea A; therefore he, who has an adequate idea or knows a thing truly (II. xxxiv.), must at the same time have an adequate idea or true knowledge of his knowledge; that is, obviously, he must be assured. Q.E.D.

Note.—I explained in the note to II. xxi. what is meant by the idea of an idea; but we may remark that the foregoing proposition is in itself sufficiently plain. No one, who has a true idea, is ignorant that a true idea involves the highest certainty. For to have a true idea is only another expression for knowing a thing perfectly, or as well as possible. No one, indeed, can doubt of this, unless he thinks that an idea is something lifeless, like a picture on a panel, and not a mode of thinking — namely, the very act of understanding. And who, I ask, can know that he understands anything, unless he do first understand it? In other words, who can know that he is sure of a thing, unless he be first sure of that thing? Further, what can there be more clear, and more certain, than a true idea as a standard of truth? Even as light displays both itself and darkness, so is truth a standard both of itself and of falsity.

I think I have thus sufficiently answered these questions — namely, if a true idea is distinguished from a false idea, only in so far as it is said to agree with its object, a true idea has no more reality or perfection than a false idea (since the two are only distinguished by an extrinsic mark); consequently, neither will a man who has true ideas have any advantage over him who has only false ideas. Further, how comes it that men have false ideas? Lastly, how can any one be sure, that he has ideas which agree with their objects? These questions, I repeat, I have, in my opinion, sufficiently answered. The difference between a true idea and a false idea is plain: from what was said in II. xxxv., the former is related to the latter as being is to not-being. The causes of falsity I have set forth very clearly in II. xix. and II. xxxv. with the note. From what is there stated, the difference between a man who has true ideas, and a man who has only false ideas, is made apparent. As for the last question — as to how a man can be sure that he has ideas that agree with their objects, I have just pointed out, with abundant clearness, that his knowledge arises from the simple fact, that he has an idea which corresponds with its object — in other words, that truth is its own standard. We may add that our mind, in so far as it perceives things truly, is part of the infinite intellect of God (II. xi. Coroll.); therefore, the clear and distinct ideas of the mind are as necessarily true as the ideas of God.

PROP. XLIV. It is not in the nature of reason to regard things as contingent, but as necessary.

Proof.— It is in the nature of reason to perceive things truly (II. xli.), namely (I. Ax. vi.), as they are in themselves — that is (I. xxix.), not as contingent, but as necessary. Q.E.D.

Corollary I.— Hence it follows, that it is only through our imagination that we consider things, whether in respect to the future or the past, as contingent.

Note.— How this way of looking at things arises, I will briefly explain. We have shown above (II. xvii. and Coroll.) that the mind always regards things as present to itself, even though they be not in existence, until some causes arise which exclude their existence and presence. Further (II. xviii.), we showed that, if the human body has once been affected by two external bodies simultaneously, the mind, when it afterward imagines one of the said external bodies, will straightway remember the other — that is, it will regard both as present to itself, unless there arise causes which exclude their existence and presence. Further, no one doubts that we imagine time, from the fact that we imagine bodies to be moved some more slowly than others, some more quickly, some at equal speed. Thus, let us suppose that a child yesterday saw Peter for the first time in the morning, Paul at noon, and Simon in the evening; then that to-day he again sees Peter in the morning. It is evident, from II. Prop. xviii., that, as soon as he sees the morning light, he will imagine that the sun will traverse the same parts of the sky, as it did when he saw it on the preceding day; in other words, he will imagine a complete day, and, together with his imagination of the morning, he will imagine Peter; with noon, he will imagine Paul; and with evening, he will imagine Simon — that is, he will imagine the existence of Paul and Simon in relation to a future time; on the other hand, if he sees Simon in the evening, he will refer Peter and Paul to a past time, by imagining them simultaneously with the imagination of a past time. If it should at any time happen, that on some other evening the child should see James instead of Simon, he will, on the following morning, associate with his imagination of evening sometimes Simon, sometimes James, not both together: for the child is supposed to have seen, at evening, one or other of them, not both together. His imagination will therefore waver; and, with the imagination of future evenings, he will associate first one, then the other — that is, he will imagine them in the future, neither of them as certain, but both as contingent. This wavering of the imagination will be the same, if the imagination be concerned with things which we thus contemplate, standing in relation to time past or time present: consequently, we may imagine things as contingent, whether they be referred to time present, past, or future.

Corollary II.—It is in the nature of reason to perceive things under a certain form of eternity (*sub quâdam æternitatis specie*).

Proof.—It is in the nature of reason to regard things, not as contingent, but as necessary (II. xliv.). Reason perceives this necessity of things (II. xli.) truly — that is (I. Ax. vi.), as it is in itself. But (I. xvi.) this necessity of things is the very necessity of the eternal nature of God; therefore, it is in the nature of reason to regard things under this form of eternity. We may add that the bases of reason are the notions (II. xxxviii.) which answer to things common to all, and which (II xxxvii.) do not answer to the essence of any particular thing: which must therefore be conceived without any relation to time, under a certain form of eternity.

PROP. XLV. Every idea of everybody, or of every particular thing actually existing, necessarily involves the eternal and infinite essence of God.

Proof.— The idea of a particular thing actually existing necessarily involves both the existence and the essence of the said thing (II. viii.). Now particular things cannot be conceived without God (I. xv.); but, inasmuch as (II. vi.) they have God for their cause, in so far as he is regarded under the attribute of which the things in question are modes, their ideas must necessarily involve (I. Ax. iv.) the conception of the attribute of those ideas—that is (I. vi.), the eternal and infinite essence of God. Q.E.D.

Note.— By existence I do not here mean duration—that is, existence in so far as it is conceived abstractedly, and as a certain form of quantity. I am speaking of the very nature of existence, which is assigned to particular things, because they follow in infinite numbers and in infinite ways from the eternal necessity of God's nature (I. xvi.). I am speaking, I repeat, of the very existence of particular things, in so far as they are in God. For although each particular thing be conditioned by another particular thing to exist in a given way, yet the force whereby each particular thing perseveres in existing follows from the eternal necessity of God's nature (*cf.* I. xxiv., Coroll.).

PROP. XLVI. The knowledge of the eternal and infinite essence of God which every idea involves is adequate and perfect.

Proof.— The proof of the last proposition is universal; and whether a thing be considered as a part or a whole, the idea thereof, whether of the whole or of a part (by the last Prop.), will involve God's eternal and infinite essence. Wherefore, that, which gives knowledge of the eternal and infinite essence of God, is common to all, and is equally in the part and in the whole; therefore (II. xxxviii.) this knowledge will be adequate. Q.E.D.

PROP. XLVII. The human mind has an adequate knowledge of the eternal and infinite essence of God.

Proof.— The human mind has ideas (II. xxii.) from which (II. xxiii.) it perceives itself and its own body

(II. xix.) and external bodies (II. xvi. Coroll. I. and II. xvii.) as actually existing; therefore (II. xlv. xlvi.) it has an adequate knowledge of the eternal and infinite essence of God. Q.E.D.

Note.— Hence we see, that the infinite essence and the eternity of God are known to all. Now as all things are in God, and are conceived through God, we can from this knowledge infer many things, which we may adequately know, and we may form that third kind of knowledge of which we spoke in the note to II. xl., and of the excellence and use of which we shall have occasion to speak in Part V. Men have not so clear a knowledge of God as they have of general notions, because they are unable to imagine God as they do bodies, and also because they have associated the name of God with images of things that they are in the habit of seeing, as indeed they can hardly avoid doing, being, as they are, men, and continually affected by external bodies. Many errors, in truth, can be traced to this head, namely, that we do not apply names to things rightly. For instance, when a man says that the lines drawn from the centre of a circle to its circumference are not equal, he then, at all events, assuredly attaches a meaning to the word circle different from that assigned by mathematicians. So again, when men make mistakes in calculation, they have one set of figures in their mind, and another on the paper. If we could see into their minds, they do not make a mistake; they seem to do so, because we think that they have the same numbers in their mind as they have on the paper. If this were not so, we should not believe them to be in error, any more than I thought that a man was in error, whom I lately heard exclaiming that his entrance hall had flown into a neighbor's hen, for his meaning seemed to me sufficiently clear. Very many controversies have arisen from the fact, that men do not rightly explain their meaning, or do not rightly interpret the meaning of others. For, as a matter of fact, as they flatly contradict themselves, they assume now one side, now another, of the argument, so as to oppose the opinions, which they consider mistaken and absurd in their opponents.

PROP. XLVIII. In the mind there is no absolute or free will; but the mind is determined to wish this or that by a cause, which has also been determined by another cause, and this last by another cause, and so on to infinity.

Proof.— The mind is a fixed and definite mode of thought (II. xi.), therefore it cannot be the free cause of its actions (I. xvii. Coroll. ii.); in other words it cannot have an absolute faculty of positive or negative volition; but (by I. xxviii.) it must be determined by a cause, which has also been determined by another cause, and this last by another, etc. Q.E.D.

Note.— In the same way it is proved, that there is in the mind no absolute faculty of understanding, desiring, loving, etc. Whence it follows that these and similar faculties are either entirely fictitious, or are merely abstract or general terms, such as we are accustomed to put together from particular things. Thus the intellect and the will stand in the same relation to this or that idea, or this or that volition, as "lapidity" to this or that stone, or as "man" to Peter and Paul. The cause which leads men to consider themselves free has been set forth in the Appendix to Part I. But, before I proceed further, I would here remark that, by the will to affirm and decide, I mean the faculty, not the desire. I mean, I repeat, the faculty, whereby the mind affirms or denies what is true or false, not the desire, wherewith the mind wishes for or turns away from any given thing. After we have proved, that these faculties of ours are general notions, which cannot be distinguished from the particular instances on which they are based, we must inquire whether volitions themselves are anything besides the ideas of things. We must inquire, I say, whether there is in the mind any affirmation or negation beyond that, which the idea, in so far as it is an idea, involves. On which subject see the following proposition, and II. Def. iii., lest the idea of pictures should suggest itself. For by ideas I do not mean images such as are formed at the back of the eye, or in the midst of the brain, but the conceptions of thought.

Prop. XLIX. There is in the mind no volition or affirmation and negation, save that which an idea, inasmuch as it is an idea, involves.

Proof.— There is in the mind no absolute faculty of positive or negative volition, but only particular volitions, namely, this or that affirmation, and this or that negation. Now let us conceive a particular volition, namely the mode of thinking whereby the mind affirms, that the three interior angles of a triangle are equal to two right angles. This affirmation involves the conception or idea of a triangle, that is, without the idea of a triangle it cannot be conceived. It is the same thing to say, that the concept A must involve the concept B, as it is to say, that A cannot be conceived without B. Further, this affirmation cannot be made (II. Ax. iii) without the idea of a triangle. Therefore, this affirmation can neither be nor be conceived, without the idea of a triangle. Again, this idea of a triangle must involve this same affirmation, namely, that its three interior angles are equal to two right angles. Wherefore, and *vice versâ*, this idea of a triangle can neither be nor be conceived without this affirmation, therefore, this affirmation belongs to the essence of the idea of a triangle, and is nothing besides. What we have said of this volition (inasmuch as we have selected it at random) may be said of any other volition, namely, that it is nothing but an idea. Q.E.D.

Corollary.— Will and understanding are one and the same.

Proof.— Will and understanding are nothing beyond the individual volitions and ideas (II. xlviii. and note). But a particular volition and a particular idea are one and the same (by the foregoing Prop.); therefore, will and understanding are one and the same. Q.E.D.

Note.— We have thus removed the cause which is commonly assigned for error. For we have shown above, that falsity consists solely in the privation of knowledge involved in ideas which are fragmentary and confused. Wherefore a false idea, inasmuch as it is false, does not involve certainty. When we say, then, that a man acquiesces in what is false, and that he has no doubts on the subject, we do not say that he is certain, but only that he does not doubt, or that he acquiesces in what is false, inasmuch as there are no reasons, which should cause his imagination to waver (see II. xliv. note). Thus, although the man be assumed to acquiesce in what is false, we shall never say that he is certain. For by certainty we mean something positive (II. xliii. and note), not merely the absence of doubt.

However, in order that the foregoing proposition may be fully explained, I will draw attention to a few additional points, and I will furthermore answer the objections which may be advanced against our doctrine. Lastly, in order to remove every scruple, I have thought it worth while to point out some of the advantages, which follow therefrom. I say "some," for they will be better appreciated from what we shall set forth in the fifth part.

I begin, then, with the first point, and warn my readers to make an accurate distinction between an idea, or conception of the mind and the images of things which we imagine. It is further necessary that they should distinguish between idea and words, whereby we signify things. These three — namely, images, words, and ideas — are by many persons either entirely confused together, or not distinguished with sufficient accuracy or care, and hence people are generally in ignorance, how absolutely necessary is a knowledge of this doctrine of the will, both for philosophic purposes and for the wise ordering of life. Those who think that ideas consist in images which are formed in us by contact with external bodies, persuade themselves that the ideas of those things, whereof we can form no mental picture, are not ideas, but only figments, which we invent by the free decree of our will; they thus regard ideas as though they were inanimate pictures on a panel, and filled with this misconception, do not see that an idea, inasmuch as it is an idea, involves an affirmation or negation. Again, those who confuse words with ideas, or with the affirmation which an idea involves, think that they can wish something contrary to what they feel, affirm, or deny. This misconception will easily be laid aside by one who reflects on the nature of knowledge, and seeing that it in no wise involves the conception of extension, will therefore clearly understand, that an idea (being a mode of thinking) does not consist in the image of anything, nor in words. The essence of words and images is put together by bodily motions, which in no wise involve the conception of thought.

These few words on this subject will suffice: I will therefore pass on to consider the objections which may be raised against our doctrine. Of these, the first is advanced by those, who think that the will has a wider scope than the understanding, and that therefore it is different therefrom. The reason for their holding the belief, that the will has wider scope than the understanding, is that they assert, that they have no need of an increase in their faculty of assent, that is of affirmation or negation, in order to assent to an infinity of things which we do not perceive, but that they have need of an increase in their faculty of understanding. The will is thus distinguished from the intellect, the latter being finite and the former infinite. Secondly, it may be objected that experience seems to teach us especially clearly, that we are able to suspend our judgment before assenting to things which we perceive, this is confirmed by the fact that no one is said to be deceived; in so far as he perceives anything, but only in so far as he assents or dissents.

For instance, he who feigns a winged horse, does not therefore admit that a winged horse exists; that is, he is not deceived, unless he admits in addition that a winged horse does exist. Nothing therefore seems to be taught more clearly by experience, than that the will or faculty of assent is free and different from the faculty of understanding. Thirdly, it may be objected that one affirmation does not apparently contain more reality than another; in other words, that we do not seem to need for affirming, that what is true is true, any greater power than for affirming, that what is false is true. We have, however, seen that one idea has more reality or perfection than another, for as objects are some more excellent than others, so also are the ideas of them some more excel-

lent than others; this also seems to point to a difference
between the understanding and the will. Fourthly, it
may be objected, if man does not act from free will,
what will happen if the incentives to action are equally
balanced as in the case of Buridan's ass? Will he perish of hunger and thirst? If I say that he would, I shall
seem to have in my thoughts an ass or the statue of a
man rather than actual man. If I say that he would not,
he would then determine his own action, and would consequently possess the faculty of going and doing whatever
he liked. Other objections might also be raised, but, as
I am not bound to put in evidence everything that any
one may dream, I will only set myself to the task of refuting those I have mentioned, and that as briefly as
possible.

To the FIRST objection I answer, that I admit that the
will has a wider scope than the understanding, if by the
understanding be meant only clear and distinct ideas;
but I deny that the will has a wider scope than the perceptions, and the faculty of forming conceptions; nor do
I see why the faculty of volition should be called infinite,
any more than the faculty of feeling: for, as we are
able by the same faculty of volition to affirm an infinite
number of things (one after the other, for we cannot
affirm an infinite number simultaneously), so also can
we, by the same faculty of feeling, feel or perceive (in
succession) an infinite number of bodies. If it be said
that there is an infinite number of things which we cannot perceive, I answer, that we cannot attain to such
things by any thinking, nor, consequently, by any faculty
of volition. But, it may still be urged, if God wished
to bring it about that we should perceive them, he would
be obliged to endow us with a greater faculty of perception, but not a greater faculty of volition than we
have already. This is the same as to say that, if God
wished to bring it about that we should understand an
infinite number of other entities, it would be necessary
for him to give us a greater understanding, but not a
more universal idea of entity than that which we have
already, in order to grasp such infinite entities. We have

shown that will is a universal entity or idea, whereby we explain all particular volitions — in other words, that which is common to all such volitions.

As, then, our opponents maintain that this idea, common or universal to all volitions, is a faculty, it is little to be wondered at that they assert, that such a faculty extends itself into the infinite, beyond the limits of the understanding: for what is universal is predicated alike of one, of many, and of an infinite number of individuals.

To the SECOND objection I reply by denying, that we have a free power of suspending our judgment; for, when we say that any one suspends his judgment, we merely mean that he sees, that he does not perceive the matter in question adequately. Suspension of judgment is, therefore, strictly speaking, a perception, and not free will. In order to illustrate the point, let us suppose a boy imagining a horse, and perceiving nothing else. Inasmuch as this imagination involves the existence of the horse (II. xvii. Coroll.), and the boy does not perceive anything which would exclude the existence of the horse, he will necessarily regard the horse as present; he will not be able to doubt of its existence, although he be not certain thereof. We have daily experience of such a state of things in dreams; and I do not suppose that there is any one, who would maintain that, while he is dreaming, he has the free power of suspending his judgment concerning the things in his dream, and bringing it about that he should not dream those things, which he dreams that he sees; yet it happens, notwithstanding, that even in dreams we suspend our judgment, namely, when we dream that we are dreaming.

Further, I grant that no one can be deceived, so far as actual perception extends — that is, I grant that the mind's imaginations, regarded in themselves, do not involve error (II. xvii., note); but I deny, that a man does not, in the act of perception, make any affirmation. For what is the perception of a winged horse, save affirming that a horse has wings? If the mind could perceive nothing else but the winged horse, it would regard the same as present to itself; it would have no reasons for doubting its existence, nor any faculty of dissent, unless the imagination of a winged horse be joined to an idea which precludes the existence of the said horse, or unless the mind perceives that the idea which it possesses of a winged horse is inadequate, in which case it will either necessarily deny the existence of such a horse, or will necessarily be in doubt on the subject.

I think that I have anticipated my answer to the THIRD objection, namely, that the will is something universal which is predicated of all ideas, and that it only signifies that which is common to all ideas, namely, an affirmation, whose adequate essence must, therefore, in so for as it is thus conceived in the abstract, be in every idea, and be, in this respect alone, the same in all, not in so far as it is considered as constituting the idea's essence: for, in this respect, particular affirmations differ one from the other, as much as do ideas. For instance, the affirmation which involves the idea of a circle, differs from that which involves the idea of a triangle, as much as the idea of a circle differs from the idea of a triangle.

Further, I absolutely deny, that we are in need of an equal power of thinking, to affirm that that which is true is true, and to affirm that that which is false is true. These two affirmations, if we regard the mind, are in the same relation to one another as being and not being; for there is nothing positive in ideas, which constitutes the actual reality of falsehood (II. xxxv. note, and xlvii. note).

We must therefore conclude that we are easily deceived, when we confuse universals with singulars, and the entities of reason and abstractions with realities. As for the FOURTH objection, I am quite ready to admit, that a man placed in the equilibrium described (namely, as perceiving nothing but hunger and thirst, a certain food and a certain drink, each equally distant from him) would die of hunger and thirst. If I am asked, whether such an one should not rather be considered an ass than a man; I answer, that I do not know, neither do I know how a man should be considered, who hangs himself, or how we should consider children, fools, madmen, etc.

It remains to point out the advantages of a knowledge of this doctrine as bearing on conduct, and this may be easily gathered from what has been said. The doctrine is good.

1. Inasmuch as it teaches us to act solely according to the decree of God, and to be partakers in the Divine nature, and so much the more, as we perform more perfect actions and more and more understand God. Such a doctrine not only completely tranquillizes our spirit, but also shows us where our highest happiness and blessedness is, namely, solely in the knowledge of God, whereby we are led to act only as love and piety shall bid us. We may thus clearly understand, how far astray from a true estimate of virtue are those who expect to be decorated by God with high rewards for their virtue, and their best actions, as for having endured the direst slavery; as if virtue and the service of God were not in itself happiness and perfect freedom.

2. Inasmuch as it teaches us, how we ought to conduct ourselves with respect to the gifts of fortune, or matters which are not in our own power, and do not follow from our nature. For it shows us that we should await and endure fortune's smiles or frowns with an equal mind, seeing that all things follow from the eternal decree of God by the same necessity, as it follows from the essence of a triangle, that the three angles are equal to two right angles.

3. This doctrine raises social life, inasmuch as it teaches us to hate no man, neither to despise, to deride, to envy, or to be angry with any. Further, as it tells us that each should be content with his own, and helpful to his neighbor, not from any womanish pity, favor, or superstition, but solely by the guidance of reason, according as the time and occasion demand, as I will show in Part III.

4. Lastly, this doctrine confers no small advantage on the commonwealth; for it teaches how citizens should be governed and led, not so as to become slaves, but so that they may freely do whatsoever things are best.

I have thus fulfilled the promise made at the beginning of this note, and I thus bring the second part of my treatise to a close. I think I have therein explained the nature and properties of the human mind at sufficient length, and, considering the difficulty of the subject, with sufficient clearness. I have laid a foundation, whereon may be raised many excellent conclusions of the highest utility and most necessary to be known, as will, in what follows, be partly made plain.

PART III.

ON THE ORIGIN AND NATURE OF THE EMOTIONS.

MOST writers on the emotions and on human conduct seem to be treating rather of matters outside nature than of natural phenomena following nature's general laws. They appear to conceive man to be situated in nature as a kingdom within a kingdom: for they believe that he disturbs rather than follows nature's order, that he has absolute control over his actions, and that he is determined solely by himself. They attribute human infirmities and fickleness, not to the power of nature in general, but to some mysterious flaw in the nature of man, which accordingly they bemoan, deride, despise, or, as usually happens, abuse: he, who succeeds in hitting off the weakness of the human mind more eloquently or more acutely than his fellows is looked upon as a seer. Still there has been no lack of very excellent men (to whose toil and industry I confess myself much indebted), who have written many noteworthy things concerning the right way of life, and have given much sage advice to mankind. But no one, so far as I know, has defined the nature and strength of the emotions, and the power of the mind against them for their restraint.

I do not forget, that the illustrious Descartes, though he believed, that the mind has absolute power over its actions, strove to explain human emotions by their primary causes, and, at the same time, to point out a way, by which the mind might attain to absolute dominion over them. However, in my opinion, he accomplishes nothing beyond a display of the acuteness of his own great intellect, as I will show in the proper place. For the present I wish to revert to those, who would rather

127

abuse or deride human emotions than understand them. Such persons will doubtless think it strange that I should attempt to treat of human vice and folly geometrically, and should wish to set forth with rigid reasoning those matters which they cry out against as repugnant to reason, frivolous, absurd, and dreadful. However, such is my plan. Nothing comes to pass in nature, which can be set down to a flaw therein; for nature is always the same, and everywhere one and the same in her efficacy and power of action; that is, nature's laws and ordinances, whereby all things come to pass and change from one form to another, are everywhere and always the same; so that there should be one and the same method of understanding the nature of all things whatsoever, namely, through nature's universal laws and rules. Thus the passions of hatred, anger, envy, and so on, considered in themselves, follow from this same necessity and efficacy of nature; they answer to certain definite causes, through which they are understood, and possess certain properties as worthy of being known as the properties of anything else, whereof the contemplation in itself affords us delight. I shall, therefore, treat of the nature and strength of the emotions according to the same method, as I employed heretofore in my investigations concerning God and the mind. I shall consider human actions and desires in exactly the same manner, as though I were concerned with lines, planes, and solids.

Definitions.

I. By an ADEQUATE cause, I mean a cause through which its effect can be clearly and distinctly perceived. By an INADEQUATE or partial cause, I mean a cause through which, by itself, its effect cannot be understood.

II. I say that we ACT when anything takes place, either within us or externally to us, whereof we are the adequate cause; that is (by the foregoing definition) when through our nature something takes place within us or externally to us, which can through our nature alone be clearly and distinctly understood. On the other hand, I say that we are passive as regards something when that something takes place within us, or follows from our nature externally, we being only the partial cause.

III. By EMOTION I mean the modifications of the body, whereby the active power of the said body is increased or diminished, aided or constrained, and also the ideas of such modifications.

N. B. If we can be the adequate cause of any of these modifications, I then call the emotion an activity, otherwise I call it a passion, or state wherein the mind is passive.

POSTULATES.

I. The human body can be affected in many ways, whereby its power of activity is increased or diminished, and also in other ways which do not render its power of activity either greater or less.

N. B. This postulate or axiom rests on Postulate i. and Lemmas v. and vii., which see after II. xiii.

II. The human body can undergo many changes, and, nevertheless, retain the impressions or traces of objects (*cf.* II. Post. v.) and, consequently, the same images of things (see note II. xvii.).

PROP. I. Our mind is in certain cases active, and in certain cases passive. In so far as it has adequate ideas it is necessarily active, and in so far as it has inadequate ideas, it is necessarily passive.

Proof.— In every human mind there are some adequate ideas, and some ideas that are fragmentary and confused (II. xl. note). Those ideas which are adequate in the mind are adequate also in God, inasmuch as he constitutes the essence of the mind (II. xl. Coroll.), and those which are inadequate in the mind are likewise (by the same Coroll.) adequate in God, not inasmuch as he contains in himself the essence of the given mind alone, but as he, at the same time, contains the minds of other things. Again, from any given idea some effect must necessarily follow (I. 36); of this effect God is the adequate cause (III. Def. i.) not inasmuch as he is infinite, but inasmuch as he is conceived as affected by the given idea (II. ix.). But of that effect whereof God is the cause, inasmuch as he is affected by an idea which is ade-

quate in a given mind, of that effect, I repeat, the mind
in question is the adequate cause (II. xi. Coroll.).
Therefore our mind, in so far as it has adequate ideas
(III. Def. ii.), is in certain cases necessarily active; this
was our first point. Again, whatsoever necessarily follows from the idea which is adequate in God, not by
virtue of his possessing in himself the mind of one man
only, but by virtue of his containing, together with the
mind of that one man, the minds of other things also,
of such an effect (II. xi. Coroll.) the mind of the given
man is not an adequate, but only a partial cause; thus
(III. Def. ii.) the mind, inasmuch as it has inadequate
ideas, is in certain cases necessarily passive; this was our
second point. Therefore our mind, etc. Q. E. D.

Corollary.— Hence it follows that the mind is more or
less liable to be acted upon, in proportion as it possesses inadequate ideas, and contrariwise, is more or less active in proportion as it possesses adequate ideas.

PROP. II. Body cannot determine mind to think, neither
can mind determine body to motion or rest or any state
different from these, if such there be.

Proof.— All modes of thinking have for their cause
God, by virtue of his being a thinking thing, and not by
virtue of his being displayed under any other attribute
(II. vi.). That, therefore, which determines the mind
to thought is a mode of thought, and not a mode of extension; that is (II. Def. i.), it is not body. This was
our first point. Again, the motion and rest of a body
must arise from another body, which has also been determined to a state of motion or rest by a third body,
and absolutely everything which takes place in a body
must spring from God, in so far as he is regarded as
affected by some mode of extension, and not by some
mode of thought (II. vi.); that is, it cannot spring from
the mind, which is a mode of thought. This was our
second point. Therefore body cannot determine mind,
etc. Q. E. D.

Note.— This is made more clear by what was said in
the note to II. vii., namely, that mind and body are one
and the same thing, conceived first under the attribute

of thought, secondly, under the attribute of extension. Thus it follows that the order or concatenation of things is identical, whether nature be conceived under the one attribute or the other; consequently the order of states of activity and passivity in our body is simultaneous in nature with the order of states of activity and passivity in the mind. The same conclusion is evident from the manner in which we proved II. xii.

Nevertheless, though such is the case, and though there be no further room for doubt, I can scarcely believe, until the fact is proved by experience, that men can be induced to consider the question calmly and fairly, so firmly are they conceived that it is merely at the bidding of the mind that the body is set in motion or at rest, or performs a variety of actions depending solely on the mind's will or the exercise of thought. However, no one has hitherto laid down the limits to the powers of the body, that is, no one has as yet been taught by experience what the body can accomplish solely by the laws of nature, in so far as she is regarded as extension. No one hitherto has gained such an accurate knowledge of the bodily mechanism, that he can explain all its functions; nor need I call attention to the fact that many actions are observed in the lower animals, which far transcend human sagacity, and that somnambulists do many things in their sleep, which they would not venture to do when awake: these instances are enough to show, that the body can by the sole laws of its nature do many things which the mind wonders at.

Again, no one knows how or by what means the mind moves the body, nor how many various degrees of motion it can impart to the body, nor how quickly it can move it. Thus, when men say that this or that physical action has its origin in the mind, which latter has dominion over the body, they are using words without meaning, or are confessing in specious phraseology that they are ignorant of the cause of the said action, and do not wonder at it.

But, they will say, whether we know or do not know the means whereby the mind acts on the body, we have, at any rate, experience of the fact that unless the human mind is in a fit state to think, the body remains inert. Moreover, we have experience, that the mind alone can determine whether we speak or are silent, and a variety of similar states which, accordingly, we say depend on the mind's decree. But, as to the first point, I ask such objectors, whether experience does not also teach, that if the body be inactive the mind is simultaneously unfitted for thinking? For when the body is at rest in sleep, the mind simultaneously is in a state of torpor also, and has no power of thinking, such as it possesses when the body is awake. Again, I think everyone's experience will confirm the statement, that the mind is not at all times equally fit for thinking on a given subject, but according as the body is more or less fitted for being stimulated by the image of this or that object, so also is the mind more or less fitted for contemplating the said object.

But, it will be urged, it is impossible that solely from the laws of nature considered as extended substance, we should be able to deduce the causes of buildings, pictures, and things of that kind, which are produced only by human art; nor would the human body, unless it were determined and led by the mind, be capable of building a single temple. However, I have just pointed out that the objectors cannot fix the limits of the body's power, or say what can be concluded from a consideration of its sole nature, whereas they have experience of many things being accomplished solely by the laws of nature, which they would never have believed possible except under the direction of mind: such are the actions performed by somnambulists while asleep, and wondered at by their performers when awake. I would further call attention to the mechanism of the human body which far surpasses in complexity all that has been put together by human art, not to repeat what I have already shown, namely, that from nature, under whatever attribute she be considered, infinite results follow. As for the second objection, I submit that the world would be much happier, if men were as fully able to keep silence as they are to speak. Experience abundantly shows that men can govern anything more easily than their tongues, and restrain anything more easily than their appetites; whence it comes about that many believe, that we are only free in respect to objects which we moderately desire, because our desire for such can easily be controlled by the thought of something else frequently remembered, but that we are by no means free in respect to what we seek with violent emotion, for our desire cannot then be allayed with the remembrance of anything else. However, unless such persons had proved by experience that we do many things which we afterward repent of, and again that we often, when assailed by contrary emotions, see the better and follow the worse, there would be nothing to prevent their believing that we are free in all things. Thus an infant believes that of its own free will it desires milk, an angry child believes that it freely desires vengeance, a timid child believes that it freely desires to run away; further, a drunken man believes that he utters from the free decision of his mind words which, when he is sober, he would willingly have withheld: thus, too, a delirious man, a garrulous woman, a child, and others of like complexion, believe that they speak from the free decision of their mind, when they are in reality unable to restrain their impulse to talk. Experience teaches us no less clearly than reason, that men believe themselves to be free, simply because they are conscious of their actions, and unconscious of the causes whereby those actions are determined; and, further, it is plain that the dictates of the mind are but another name for the appetites, and therefore vary according to the varying state of the body. Every one shapes his actions according to his emotion, those who are assailed by conflicting emotions know not what they wish; those who are not attacked by any emotion are readily swayed this way or that. All these considerations clearly show that a mental decision and a bodily appetite, or determined state, are simultaneous, or rather are one and the same thing, which we call decision, when it is regarded under and explained through the attribute of thought, and a conditioned state, when it is regarded under the attribute of extension, and deduced from the laws of motion and rest. This will appear yet more plainly in the sequel. For the present I wish to call attention to another point, namely, that we cannot act by the decision of the mind, unless we have a remembrance of having done so. For instance, we cannot say a word without remembering that we have done so. Again, it is not within the free power of the mind to remember or forget a thing at will. Therefore the freedom of the mind must in any case be limited to the power of uttering or not uttering something which it remembers. But when we dream that we speak, we believe that we speak from a free decision of the mind, yet we do not speak, or, if we do, it is by a spontaneous motion of the body. Again, we dream that we are concealing something, and we seem to act from the same decision of the mind as that, whereby we keep silence when awake concerning something we know. Lastly, we dream that from the free decision of our mind we do something, which we should not dare to do when awake.

Now I should like to know whether there be in the mind two sorts of decisions, one sort illusive, and the other sort free? If our folly does not carry us so far as this, we must necessarily admit, that the decision of the mind which is believed to be free, is not distinguishable from the imagination or memory, and is nothing more than the affirmation, which an idea, by virtue of being an idea, necessarily involves (II. xlix.). Wherefore these decisions of the mind arise in the mind by the same necessity, as the ideas of things actually existing. Therefore, those who believe, that they speak or keep silence or act in any way from the free decision of their mind, do but dream with their eyes open.

Prop. III. The activities of the mind arise solely from adequate ideas; the passive states of the mind depend solely on inadequate ideas.

Proof.—The first element, which constitutes the essence of the mind, is nothing else but the idea of the actually existent body (II. xi. and xiii.), which (II. xv.) is compounded of many other ideas, whereof some are adequate

and some inadequate (II. xxix. Coroll., II. xxxviii Coroll.).
Whatsoever therefore follows from the nature of mind,
and has mind for its proximate cause, through which it
must be understood, must necessarily follow either from
an adequate or from an inadequate idea.   But in so far
as the mind (III. i.) has inadequate ideas, it is necessarily
passive: wherefore the activities of the mind follow solely
from adequate ideas, and accordingly the mind is only
passive in so far as it has inadequate ideas.   Q. E. D.

Note.—Thus we see, that passive states, are not attributed to the mind, except in so far as it contains something involving negation, or in so far as it is regarded as
a part of nature which cannot be clearly and distinctly
perceived through itself without other parts: I could thus
show, that passive states are attributed to individual
things in the same way that they are attributed to
the mind, and that they cannot otherwise be perceived,
but my purpose is solely to treat of the human mind.

PROP. IV. Nothing can be destroyed, except by a cause
external to itself.

Proof.—This proposition is self-evident, for the definition of anything affirms the essence of that thing, but
does not negative it; in other words, it postulates the
essence of the thing, but does not take it away.   So long
therefore as we regard only the thing itself, without
taking into account external causes, we shall not be able
to find in it anything which could destroy it.   Q. E. D.

PROP. V. Things are naturally contrary, that is, cannot
exist in the same object, in so far as one is capable of
destroying the other.

Proof.—If they could agree together or coexist in the
same object, there would then be in the said object
something which could destroy it; but this, by the foregoing proposition, is absurd; therefore things, etc.   Q. E. D.

PROP. VI. Everything, in so far as it is in itself,
endeavors to persist in its own being.

Proof.—Individual things are modes whereby the attributes of God are expressed in a given determinate manner (I. xxv. Coroll.), that is (I. xxxiv.), they are things
which express in a given determinate manner the power

of God, whereby God is and acts; now no thing contains in itself anything whereby it can be destroyed, or which can take away its existence (III. iv.); but contrariwise it is opposed to all that could take away its existence (III. v.). Therefore, in so far as it can, and in so far as it is in itself, it endeavors to persist in its own being. Q.E.D.

PROP. VII. The endeavor, wherewith everything endeavors to persist in its own being, is nothing else but the actual essence of the thing in question.

Proof.— From the given essence of anything certain consequences necessarily follow (I. xxxvi.), nor have things any power save such as necessarily follows from their nature as determined (I. xxix.); wherefore the power of any given thing, or the endeavor whereby, either alone or with other things, it acts, or endeavors to act, that is (III. vi.), the power or endeavor, wherewith it endeavors to persist in its own being, is nothing else but the given or actual essence of the thing in question. Q.E.D.

PROP. VIII. The endeavor, whereby a thing endeavors to persist in its being, involves no finite time, but an indefinite time.

Proof.— If it involved a limited time, which should determine the duration of the thing, it would then follow solely from that power whereby the thing exists, that the thing could not exist beyond the limits of that time, but that it must be destroyed; but this (III. iv.) is absurd. Wherefore the endeavor wherewith a thing exists involves no definite time; but, contrariwise, since (III. iv.) it will, by the same power whereby it already exists, always continue to exist, unless it be destroyed by some external cause, this endeavor involves an indefinite time.

PROP. IX. The mind, both in so far as it has clear and distinct ideas, and also in so far as it has confused ideas, endeavors to persist in its being for an indefinite period, and of this endeavor it is conscious.

Proof.— The essence of the mind is constituted by adequate and inadequate ideas (III. iii.); therefore (III. vii.), both in so far as it possesses the former, and in so far as it possesses the latter, it endeavors to persist in its own being, and that for an indefinite time (III. viii.). Now as the mind (II. xxiii.) is necessarily conscious of itself through the ideas of the modifications of the body, the mind is therefore (III. vii.) concious of its own endeavor.

Note.— This endeavor, when referred solely to the mind, is called WILL, when referred to the mind and body in conjunction it is called APPETITE; it is, in fact, nothing else but man's essence, from the nature of which necessarily follow all those results which tend to its preservation; and which man has thus been determined to perform.

Further, between appetite and desire there is no difference, except that the term desire is generally applied to men, in so far as they are conscious of their appetite, and may accordingly be thus defined: DESIRE IS APPETITE WITH CONSCIOUSNESS THEREOF. It is thus plain from what has been said, that in no case do we strive for, wish for, long for, or desire anything, because we deem it to be good, but on the other hand we deem a thing to be good, because we strive for it, wish for it, long for it, or desire it.

PROP. X. An idea, which excludes the existence of our body, cannot be postulated in our mind, but is contrary thereto.

Proof.— Whatsoever can destroy our body, cannot be postulated therein (III. v.). Therefore, neither can the idea of such a thing occur in God, in so far as he has the idea of our body (II. ix. Coroll.); that is (II. xi. xiii.), the idea of that thing cannot be postulated as in our mind, but contrariwise, since (II. xi. xiii.,) the first element, that constitutes the essence of the mind, is the idea of the human body as actually existing, it follows that the first and chief endeavor of our mind is the endeavor to affirm the existence of our body; thus, an idea, which negatives the existence of our body, is contrary to our mind, etc. Q.E.D.

PROP. XI. Whatsoever increases or diminishes, helps or hinders the power of activity in our body, the idea thereof increases or diminishes, helps or hinders the power of thought in our mind.

Proof.— This proposition is evident from II. vii. or from II. xiv.

Note. — Thus we see, that the mind can undergo many changes, and can pass sometimes to a state of greater perfection, sometimes to a state of lesser perfection. These passive states of transition explain to us the emotions of pleasure and pain. By PLEASURE therefore in the following propositions I shall signify A PASSIVE STATE WHEREIN THE MIND PASSES TO A GREATER PERFECTION. By PAIN I shall signify A PASSIVE STATE WHEREIN THE MIND PASSES TO A LESSER PERFECTION. Further, the emotion of pleasure in reference to the body and mind together I shall call STIMULATION (*titillatio*) or MERRIMENT (*hilaritas*), the emotion of pain in the same relation I shall call SUFFERING or MELANCHOLY. But we must bear in mind, that stimulation and suffering are attributed to man, when one part of his nature is more affected than the rest, merriment and melancholy, when all parts are alike affected. What I mean by desire I have explained in the note to Prop. ix. of this part; beyond these three I recognize no other primary emotion; I will show as I proceed, that all other emotions arise from these three. But, before I go further, I should like here to explain at greater length Prop. x. of this part, in order that we may clearly understand how one idea is contrary to another. In the note to II. xvii. we showed that the idea, which constitutes the essence of mind, involves the existence of body, so long as the body itself exists. Again, it follows from what we have pointed out in the Coroll. to II. viii., that the present existence of our mind depends solely on the fact, that the mind involves the actual existence of the body. Lastly, we showed (II. xvii. xviii. and note) that the power of the mind, whereby it imagines and remembers things, also depends on the fact, that it involves the actual existence of the body. Whence it follows, that the present existence of the mind and its power of imagining are removed, as soon as the mind ceases to affirm the present existence of the body. Now the cause, why the mind ceases to affirm this existence of the body, cannot be the mind itself (III. iv.), nor again the fact that the body ceases to exist.   For (by II. vi.) the cause, why the mind affirms the existence of the body, is not that the body began to exist; therefore, for the same reason, it does not cease to affirm the existence of the body, because the body ceases to exist; but (II. xvii.) this result follows from another idea, which excludes the present existence of our body and, consequently of our mind, and which is therefore contrary to the idea constituting the essence of our mind.

PROP. XII. The mind, as far as it can, endeavors to conceive those things, which increase or help the power of activity in the body.

Proof.— So long as the human body is affected in a mode, which involves the nature of any external body, the human mind will regard that external body as present (II. xvii.), and consequently (II. vii.), so long as the human mind regards an external body as present, that is (II. xvii. note), conceives it, the human body is affected in a mode, which involves the nature of the said external body; thus so long as the mind conceives things, which increase or help the power of activity in our body, the body is affected in modes which increase or help its power of activity (III. Post. i.); consequently (III. xi.) the mind's power of thinking is for that period increased or helped.   Thus (III. vi. ix.) the mind, as far as it can, endeavors to imagine such things.   Q.E.D.

PROP. XIII. When the mind conceives things which diminish or hinder the body's power of activity, it endeavors, as far as possible, to remember things which exclude the existence of the first-named things.

Proof.— So long as the mind conceives anything of the kind alluded to, the power of the mind and body is diminished or constrained (*cf.* III. xii. Proof); nevertheless it will continue to conceive it, until the mind conceives something else, which excludes the present existence thereof (II. xvii.); that is (as I have just shown), the power of the mind and of the body is diminished, or constrained, until the mind conceives something else, which excludes the existence of the former thing conceived: therefore the mind (III. ix.), as far as it can, will endeavor to conceive or remember the latter. Q. E. D.

Corollary.—Hence it follows, that the mind shrinks from conceiving those things, which diminish or constrain the power of itself and of the body.

Note.—From what has been said we may clearly understand the nature of Love and Hate. LOVE is nothing else but PLEASURE ACCOMPANIED BY THE IDEA OF AN EXTERNAL CAUSE: HATE is nothing else but PAIN ACCOMPANIED BY THE IDEA OF AN EXTERNAL CAUSE. We further see, that he who loves necessarily endeavors to have, and to keep present to him, the object of his love; while he who hates endeavors to remove and destroy the object of his hatred. But I will treat of these matters at more length hereafter.

PROP. XIV. If the mind has once been affected by two emotions at the same time, it will, whenever it is afterward affected by one of the two, be also affected by the other.

Proof.—If the human body has once been affected by two bodies at once, whenever afterward the mind conceives one of them, it will straightway remember the other also (II. xviii.). But the mind's conceptions indicate rather the emotions of our body than the nature of external bodies (II. xvi. Coroll. ii.); therefore, if the body, and consequently the mind (III. Def. iii.) has been once affected by two emotions at the same time, it will, whenever it is afterward affected by one of the two, be also affected by the other.

PROP. XV. Anything can accidentally be the cause of pleasure, pain, or desire.

Proof.—Let it be granted that the mind is simultaneously affected by two emotions, of which one neither increases nor diminishes its power of activity, and the other does either increase or diminish the said power (III. Post. i.). From the foregoing proposition it is evident that, whenever the mind is afterward affected by the former, through its true cause, which (by hypothesis) neither increases nor diminishes its power of action, it will be at the same time affected by the latter, which does increase or diminish its power of activity, that is (III. xi. note), it will be affected with pleasure or pain. Thus the former of the two emotions will, not through itself, but accidentally, be the cause of pleasure or pain. In the same way also it can be easily shown, that a thing may be accidentally the cause of desire. Q. E. D.

Corollary.—Simply from the fact that we have regarded a thing with the emotion of pleasure or pain, though that thing be not the efficient cause of the emotion, we can either love or hate it.

Proof.—For from this fact alone it arises (III. xiv.), that the mind afterward conceiving the said thing is affected with the emotion of pleasure or pain, that is (III. xi. note), according as the power of the mind and body may be increased or diminished, etc.; and consequently (III. xii.), according as the mind may desire or shrink from the conception of it (III. xiii. Coroll.), in other words (III. xiii. note), according as it may love or hate the same.   Q. E. D.

Note.—Hence we understand how it may happen, that we love or hate a thing without any cause for our emotion being known to us; merely, as the phrase is, from SYMPATHY or ANTIPATHY. We should refer to the same category those objects, which affect us pleasurably or painfully, simply because they resemble other objects which affect us in the same way. This I will show in the next proposition. I am aware that certain authors, who were the first to introduce these terms "sympathy" and "antipathy," wished to signify thereby some occult qualities in things; nevertheless I think we may be permitted to use the same terms to indicate known or manifest qualities.

PROP. XVI. Simply from the fact that we conceive that a given object has some point of resemblance with another object which is wont to affect the mind pleasurably or painfully, although the point of resemblance be not the efficient cause of the said emotions, we shall still regard the first-named object with love or hate.

Proof.—The point of resemblance was in the object (by

hypothesis), when we regarded it with pleasure or pain, thus (III. xiv.), when the mind is affected by the image thereof, it will straightway be affected by one or the other emotion, and consequently the thing, which we perceive to have the same point of resemblance, will be accidentally (III. xv.) a cause of pleasure or pain. Thus (by the foregoing Corollary), although the point in which the two objects resemble one another be not the efficient cause of the emotion, we shall still regard the first-named object with love or hate. Q.E.D.

PROP. XVII. If we conceive that a thing which is wont to affect us painfully, has any point of resemblance with another thing which is wont to affect us with an equally strong emotion of pleasure, we shall hate the first-named thing, and at the same time we shall love it.

Proof.— The given thing is (by hypothesis) in itself a cause of pain, and (III. xiii. note), in so far as we imagine it with this emotion, we shall hate it: further, inasmuch as we conceive that it has some point of resemblance to something else, which is wont to affect us with an equally strong emotion of pleasure, we shall with an equally strong impulse of pleasure love it (III. xvi.); thus we shall both hate and love the same thing. Q.E.D.

Note.— This disposition of the mind, which arises from two contrary emotions, is called VACILLATION; it stands to the emotions in the same relation as doubt does to the imagination (II. xliv. note); vacillation and doubt do not differ one from the other except as greater differs from less. But we must bear in mind that I have deduced this vacillation from causes, which give rise through themselves to one of the emotions, and to the other accidentally. I have done this, in order that they might be more easily deduced from what went before; but I do not deny that vacillation of the disposition generally arises from an object, which is the efficient cause of both emotions. The human body is composed (II. Post. i.) of a variety of individual parts of different nature, and may therefore (Ax. i. after Lemma iii. after II. xiii.) be affected in a variety of different ways by one and the same body; and contrariwise, as one and the same thing can be affected

In many ways, it can also in many different ways affect one and the same part of the body. Hence we can easily conceive, that one and the same object may be the cause of many and conflicting emotions.

PROP. XVIII. A man is as much affected pleasurably or painfully by the image of a thing past or future as by the image of a thing present.

Proof.—So long as a man is affected by the image of anything, he will regard that thing as present, even though it be non-existent (II. xvii. and Coroll.), he will not conceive it as past or future, except in so far as its image is joined to the image of time past or future (II. xliv. note). Wherefore the image of a thing, regarded in itself alone, is identical, whether it be referred to time past, time future, or time present; that is (II. xvi. Coroll.), the disposition or emotion of the body is identical, whether the image be of a thing past, future, or present. Thus the emotion of pleasure or pain is the same, whether the image be of a thing past or future. Q. E. D.

Note I.—I call a thing past or future, according as we either have been or shall be affected thereby. For instance, according as we have seen it, or are about to see it, according as it has recreated us, or will recreate us, according as it has harmed us, or will harm us. For, as we thus conceive it, we affirm its existence; that is, the body is affected by no emotion which excludes the existence of the thing, and therefore (II. xvii.) the body is affected by the image of the thing, in the same way as if the thing were actually present. However, as it generally happens that those, who have had many experiences, vacillate, so long as they regard a thing as future or past, and are usually in doubt about its issue (II. xliv. note); it follows that the emotions which arise from similar images of things are not so constant, but are generally disturbed by the images of other things, until men become assured of the issue.

Note II.—From what has just been said, we understand what is meant by the terms Hope, Fear, Confidence, Despair, Joy, and Disappointment. HOPE is nothing else but an inconstant pleasure, arising from the image of something future or past, whereof we do not yet know the issue. FEAR on the other hand, is an inconstant pain also arising from the image of something concerning which we are in doubt. If the element of doubt be removed from these emotions, hope becomes CONFIDENCE and fear becomes DESPAIR. In other words, PLEASURE or PAIN arising from the image of something concerning which we have hoped or feared. Again, JOY is PLEASURE arising from the image of something past whereof we doubted the issue. DISAPPOINTMENT is the PAIN opposed to JOY.

PROP. XIX. He who conceives that the object of his love is destroyed will feel pain; if he conceives that it is preserved he will feel pleasure.

Proof.—The mind, as far as possible, endeavors to conceive those things which increase or help the body's power of activity (III. xii.); in other words (III. xii. note), those things which it loves. But conception is helped by those things which postulate the existence of a thing, and contrariwise is hindered by those which exclude the existence of a thing (II. xvii.); therefore the images of things, which postulate the existence of an object of love, help the mind's endeavor to conceive the object of love, in other words (III. xi. note), affect the mind pleasurably; contrariwise those things, which exclude the existence of an object of love, hinder the aforesaid mental endeavor; in other words, affect the mind painfully. He, therefore, who conceives that the object of his love is destroyed will feel pain, etc. Q. E. D.

PROP. XX. He who conceives that the object of his hate is destroyed will feel pleasure.

Proof.—The mind (III. xiii.) endeavors to conceive those things, which exclude the existence of things whereby the body's power of activity is diminished or constrained; that is (III. xiii. note), it endeavors to conceive such things as exclude the existence of what it hates; therefore the image of a thing, which excludes the existence of what the mind hates, helps the aforesaid mental effort, in other words (III. xi. note), affects the mind pleasurably. Thus he who conceives that the object of his hate is destroyed will feel pleasure. Q.E.D.

PROP. XXI. He who conceives that the object of his love is affected pleasurably or painfully, will himself be affected pleasurably or painfully; and the one or the other emotion will be greater or less in the lover according as it is greater or less in the thing loved.

Proof.— The images of things (as we showed in III. xix.) which postulate the existence of the object of love, help the mind's endeavor to conceive the said object. But pleasure postulates the existence of something feeling pleasure, so much the more in proportion as the emotion of pleasure is greater; for it is (III. xi. note) a transition to a greater perfection; therefore the image of pleasure in the object of love helps the mental endeavor of the lover; that is, it affects the lover pleasurably, and so much the more, in proportion as this emotion may have been greater in the object of love. This was our first point. Further, in so far as a thing is affected with pain, it is to that extent destroyed, the extent being in proportion to the amount of pain (III. xi. note); therefore (III. xix.) he who conceives, that the object of his love is affected painfully, will himself be affected painfully, in proportion as the said emotion is greater or less in the object of love. Q.E.D.

PROP. XXII. If we conceive that anything pleasurably affects some object of our love, we shall be affected with love toward that thing. Contrariwise, if we conceive that it affects an object of our love painfully, we shall be affected with hatred toward it.

Proof.— He, who affects pleasurably or painfully the object of our love, affects us also pleasurably or painfully — that is, if we conceive the loved object as affected with the said pleasure or pain (III. xxi.). But this pleasure or pain is postulated to come to us accompanied by the idea of an external cause; therefore (III. xiii. note), if we conceive that any one affects an object of our love pleasurably or painfully, we shall be affected with love or hatred toward him. Q.E.D.

Note.— Prop. xxi. explains to us the nature of PITY, which we may define as PAIN ARISING FROM ANOTHER'S HURT. What term we can use for pleasure arising from another's gain, I know not.

We will call the LOVE TOWARD HIM WHO CONFERS A BENEFIT ON ANOTHER, APPROVAL; and the HATRED TOWARD HIM WHO INJURES ANOTHER, we will call INDIGNATION. We must further remark, that we not only feel pity for a thing which we have loved (as shown in III. xxi.), but also for a thing which we have hitherto regarded without emotion, provided that we deem that it resembles ourselves (as I will show presently). Thus, we bestow approval on one who has benefited anything resembling ourselves, and, contrariwise, are indignant with him who has done it an injury.

PROP. XXIII. He who conceives, that an object of his hatred is painfully affected, will feel pleasure. Contrariwise, if he thinks that the said object is pleasurably affected, he will feel pain. Each of these emotions will be greater or less, according as its contrary is greater or less in the object of hatred.

Proof.— In so far as an object of hatred is painfully affected, it is destroyed to an extent proportioned to the strength of the pain (III. xi. note). Therefore, he (III. xx.) who conceives, that some object of his hatred is painfully affected, will feel pleasure to an extent proportioned to the amount of pain he conceives in the object of his hatred. This was our first point. Again, pleasure postulates the existence of the pleasurably affected thing (III. xi. note), in proportion as the pleasure is greater or less. If anyone imagines that an object of his hatred is pleasurably affected, this conception (III. xiii.) will hinder his own endeavor to persist; in other words (III. xi. note), he who hates will be painfully affected. Q.E.D.

Note.— This pleasure can scarcely be felt unalloyed, and without any mental conflict. For (as I am about to show in Prop. xxvii.), in so far as a man conceives that something similar to himself is affected by pain, he will himself be affected in like manner; and he will have the contrary emotion in contrary circumstances. But here we are regarding hatred only.

PROP. XXIV. If we conceive that anyone pleasurably affects an object of our hate, we shall feel hatred toward him also. If we conceive that he painfully affects the said object, we shall feel love toward him.

Proof.— This proposition is proved in the same way as III. xxii., which see.

Note.— These and similar emotions of hatred are attributable to ENVY, which, accordingly, is nothing else but HATRED, IN SO FAR AS IT IS REGARDED AS DISPOSING A MAN TO REJOICE IN ANOTHER'S HURT, AND TO GRIEVE AT ANOTHER'S ADVANTAGE.

PROP. XXV. We endeavor to affirm, concerning ourselves, and concerning what we love, everything that we conceive to affect pleasurably ourselves, or the loved object. Contrariwise, we endeavor to negative everything, which we conceive to affect painfully ourselves or the loved object.

Proof.—That, which we conceive to affect an object of our love pleasurably or painfully, affects us also pleasurably or painfully (III. xxi.). But the mind (III. xii.) endeavors, as far as possible, to conceive those things which affect us pleasurably; in other words (II. xvii. and Coroll.), it endeavors to regard them as present. And, contrariwise (III. xiii.), it endeavors to exclude the existence of such things as affect us painfully; therefore, we endeavor to affirm concerning ourselves, and concerning the loved object, whatever we conceive to affect ourselves, or the loved object pleasurably. Q.E.D.

PROP. XXVI. We endeavor to affirm, concerning that which we hate, everything which we conceive to affect it painfully; and, contrariwise, we endeavor to deny, concerning it, everything which we conceive to affect it pleasurably.

Proof.— This proposition follows from III. xxiii., as the foregoing proposition followed from III. xxi.

Note.— Thus we see that it may readily happen, that a man may easily think too highly of himself, or a loved object, and, contrariwise, too meanly of a hated object.

This feeling is called PRIDE, in reference to the man who thinks too highly of himself, and is a species of madness, wherein a man dreams with his eyes open, thinking that he can accomplish all things that fall within the scope of his conception, and thereupon accounting them real, and exulting in them, so long as he is unable to conceive anything which excludes their existence, and determines his own power of action. PRIDE, therefore, is PLEASURE SPRINGING FROM A MAN THINKING TOO HIGHLY OF HIMSELF. Again, the PLEASURE WHICH ARISES FROM A MAN THINKING TOO HIGHLY OF ANOTHER is called OVER-ESTEEM. Whereas the PLEASURE WHICH ARISES FROM THINKING TOO LITTLE OF A MAN is called DISDAIN.

PROP. XXVII. By the very fact that we conceive a thing, which is like ourselves, and which we have not regarded with any emotion, to be affected with any emotion, we are ourselves affected with a like emotion (*affectus*).

Proof.—The images of things are modifications of the human body, whereof the ideas represent external bodies as present to us (II. xvii.); in other words (II. x.), whereof the ideas involve the nature of our body, and, at the same time, the nature of external bodies as present. If, therefore, the nature of the external body be similar to the nature of our body, then the idea which we form of the external body will involve a modification of our own body similar to the modification of the external body. Consequently, if we conceive anyone similar to ourselves as affected by any emotion, this conception will express a modification of our body similar to that emotion. Thus, from the fact of conceiving a thing like ourselves to be affected with any emotion, we are ourselves affected with a like emotion. If, however, we hate the said thing like ourselves, we shall, to that extent, be affected by a contrary, and not similar, emotion. Q.E.D.

Note I.—This imitation of emotions, when it is referred to pain, is called COMPASSION (*cf.* III. xxii. note); when it is referred to desire, it is called EMULATION, which is nothing else but THE DESIRE OF ANYTHING

ENGENDERED IN US BY THE FACT THAT WE CONCEIVE THAT
OTHERS HAVE THE LIKE DESIRE.

Corollary I.— If we conceive that anyone, whom we
have hitherto regarded with no emotion, pleasurably affects something similar to ourselves, we shall be affected
with love toward him. If, on the other hand, we conceive that he painfully affects the same, we shall be
affected with hatred toward him.

Proof.— This is proved from the last proposition in the
same manner as III. xxii. is proved from III. xxi.

Corollary II.— We cannot hate a thing which we pity,
because its misery affects us painfully.

Proof.— If we could hate it for this reason, we should
rejoice in its pain, which is contrary to the hypothesis.

Corollary III.—We seek to free from misery, as far as
we can, a thing which we pity.

Proof.— That, which painfully affects the object of our
pity, affects us also with similar pain (by the foregoing
proposition); therefore, we shall endeavor to recall everything which removes its existence, or which destroys it
(*cf.* III. xiii); in other words (III. ix. note), we shall
desire to destroy it, or we shall be determined for its
destruction; thus, we shall endeavor to free from misery
a thing which we pity. Q. E. D.

Note II.— This will or appetite for doing good, which
arises from pity of the thing whereon we would confer a
benefit, is called BENEVOLENCE, and is nothing else but
DESIRE ARISING FROM COMPASSION. Concerning love or hate
toward him who has done good or harm to something,
which we conceive to be like ourselves, see III. xxii.
note.

PROP. XXVIII. We endeavor to bring about whatsoever we concede to conduce to pleasure; but we endeavor
to remove or destroy whatsoever we conceive to be truly
repugnant thereto, or to conduce to pain.

Proof.— We endeavor, as far as possible, to conceive
that which we imagine to conduce to pleasure (III. xii.);
in other words (II. xvii.) we shall endeavor to conceive
it as far as possible as present or actually existing. But
the endeavor of the mind, or the mind's power of thought,

is equal to and simultaneous with, the endeavor of the body, or the body's power of action. (This is clear from II. vii. Coroll. and II. xi. Coroll.) Therefore we make an absolute endeavor for its existence, in other words (which by III. ix. note come to the same thing) we desire and strive for it; this was our first point. Again, if we conceive that something, which we believe to be the cause of pain, that is (III. xiii. note), which we hate, is destroyed, we shall rejoice (III. xx.). We shall, therefore (by the first part of this proof), endeavor to destroy the same, or (III. xiii.) to remove it from us, so that we may not regard it as present; this was our second point. Wherefore whatsoever conduces to pleasure, etc. Q. E. D.

Prop. XXIX. We shall also endeavor to do whatsoever we conceive men* to regard with pleasure, and contrariwise we shall shrink from doing that which we conceive men to shrink from.

Proof.— From the fact of imagining, that men love or hate anything, we shall love or hate the same thing (III. xxvii.). That is (III. xiii. note), from this mere fact we shall feel pleasure or pain at the thing's presence. And so we shall endeavor to do whatever we conceive men to love or regard with pleasure, etc. Q. E. D.

Note.— This endeavor to do a thing or leave it undone, solely in order to please men, we call AMBITION, especially when we so eagerly endeavor to please the vulgar, that we do or omit certain things to our own or another's hurt: in other cases it is generally called KINDLINESS. Furthermore I give the name of PRAISE to the PLEASURE, WITH WHICH WE CONCEIVE THE ACTION OF ANOTHER, WHEREBY HE HAS ENDEAVORED TO PLEASE US; but of BLAME to the PAIN WHEREWITH WE FEEL AVERSION TO HIS ACTION.

Prop. XXX. If anyone has done something which he conceives as affecting other men pleasurably, he will be affected by pleasure, accompanied by the idea of himself as cause; in other words, he will regard himself with

* N.B. By "men" in this and the following propositions, I mean men whom we regard without any particular emotion.

pleasure. On the other hand, if he has done anything which he conceives as affecting others painfully, he will regard himself with pain.

Proof.— He who conceives, that he affects others with pleasure or pain, will, by that very fact, himself be affected with pleasure or pain (III. xxvii.), but, as a man, (II. xix. and xxiii.) is conscious of himself through the modifications whereby he is determined to action, it follows that he who conceives, that he affects others pleasurably, will be affected with pleasure accompanied by the idea of himself as cause; in other words, will regard himself with pleasure. And so *mutatis mutandis* in the case of pain. Q.E.D.

Note.— As love (III. xiii.) is pleasure accompanied by the idea of an external cause, and hatred is pain accompanied by the idea of an external cause; the pleasure and pain in question will be a species of love and hatred. But, as the terms love and hatred are used in reference to external objects, we will employ other names for the emotions now under discussion: pleasure accompanied by the idea of an external cause we will style HONOR, and the emotion contrary thereto we will style SHAME: I mean in such cases as where pleasure or pain arises from a man's belief, that he is being praised or blamed: otherwise pleasure accompanied by the idea of an external cause is called SELF-COMPLACENCY, and its contrary pain is called REPENTANCE. Again, as it may happen (II. xvii. Coroll.) that the pleasure, wherewith a man conceives that he affects others, may exist solely in his own imagination, and as (III. xxv.) everyone endeavors to conceive concerning himself that which he conceives will affect him with pleasure, it may easily come to pass that a vain man may be proud and may imagine that he is pleasing to all, when in reality he may be an annoyance to all.

PROP. XXXI. If we conceive that anyone loves, desires, or hates anything which we ourselves love, desire, or hate, we shall thereupon regard the thing in question with more steadfast love, etc. On the contrary, if we think that anyone shrinks from something that we love, we shall undergo vacillation of soul.

Proof.— From the mere fact of conceiving that anyone loves anything we shall ourselves love that thing (III. xxvii.): but we are assumed to love it already; there is, therefore, a new cause of love, whereby our former emotion is fostered; hence we shall thereupon love it more steadfastly. Again, from the mere fact of conceiving that anyone shrinks from anything, we shall ourselves shrink from that thing (III. xxvii.). If we assume that we at the same time love it, we shall then simultaneously love it and shrink from it; in other words, we shall be subject to vacillation (III. xvii. note). Q.E.D.

Corollary.— From the foregoing, and also from III. xxviii. it follows that everyone endeavors, as far as possible, to cause others to love what he himself loves, and to hate what he himself hates: as the poet says: "As lovers let us share every hope and every fear: iron-hearted were he who should love what the other leaves."

Note.— This endeavor to bring it about, that our own likes and dislikes should meet with universal approval, is really ambition (see III. xxix. note); wherefore we see that every one by nature desires (*appetere*), that the rest of mankind should live according to his own individual disposition: when such a desire is equally present in all, every one stands in every one else's way, and in wishing to be loved or praised by all, all become mutually hateful.

Prop. XXXII. If we conceive that any one takes delight in something, which only one person can possess, we shall endeavor to bring it about that the man in question shall not gain possession thereof.

Proof.— From the mere fact of our conceiving that another person takes delight in a thing (III. xxvii. and Coroll.) we shall ourselves love that thing and desire to take delight therein. But we assumed that the pleasure in question would be prevented by another's delight in its object; we shall, therefore, endeavor to prevent his possession thereof (III. xxviii.). Q.E.D.

Note.— We thus see that man's nature is generally so constituted, that he takes pity on those who fare ill, and envies those who fare well with an amount of hatred

proportioned to his own love for the goods in their possession.   Further, we see that from the same property of
human nature, whence it follows that men are merciful,
it follows also that they are envious and ambitious.
Lastly, if we make appeal to Experience, we shall find that
she entirely confirms what we have said; more especially
if we turn our attention to the first years of our life.   We
find that children, whose body is continually, as it were,
in equilibrium, laugh or cry simply because they see
others laughing or crying; moreover, they desire forthwith to imitate whatever they see others doing, and to
possess themselves whatever they conceive as delighting
others: inasmuch as the images of things are, as we have
said, modifications of the human body, or modes wherein
the human body is affected and disposed by external
causes to act in this or that manner.

PROP. XXXIII. When we love a thing similar to ourselves we endeavor, as far as we can, to bring about that
it should love us in return.

Proof.— That which we love we endeavor, as far as we
can, to conceive in preference to anything else (III. xii.).
If the thing be similar to ourselves, we shall endeavor to
affect it pleasurably in preference to anything else (III.
xxix.).   In other words, we shall endeavor, as far as we
can, to bring it about, that the thing should be affected
with pleasure, accompanied by the idea of ourselves,
that is (III. xiii. note) that it should love us in return.
Q.E.D.

PROP. XXXIV. The greater the emotion with which we
conceive a loved object to be affected toward us, the
greater will be our complacency.

Proof.— We endeavor (III. xxxiii.), as far as we can,
to bring about, that what we love should love us in return; in other words, that what we love should be affected
with pleasure accompanied by the idea of ourself as
cause.   Therefore, in proportion as the loved object is
more pleasurably affected because of us, our endeavor
will be assisted—that is (III. xi. and note) the greater
will be our pleasure.   But when we take pleasure in the
fact, that we pleasurably affect something similar to our-

selves, we regard ourselves with pleasure (III. 30);
therefore the greater the emotion with which we conceive a loved object to be affected, etc. Q.E.D.

Prop. XXXV. If any one conceive, that an object of his
love joins itself to another with closer bonds of friendship than he himself has attained to, he will be affected
with hatred toward the loved object and with envy
toward his rival.

Proof.—In proportion as a man thinks that a loved
object is well affected toward him, will be the strength
of his self-approval (by the last Prop.), that is (III. xxx.
note), of his pleasure; he will, therefore (III. xxviii.), endeavor, as far as he can, to imagine the loved object as
most closely bound to him: this endeavor or desire will
be increased, if he thinks that some one else has a similar
desire (III. xxxi.).   But this endeavor or desire is assumed
to be checked by the image of the loved object in conjunction with the image of him whom the loved object has
joined to itself; therefore (III. xi. note) he will for that
reason be affected with pain, accompanied by the idea of
the loved object as a cause in conjunction with the image
of his rival; that is, he will be (III. xiii.) affected with
hatred toward the loved object and also toward his rival
(III. xv. Coroll.), which latter he will envy as enjoying the
beloved object. Q.E.D.

Note.—This hatred toward an object of love joined with
envy is called Jealousy, which accordingly is nothing else
but a wavering of the disposition arising from combined
love and hatred, accompanied by the idea of some rival
who is envied.   Further, this hatred toward the object of
love will be greater, in proportion to the pleasure which
the jealous man had been wont to derive from the reciprocated love of the said object; and also in proportion to
the feelings he had previously entertained toward his
rival.   If he had hated him, he will forthwith hate the
object of his love, because he conceives it is pleasurably
affected by one whom he himself hates: and also because
he is compelled to associate the image of his loved one
with the image of him whom he hates. This condition
generally comes into play in the case of love for a woman:

for he who thinks, that a woman whom he loves prostitutes herself to another, will feel pain, not only because his own desire is restrained, but also because, being compelled to associate the image of her he loves with the parts of shame and the excreta of another, he therefore shrinks from her.

We must add, that a jealous man is not greeted by his beloved with the same joyful countenance as before, and this also gives him pain as a lover, as I will now show.

PROP. XXXVI. He who remembers a thing, in which he has once taken delight, desires to possess it under the same circumstances as when he first took delight therein.

Proof.— Everything, which a man has seen in conjunction with the object of his love, will be to him accidentally a cause of pleasure (III. xv.); he will, therefore, desire to possess it in conjunction with that wherein he has taken delight; in other words, he will desire to possess the object of his love under the same circumstances as when he first took delight therein.   Q. E. D.

Corollary.— A lover will, therefore, feel pain if one of the aforesaid attendant circumstances be missing.

Proof.— For, in so far as he finds some circumstances to be missing, he conceives something which excludes its existence.   As he is assumed to be desirous for love's sake of that thing or circumstance (by the last Prop.), he will, in so far as he conceives it to be missing, feel pain (III. xix.).   Q. E. D.

Note.— This pain, in so far as it has reference to the absence of the object of love, is called REGRET.

PROP. XXXVII. Desire arising through pain or pleasure, hatred or love, is greater in proportion as the emotion is greater.

Proof.— Pain diminishes or constrains man's power of activity (III. xi. note), in other words (III. vii.), diminishes or constrains the effort, wherewith he endeavors to persist in his own being; therefore (III. v.) it is contrary to the said endeavor: thus all the endeavors of a man affected by pain are directed to removing that pain. But (by the definition of pain), in proportion as the pain is greater, so also is it necessarily opposed to a greater part of man's power of activity; therefore the greater the pain, the greater the power of activity employed to remove it; that is, the greater will be the desire or appetite in endeavoring to remove it. Again, since pleasure (III. xi. note) increases or aids a man's power of activity, it may easily be shown in like manner, that a man affected by pleasure has no desire further than to preserve it, and his desire will be in proportion to the magnitude of the pleasure.

Lastly, since hatred and love are themselves emotions of pain and pleasure, it follows in like manner that the endeavor, appetite, or desire, which arises through hatred or love, will be greater in proportion to the hatred or love. Q.E.D.

Prop. XXXVIII. If a man has begun to hate an object of his love, so that love is thoroughly destroyed, he will, causes being equal, regard it with more hatred than if he had never loved it, and his hatred will be in proportion to the strength of his former love.

Proof.—If a man begins to hate that which he had loved, more of his appetites are put under restraint than if he had never loved it. For love is a pleasure (III. xiii. note) which a man endeavors as far as he can to render permanent (III. xxviii.); he does so by regarding the object of his love as present, and by affecting it as far as he can pleasurably; this endeavor is greater in proportion as the love is greater, and so also is the endeavor to bring about that the beloved should return his affection (III. xxxiii.). Now these endeavors are constrained by hatred toward the object of love (III. xiii. Coroll. and III. xxiii.); wherefore the lover (III. xi. note) will for this cause also be affected with pain, the more so in proportion as his love has been greater; that is, in addition to the pain caused by hatred, there is a pain caused by the fact that he has loved the object; wherefore the lover will regard the beloved with greater pain, or in other words, will hate it more than if he had never loved it, and with the more intensity in proportion as his former love was greater. Q.E.D.

PROP. XXXIX. He who hates anyone will endeavor to do him an injury, unless he fears that a greater injury will thereby accrue to himself; on the other hand, he who loves anyone will, by the same law, seek to benefit him.

Proof.—To hate a man is (III. xiii. note) to conceive him as a cause of pain; therefore he who hates a man will endeavor to remove or destroy him. But if anything more painful, or, in other words, a greater evil, should accrue to the hater thereby—and if the hater thinks he can avoid such evil by not carrying out the injury, which he planned against the object of his hate—he will desire to abstain from inflicting that injury (III. xxviii.), and the strength of his endeavor (III. xxxvii.), will be greater than his former endeavor to do injury, and will therefore prevail over it, as we asserted. The second part of this proof proceeds in the same manner. Wherefore he who hates another, etc. Q.E.D.

Note.—By GOOD I here mean every kind of pleasure, and all that conduces thereto, especially that which satisfies our longings, whatsoever they may be. By EVIL, I mean every kind of pain, especially that which frustrates our longings. For I have shown (III. ix. note) that we in no case desire a thing because we deem it good, but, contrariwise, we deem a thing good because we desire it: consequently we deem evil that which we shrink from; every one, therefore, according to his particular emotions, judges or estimates what is good, what is bad, what is better, what is worse, lastly, what is best, and what is worst. Thus a miser thinks that abundance of money is the best, and want of money the worst; an ambitious man desires nothing so much as glory, and fears nothing so much as shame. To an envious man nothing is more delightful than another's misfortune, and nothing more painful than another's success. So every man, according to his emotions, judges a thing to be good or bad, useful or useless. The emotion, which induces a man to turn from that which he wishes, or to wish for that which he turns from, is called TIMIDITY, which may accordingly be defined as THE FEAR WHEREBY A MAN IS INDUCED TO AVOID

AN EVIL WHICH HE REGARDS AS FUTURE BY ENCOUNTERING A LESSER EVIL (III. xxviii.). But if the evil which he fears be shame, timidity becomes BASHFULNESS. Lastly, if·the desire to avoid a future evil be checked by the fear of another evil, so that the man knows not which to choose, fear becomes CONSTERNATION, especially if both the evils feared be very great.

PROP. XL. He, who conceives himself to be hated by another, and believes that he has given him no cause for hatred, will hate that other in return.

Proof.— He who conceives another as affected with hatred, will thereupon be affected himself with hatred (III. xxvii.), that is, with pain, accompanied by the idea of an external cause. But, by the hypothesis, he conceives no cause for this pain except him who is his enemy; therefore, from conceiving that he is hated by some one, he will be affected with pain, accompanied by the idea of his enemy; in other words, he will hate his enemy in return.   Q.E.D.

Note.— He who thinks that he has given just cause for hatred will (III. xxx. and note) be affected with shame; but this case (III. xxv.) rarely happens. This reciprocation of hatred may also arise from the hatred, which follows an endeavor to injure the object of our hate (III. xxxix.). He therefore who conceives that he is hated by another will conceive his enemy as the cause of some evil or pain; thus he will be affected with pain or fear, accompanied by the idea of his enemy as cause; in other words, he will be affected with hatred toward his enemy, as I said above.

Corollary I.— He who conceives, that one whom he loves hates him, will be a prey to conflicting hatred and love. For, in so far as he conceives that he is an object of hatred, he is determined to hate his enemy in return. But, by the hypothesis, he nevertheless loves him: wherefore he will be a prey to conflicting hatred and love.

Corollary II.— If a man conceives that one, whom he has hitherto regarded without emotion, has done him any injury from motives of hatred, he will forthwith seek to repay the injury in kind.

Proof.—He who conceives, that another hates him, will (by the last proposition) hate his enemy in return, and (III. xxvi.) will endeavor to recall everything which can affect him painfully; he will moreover, endeavor to do him an injury (III. xxxix.). Now the first thing of this sort which he conceives is the injury done to himself; he will, therefore, forthwith endeavor to repay it in kind. Q.E.D.

Note.—The endeavor to injure one whom we hate is called ANGER; the endeavor to repay in kind injury done to ourselves is called REVENGE.

PROP. XLI. If any one conceives that he is loved by another, and believes that he has given no cause for such love, he will love that other in return. (*cf.* III. xv. Coroll., and III. xvi.).

Proof.—This proposition is proved in the same way as the preceding one. See also the note appended thereto.

Note.—If he believes that he has given just cause for the love, he will take pride therein (III. xxx. and note); this is what most often happens (III. xxv.), and we said that its contrary took place whenever a man conceives himself to be hated by another. (See note to preceding proposition). This reciprocal love, and consequently the desire of benefiting him who loves us (III. xxxix.), and who endeavors to benefit us, is called GRATITUDE or THANKFULNESS. It thus appears that men are much more prone to take vengeance than to return benefits.

Corollary.—He who imagines, that he is loved by one whom he hates, will be a prey to conflicting hatred and love. This is proved in the same way as the first corollary of the preceding proposition.

Note.—If hatred be the prevailing emotion, he will endeavor to injure him who loves him; this emotion is called cruelty, especially if the victim be believed to have given no ordinary cause for hatred.

PROP. XLII. He who has conferred a benefit on any one from motives of love or honor will feel pain, if he sees that the benefit is received without gratitude.

Proof.—When a man loves something similar to himself, he endeavors, as far as he can, to bring it about that he should be loved thereby in return (III. xxxiii.). Therefore he who has conferred a benefit confers it in obedience to the desire, which he feels of being loved in return; that is (III. xxxiv,) from the hope of honor or (III. xxx. note) pleasure; hence he will endeavor, as far as he can, to conceive this cause of honor, or to regard it as actually existing. But, by the hypothesis, he conceives something else, which excludes the existence of the said cause of honor: wherefore he will thereat feel pain (III. xix.) Q. E. D.

PROP. XLIII. Hatred is increased by being reciprocated, and can on the other hand be destroyed by love.

Proof.— He who conceives, that an object of his hate hates him in return, will thereupon feel a new hatred, while the former hatred (by hypothesis) still remains (III. xl.). But if on the other hand, he conceives that the object of hate loves him, he will to this extent (III. xxxviii.) regard himself with pleasure, and (III. xxix.) will endeavor to please the cause of his emotion. In other words, he will endeavor not to hate him (III. xli.), and not to affect him painfully; this endeavor (III. xxxvii.) will be greater or less in proportion to the emotion from which it arises. Therefore, if it be greater than that which arises from hatred, and through which the man endeavors to affect painfully the thing which he hates, it will get the better of it and banish the hatred from his mind. Q. E. D.

PROP. XLIV. Hatred which is completely vanquished by love passes into love: and love is thereupon greater than if hatred had not preceded it.

Proof.— The proof proceeds in the same way as Prop. xxxviii. of this Part: for he who begins to love a thing, which he was wont to hate or regard with pain, from the very fact of loving feels pleasure. To this pleasure involved in love is added the pleasure arising from aid given to the endeavor to remove the pain involved in hatred (III. xxxvii.), accompanied by the idea of the former object of hatred as cause.

Note.— Though this be so, no one will endeavor to hate anything, or to be affected with pain for the sake of enjoying this greater pleasure; that is, no one will desire that he should be injured, in the hope of recovering from the injury, nor long to be ill for the sake of getting well. For every one will always endeavor to persist in his being, and to ward off pain as far as he can. If the contrary is conceivable, namely, that a man should desire to hate some one, in order that he might love him the more thereafter, he will always desire to hate him. For the strength of the love is in proportion to the strength of the hatred, wherefore the man would desire, that the hatred be continually increased more and more, and, for a similar reason, he would desire to become more and more ill, in order that he might take greater pleasure in being restored to health; in such a case he would always endeavor to be ill, which (III. vi.) is absurd.

Prop. XLV. If a man conceives, that any one similar to himself hates anything also similar to himself, which he loves, he will hate that person.

Proof.—The beloved object feels reciprocal hatred toward him who hates it (III. xl.); therefore the lover, in conceiving that any one hates the beloved object, conceives the beloved thing as affected by hatred, in other words (III. xiii.), by pain; consequently he is himself affected by pain accompanied by the idea of the hater of the beloved thing as cause; that is, he will hate him who hates anything which he himself loves (III. xiii. note). Q.E.D.

Prop. XLVI. If a man has been affected pleasurably or painfully by any one, of a class or nation different from his own, and if the pleasure or pain has been accompanied by the idea of the said stranger as cause, under the general category of the class or nation: the man will feel love or hatred not only to the individual stranger, but also to the whole class or nation whereto he belongs.

Proof.—This is evident from III. xvi.

Prop. XLVII. Joy arising from the fact, that anything we hate is destroyed, or suffers other injury, is never unaccompanied by a certain pain in us.

Proof.—This is evident from III. xxvii. For in so far as we conceive a thing similar to ourselves to be affected with pain, we ourselves feel pain.

Note.— This proposition can also be proved from the Corollary to II. xvii. Whenever we remember anything, even if it does not actually exist, we regard it only as present and the body is affected in the same manner; wherefore, in so far as the remembrance of the thing is strong, a man is determined to regard it with pain; this determination, while the image of the thing in question lasts, is indeed checked by the remembrance of other things excluding the existence of the aforesaid thing, but is not destroyed: hence, a man only feels pleasure in so far as the said determination is checked: for this reason the joy arising from the injury done to what we hate is repeated, every time we remember that object of hatred. For, as we have said, when the image of the thing in question is aroused, inasmuch as it involves the thing's existence, it determines the man to regard the thing with the same pain as he was wont to do, when it actually did exist. However, since he has joined to the image of the thing other images, which exclude its existence, this determination to pain is forthwith checked, and the man rejoices afresh as often as the repetition takes place. This is the cause of men's pleasure in recalling past evils, and delight in narrating dangers from which they have escaped. For when men conceive a danger, they conceive it as still future, and are determined to fear it; this determination is checked afresh by the idea of freedom, which became associated with the idea of the danger when they escaped therefrom: this renders them secure afresh: therefore they rejoice afresh.

PROP. XLVIII. Love or hatred toward, for instance, Peter is destroyed, if the pleasure involved in the former, or the pain involved in the latter emotion, be associated with the idea of another cause: and will be diminished in proportion as we conceive Peter not to have been the sole cause of either emotion.

Proof.—This proposition is evident from the mere definition of love and hatred (III. xiii. note). For pleasure is called love toward Peter, and pain is called hatred toward Peter, simply in so far as Peter is regarded as the cause of one emotion or the other. When this condition of causality is either wholly or partly removed, the emotion toward Peter also wholly or in part vanishes.   Q.E.D.

PROP. XLIX. Love or hatred toward a thing, which we conceive to be free, must, other conditions being similar, be greater than if it were felt toward a thing acting by necessity.

Proof.—A thing which we conceive as free must (I. Def. vii.) be perceived through itself without anything else. If, therefore, we conceive it as the cause of pleasure or pain, we shall therefore (III. xiii. note) love it or hate it, and shall do so with the utmost love or hatred that can arise from the given emotion. But if the thing which causes the emotion be conceived as acting by necessity, we shall then (by the same Def. vii. Part i.) conceive it not as the sole cause, but as one of the causes of the emotion, and therefore our love or hatred toward it will be less. Q.E.D.

Note.—Hence it follows, that men, thinking themselves to be free, feel more love or hatred toward one another than toward anything else: to this consideration we must add the imitation of emotions treated of in III. xxvii. xxxiv. xl. and xliii.

PROP. L. Anything whatever can be, accidentally, a cause of hope or fear.

Proof.—This proposition is proved in the same way as III. xv., which see, together with the note to III. xviii.

Note.—Things which are accidently the causes of hope or fear are called good or evil omens. Now, in so far as such omens are the cause of hope or fear, they are (by the definitions of hope and fear given in III. xviii. note) the causes also of pleasure and pain; consequently we, to this extent, regard them with love or hatred, and endeavor either to invoke them as means toward that which we hope for, or to remove them as obstacles, or causes of that which we fear. It follows, further, from III. xxv., that we are naturally so constituted as to believe readily in that which we hope for, and with difficulty in that which we fear; moreover, we are apt to estimate such objects above or below their true value.

Hence there have arisen superstitions, whereby men are everywhere assailed. However, I do not think it worth while to point out here the vacillations springing from hope and fear; it follows from the definition of these emotions, that there can be no hope without fear, and no fear without hope, as I will duly explain in the proper place. Further, in so far as we hope for or fear anything, we regard it with love or hatred; thus everyone can apply by himself to hope and fear what we have said concerning love and hatred.

PROP. LI. Different men may be differently affected by the same object, and the same man may be differently affected at different times by the same object.

Proof.— The human body is affected by external bodies in a variety of ways (II. Post. iii.). Two men may therefore be differently affected at the same time, and therefore (by Ax. i. after Lemma iii. after II. xiii.) may be differently affected by one and the same object. Further (by the same Post.) the human body can be affected sometimes in one way, sometimes in another; consequently (by the same Axiom) it may be differently affected at different times by one and the same object. Q.E.D.

Note.— We thus see that it is possible, that what one man loves another may hate, and that what one man fears another may not fear; or, again, that one and the same man may love what he once hated, or may be bold where he once was timid, and so on. Again, as everyone judges according to his emotions what is good, what bad, what better, and what worse (III. xxxix. note), it follows that men's judgments may vary no less than their emotions,* hence when we compare some with others, we distinguish them solely by the diversity of their emotions, and style some intrepid, others timid, others by some other epithet. For instance, I shall call a man INTREPID, if he despises an evil which I am accustomed to fear; if I further take into consideration, that, in his desire to injure his enemies and to benefit those whom

* This is possible, though the human mind is part of the divine intellect, as I have shown in II. xiii. note.

he loves, he is not restrained by the fear of an evil which is sufficient to restrain me, I shall call him DARING. Again, a man will appear TIMID to me, if he fears an evil which I am accustomed to despise; and if I further take into consideration that his desire is restrained by the fear of an evil, which is not sufficient to restrain me, I shall say that he is COWARDLY; and in like manner will everyone pass judgment.

Lastly, from this inconstancy in the nature of human judgment, inasmuch as a man often judges of things solely by his emotions, and inasmuch as the things which he believes cause pleasure or pain, and therefore endeavors to promote or prevent, are often purely imaginary, not to speak of the uncertainty of things alluded to in III. xxviii.; we may readily conceive that a man may be at one time affected with pleasure, and at another with pain, accompanied by the idea of himself as cause. Thus we can easily understand what are REPENTANCE and SELF-COMPLACENCY. REPENTANCE IS PAIN, ACCOMPANIED BY THE IDEA OF ONE'S SELF AS CAUSE; SELF-COMPLACENCY IS PLEAS-URE, ACCOMPANIED BY THE IDEA OF ONE'S SELF AS CAUSE, and these emotions are most intense because men believe themselves to be free (III. xlix.).

PROP. LII. An object which we have formerly seen in conjunction with others, and which we do not conceive to have any property that is not common to many, will not be regarded by us for so long, as an object which we conceive to have some property peculiar to itself.

Proof.—As soon as we conceive an object which we have seen in conjunction with others, we at once remember those others (II. xviii. and note), and thus we pass forthwith from the contemplation of one object to the contemplation of another object. And this is the case with the object, which we conceive to have no property that is not common to many. For we thereupon assume that we are regarding therein nothing, which we have not before seen in conjunction with other objects. But when we suppose that we conceive in an object something special, which we have never seen before, we must needs say that the mind, while regarding that object, has in itself nothing which it can fall to regarding instead thereof; therefore it is determined to the contemplation of that object only. Therefore an object, etc. Q.E.D.

Note.— This mental modification, or imagination of a particular thing, in so far as it is alone in the mind, is called WONDER; but if it be exited by an object of fear, it is called CONSTERNATION, because wonder at an evil keeps a man so engrossed in the simple contemplation thereof, that he has no power to think of anything else whereby he might avoid the evil. If, however, the object of wonder be a man's prudence, industry, or anything of that sort, inasmuch as the said man is thereby regarded as far surpassing ourselves, wonder is called VENERATION; otherwise, if a man's anger, envy, etc., be what we wonder at, the emotion is called HORROR. Again, if it be the prudence, industry, or what not, of a man we love, that we wonder at, our love will on this account be the greater (III. xii.), and when joined to wonder or veneration is called DEVOTION. We may in like manner conceive hatred, hope, confidence, and the other emotions, as associated with wonder; and we should thus be able to deduce more emotions than those which have obtained names in ordinary speech. Whence it is evident, that the names of the emotions have been applied in accordance rather with their ordinary manifestations than with an accurate knowledge of their nature.

To wonder is opposed CONTEMPT, which generally arises from the fact that, because we see someone wondering at, loving, or fearing something, or because something, at first sight, appears to be like things, which we ourselves wonder at, love, fear, etc., we are, in consequence (III. xv. Coroll. and iii. xxvii.), determined to wonder at, love, or fear that thing. But if from the presence, or more accurate contemplation of the said thing, we are compelled to deny concerning it all that can be the cause of wonder, love, fear, etc., the mind, then, by the presence of the thing, remains determined to think rather of those qualities which are not in it, than of those which are in it; whereas, on the other hand, the presence of the object would cause it more particularly to regard that which is therein. As devotion springs from wonder at a thing which we love, so does DERISION spring from contempt of a thing which we hate or fear, and SCORN from contempt of folly, as veneration from wonder at prudence. Lastly, we can conceive the emotions of love, hope, honor, etc., in association with contempt, and can thence deduce other emotions, which are not distinguished one from another by any recognized name.

PROP. LIII. When the mind regards itself and its own power of activity, it feels pleasure; and that pleasure is greater in proportion to the distinctness wherewith it conceives itself and its own power of activity.

Proof. — A man does not know himself except through the modifications of his body, and the ideas thereof (II. xix. and xxiii.). When, therefore, the mind is able to contemplate itself, it is thereby assumed to pass to a greater perfection, or (III. xi. note) to feel pleasure; and the pleasure will be greater in proportion to the distinctness, wherewith it is able to conceive itself and its own power of activity. Q.E.D.

Corollary. — This pleasure is fostered more and more, in proportion as a man conceives himself to be praised by others. For the more he conceives himself as praised by others, the more he will imagine them to be affected with pleasure, accompanied by the idea of himself (III. xxix. note); thus he is (III. xxvii.) himself affected with greater pleasure, accompanied by the idea of himself. Q.E.D.

PROP. LIV. The mind endeavors to conceive only such things as assert its power of activity.

Proof. — The endeavor or power of the mind is the actual essence thereof (III. vii.); but the essence of the mind obviously only affirms that which the mind is and can do; not that which it neither is nor can do; therefore the mind endeavors to conceive only such things as assert or affirm its power of activity. Q.E.D.

PROP. LV. When the mind contemplates its own weakness, it feels pain thereat.

Proof. — The essence of the mind only affirms that which the mind is, or can do; in other words, it is the mind's nature to conceive only such things as assert its power of activity (last Prop.). Thus, when we say that the mind contemplates its own weakness, we are merely saying that while the mind is attempting to conceive something which asserts its power of activity, it is checked in its endeavor — in other words (III. xi. note), it feels pain. Q. E. D.

Corollary. — This pain is more and more fostered, if a man conceives that he is blamed by others; this may be proved in the same way as the corollary to III. liii.

Note. — This pain, accompanied by the idea of our own weakness, is called HUMILITY; the pleasure, which springs from the contemplation of ourselves, is called SELF-LOVE or SELF-COMPLACENCY. And inasmuch as this feeling is renewed as often as a man contemplates his own virtues, or his own power of activity, it follows that every one is fond of narrating his own exploits, and displaying the force both of his body and mind, and also that for this reason, men are troublesome one to another. Again, it follows that men are naturally envious (III. xxiv. note, and III. xxxii. note), rejoicing in the shortcomings of their equals, and feeling pain at their virtues. For whenever a man conceives his own actions, he is affected with pleasure (III. liii.), in proportion as his actions display more perfection, and he conceives them more distinctly — that is (II. xl. note), in proportion as he can distinguish them from others, and regard them as something special. Therefore, a man will take most pleasure in contemplating himself, when he contemplates some quality which he denies to others. But, if that which he affirms of himself be attributable to the idea of man or animals in general, he will not be so greatly pleased; he will, on the contrary, feel pain, if he conceives that his own actions fall short when compared with those of others. This pain (III. xxviii.) he will endeavor to remove, by putting a wrong construction on the actions of his equals, or by, as far as he can, embellishing his own.

It is thus apparent that men are naturally prone to hatred and envy, which latter is fostered by their education. For parents are accustomed to incite their children to virtue solely by the spur of honor and envy. But, perhaps, some will scruple to assent to what I have said, because we not seldom admire men's virtues, and venerate their possessors. In order to remove such doubts, I append the following corollary.

Corollary.—No one envies the virtue of anyone who is not his equal.

Proof.—Envy is a species of hatred (III. xxiv. note) or (III. xiii. note) pain, that is (III. xi. note), a modification whereby a man's power of activity, or endeavor toward activity, is checked. But a man does not endeavor or desire to do anything, which cannot follow from his nature as it is given; therefore a man will not desire any power of activity or virtue (which is the same thing) to be attributed to him, that is appropriate to another's nature and foreign to his own; hence his desire cannot be checked, nor he himself pained by the contemplation of virtue in some one unlike himself, consequently he cannot envy such an one. But he can envy his equal, who is assumed to have the same nature as himself. Q.E.D.

Note.—When, therefore, as we said in the note to III. lii., we venerate a man, through wonder at his prudence, fortitude, etc., we do so, because we conceive those qualities to be peculiar to him, and not as common to our nature; we, therefore, no more envy their possessor, than we envy trees for being tall, or lions for being courageous.

PROP. LVI. There are as many kinds of pleasure, of pain, of desire, and of every emotion compounded of these, such as vacillations of spirit, or derived from these, such as love, hatred, hope, fear, etc., as there are kinds of objects whereby we are affected.

Proof.—Pleasure and pain, and consequently the emotions compounded thereof, or derived therefrom, are passions, or passive states (III. xi. note); now we are necessarily passive (III. i.), in so far as we have inadequate ideas; and only in so far as we have such ideas are we passive (III. iii.); that is, we are only necessarily passive (II. xl. note), in so far as we conceive, or (II. xvii. and note) in so far as we are affected by an emotion, which involves the nature of our own body, and the nature of an external body. Wherefore the nature of every passive state must necessarily be so explained, that the nature of the object whereby we are affected be expressed. Namely, the pleasure, which arises from, say, the object A, involves the nature of that object A, and the pleasure, which arises from the object B, involves the nature of the object B; wherefore these two pleasurable emotions are by nature different, inasmuch as the causes whence they arise are by nature different. So again the emotion of pain, which arises from one object, is by nature different from the pain arising from another object, and, similarly, in the case of love, hatred, hope, fear, vacillation, etc.

Thus, there are necessarily as many kinds of pleasure, pain, love, hatred, etc., as there are kinds of objects whereby we are affected. Now desire is each man's essence or nature, in so far as it is conceived as determined to a particular action by any given modification of itself (III. ix. note); therefore, according as a man is affected through external causes by this or that kind of pleasure, pain, love, hatred, etc., in other words, according as his nature is disposed in this or that manner, so will his desire be of one kind or another, and the nature of one desire must necessarily differ from the nature of another desire, as widely as the emotions differ, wherefrom each desire arose. Thus there are as many kinds of desire, as there are kinds of pleasure, pain, love, etc., consequently (by what has been shown) there are as many kinds of desire, as there are kinds of objects whereby we are affected. Q.E.D.

Note.—Among the kinds of emotions, which, by the last proposition, must be very numerous, the chief are LUXURY, DRUNKENNESS, LUST, AVARICE, and AMBITION, being merely species of love or desire, displaying the nature of those emotions in a manner varying according to the object, with which they are concerned. For by luxury, drunkenness, lust, avarice, ambition, etc., we simply mean the immoderate love of feasting, drinking, venery, riches, and fame. Furthermore, these emotions, in so far as we distinguish them from others merely by the objects wherewith they are concerned, have no contraries. For TEMPERANCE, SOBRIETY, and CHASTITY, which we are wont to oppose to luxury, drunkenness, and lust, are not emotions or passive states, but indicate a power of the mind which moderates the last named emotions. However, I cannot here explain the remaining kinds of emotions (seeing that they are as numerous as the kinds of objects), nor, if I could, would it be necessary. It is sufficient for our purpose, namely, to determine the strength of the emotions, and the mind's power over them, to have a general definition of each emotion. It is sufficient, I repeat, to understand the general properties of the emotions and the mind, to enable us to determine the quality and extent of the mind's power in moderating and checking the emotions. Thus, though there is a great difference between various emotions of love, hatred, or desire, for instance between love felt toward children, and love felt toward a wife, there is no need for us to take cognizance of such differences, or to track out further the nature and origin of the emotions.

PROP. LVII. Any emotion of a given individual differs from the emotion of another individual, only in so far as the essence of the one individual differs from the essence of the other.

Proof.—This proposition is evident from Ax. i. (which see after Lemma iii. Prop. xiii. Part ii.). Nevertheless, we will prove it from the nature of the three primary emotions.

All emotions are attributable to desire, pleasure, or pain, as their definitions above given show. But desire is each man's nature or essence (III. ix. note); therefore desire in one individual differs from desire in another individual, only in so far as the nature or essence of the one differs from the nature or essence of the other. Again, pleasure and pain are passive states or passions, whereby every man's power or endeavor to persist in his

being is increased or diminished, helped or hindered
(III. xi. and note). But by the endeavor to persist in its
being, in so far as it is attributable to mind and body in
conjunction, we mean appetite and desire (III. ix. note);
therefore pleasure and pain are identical with desire or
appetite, in so far as by external causes they are in-
increased or diminished, helped or hindered, in other
words, they are every man's nature; wherefore the pleasure
and pain felt by one man differ from the pleasure and
pain felt by another man, only in so far as the nature
or essence of the one man differs from the essence of the
other; consequently, any emotion of one individual only
differs, etc. Q.E.D.

Note.— Hence it follows, that the emotions of the
animals which are called irrational (for after learning
the origin of mind we cannot doubt that brutes feel),
differ only from man's emotions, to the extent that brute
nature differs from human nature. Horse and man are
alike carried away by the desire of procreation; but the
desire of the former is equine, the desire of the latter is
human. So also the lusts and appetites of insects, fishes,
and birds must needs vary according to the several natures. Thus, although each individual lives content and
rejoices in that nature belonging to him wherein he has
his being, yet the life, wherein each is content and rejoices, is nothing else but the idea, or soul, of the said
individual, and hence the joy of one differs only in nature
from the joy of another, to the extent that the essence
of one differs from the essence of another. Lastly, it
follows from the foregoing proposition, that there is no
small difference between the joy which actuates, say, a
drunkard, and the joy possessed by a philosopher, as I
just mention here by the way. Thus far I have treated
of the emotions attributable to man, in so far as he is
passive. It remains to add a few words on those attributable to him in so far as he is active.

PROP. LVIII. Besides pleasure and desire, which are
passivities or passions, there are other emotions derived
from pleasure and desire, which are attributable to us in
so far as we are active.

Proof.—When the mind conceives itself and its power of activity, it feels pleasure (III. liii.): now the mind necessarily contemplates itself, when it conceives a true or adequate idea (II. xliii). But the mind does conceive certain adequate ideas (II. xl. note 2). Therefore, it feels pleasure in so far as it conceives adequate ideas; that is, in so far as it is active (III. i). Again, the mind, both in so far as it has clear and distinct ideas, and in so far as it has confused ideas, endeavors to persist in its own being (III. ix.); but by such an endeavor we mean desire (by the note to the same Prop.); therefore, desire is also attributable to us, in so far as we understand, or (III. i.) in so far as we are active. Q.E.D.

Prop. LIX. Among all the emotions attributable to the mind as active, there are none which cannot be referred to pleasure or pain.

Proof.—All emotions can be referred to desire, pleasure, or pain, as their definitions, already given, show. Now by pain we mean that the mind's power of thinking is diminished or checked (III. xi. and note); therefore, in so far as the mind feels pain, its power of understanding, that is, of activity, is diminished or checked (III. i.); therefore, no painful emotions can be attributed to the mind in virtue of its being active, but only emotions of pleasure and desire, which (by the last Prop.) are attributable to the mind in that condition.   Q.E.D.

Note.— All actions following from emotion, which are attributable to the mind in virtue of its understanding, I set down to STRENGTH OF CHARACTER (*fortitudo*), which I divide into COURAGE (*animositas*) and HIGH-MINDEDNESS (*generositas*). By COURAGE I mean THE DESIRE WHEREBY EVERY MAN STRIVES TO PRESERVE HIS OWN BEING IN ACCORDANCE SOLELY WITH THE DICTATES OF REASON. By HIGH-MINDEDNESS I mean THE DESIRE WHEREBY EVERY MAN ENDEAVORS, SOLELY UNDER THE DICTATES OF REASON, TO AID OTHER MEN AND TO UNITE THEM TO HIMSELF IN FRIENDSHIP. Those actions, therefore, which have regard solely to the good of the agent I set down to courage, those which aim at the good of others I set down to high-mindedness. Thus temperance, sobriety, and presence of mind in danger, etc., are varieties of courage; courtesy, mercy, etc., are varieties of high-mindedness.

I think I have thus explained, and displayed through their primary causes the principal emotions and vacillations of spirit, which arise from the combination of the three primary emotions, to wit, desire, pleasure, and pain. It is evident from what I have said, that we are in many ways driven about by external causes, and that like waves of the sea driven by contrary winds we toss to and fro unwitting of the issue and of our fate. But I have said, that I have only set forth the chief conflicting emotions, not all that might be given. For, by proceeding in the same way as above, we can easily show that love is united to repentance, scorn, shame, etc. I think everyone will agree from what has been said, that the emotions may be compounded one with another in so many ways, and so many variations may arise therefrom, as to exceed all possibility of computation. However, for my purpose, it is enough to have enumerated the most important; to reckon up the rest which I have omitted would be more curious than profitable. It remains to remark concerning love, that it very often happens that while we are enjoying a thing which we longed for, the body, from the act of enjoyment, acquires a new disposition, whereby it is determined in another way, other images of things are aroused in it, and the mind begins to conceive and desire something fresh. For example, when we conceive something which generally delights us with its flavor, we desire to enjoy, that is, to eat it. But whilst we are thus enjoying it, the stomach is filled and the body is otherwise disposed. If, therefore, when the body is thus otherwise disposed, the image of the food which is present be stimulated, and consequently the endeavor or desire to eat it be stimulated also, the new disposition of the body will feel repugnance to the desire or attempt, and consequently the presence of the food which we formerly longed for will become odious. This revulsion of feeling is called SATIETY or weariness. For the rest, I have neglected the outward modifications of the body observable in emotions, such, for instance, as trembling, pallor, sobbing, laughter, etc., for these are attibutable to the body only, without any reference to the mind. Lastly, the definitions of the emotions require to be supplemented in a few points; I will therefore repeat them, interpolating such observations as I think should here and there be added.

Definitions of the Emotions.

I. DESIRE is the actual essence of man, in so far as it is conceived, as determined to a particular activity by some given modification of itself.

Explanation.—We have said above, in the note to Prop. ix. of this part, that desire is appetite, with consciousness thereof; further, that appetite is the essence of man, in so far as it is determined to act in a way tending to promote its own persistence. But, in the same note, I also remarked that, strictly speaking, I recognize no distinction between appetite and desire. For whether a man be conscious of his appetite or not, it remains one and the same appetite. Thus, in order to avoid the appearance of tautology, I have refrained from explaining desire by appetite; but I have taken care to define it in such a manner, as to comprehend, under one head, all those endeavors of human nature, which we distinguish by the terms appetite, will, desire, or impulse. I might, indeed, have said, that desire is the essence of man, in so far as it is conceived as determined to a particular activity; but from such a definition (*cf.* II. xxiii.) it would not follow that the mind can be conscious of its desire or appetite. Therefore, in order to imply the cause of such consciousness, it was necessary to add, IN SO FAR AS IT IS DETERMINED BY SOME GIVEN MODIFICATION, etc. For, by a modification of man's essence, we understand every disposition of the said essence, whether such disposition be innate, or whether it be conceived solely under the attribute of thought, or solely under the attribute of extension, or whether, lastly, it be referred simultaneously to both these attributes. By the term desire, then, I here mean all man's endeavors, impulses, appetites, and volitions, which vary according to each man's disposition, and are, therefore, not seldom opposed one to another, according as a man is drawn in different directions, and knows not where to turn.

II. PLEASURE is the transition of a man from a less to a greater perfection.

III. PAIN is the transition of a man from a greater to a less perfection.

Explanation.— I say transition: for pleasure is not perfection itself. For, if man were born with the perfection to which he passes, he would possess the same, without the emotion of pleasure. This appears more clearly from the consideration of the contrary emotion, pain. No one can deny that pain consists in the transition to a less perfection and not in the less perfection itself : for a man cannot be pained, in so far as he partakes of perfection of any degree. Neither can we say that pain consists in the absence of a greater perfection. For absence is nothing, whereas the emotion of pain is an activity; wherefore this activity can only be the activity of transition from a greater to a less perfection — in other words, it is an activity whereby a man's power of action is lessened or constrained (*cf.* III. xi. note). I pass over the definitions of merriment, stimulation, melancholy, and grief, because these terms are generally used in reference to the body, and are merely kinds of pleasure or pain.

IV. WONDER is the conception (*imaginatio*) of anything, wherein the mind comes to a stand, because the particular concept in question has no connection with other concepts (*cf.* III. lii. and note).

Explanation.— In the note to II. xviii. we showed the reason why the mind, from the contemplation of one thing, straightway falls to the contemplation of another thing, namely, because the images of the two things are so associated and arranged, that one follows the other. This state of association is impossible, if the image of the thing be new; the mind will then be at a stand in the contemplation thereof, until it is determined by other causes to think of something else.

Thus the conception of a new object, considered in itself, is of the same nature as other conceptions; hence, I do not include wonder among the emotions, nor do I see why I should so include it, inasmuch as this distraction of the mind arises from no positive cause drawing away the mind from other objects, but merely from the absence of a cause, which should determine the mind to pass from the contemplation of one object to the contemplation of another.

I, therefore, recognize only three primitive or primary emotions (as I said in the note to III. xi.), namely, pleasure, pain, and desire. I have spoken of wonder, simply because it is customary to speak of certain emotions springing from the three primitive ones by different names, when they are referred to the objects of our wonder. I am led by the same motive to add a definition of contempt.

V. CONTEMPT is the conception of anything which touches the mind so little, that its presence leads the mind to imagine those qualities which are not in it, rather than such as are in it (*cf.* III. lii. note).

The definitions of veneration and scorn I here pass over, for I am not aware that any emotions are named after them.

VI. LOVE is pleasure, accompanied by the idea of an external cause.

Explanation.— This definition explains sufficiently clearly the essence of love; the definition given by those authors who say that love is THE LOVER'S WISH TO UNITE HIMSELF TO THE LOVED OBJECT expresses a property, but not the essence of love; and, as such authors have not sufficiently discerned love's essence, they have been unable to acquire a true conception of its properties, accordingly their definition is on all hands admitted to be very obscure. It must, however, be noted, that when I say that it is a property of love, that the lover should wish to unite himself to the beloved object, I do not here mean by WISH consent, or conclusion, or a free decision of the mind (for I have shown such, in II. xlviii. to be fictitious); neither do I mean a desire of being united to the loved object when it is absent, or of continuing in its presence when it is at hand; for love can be conceived without either of these desires; but by WISH I mean the contentment, which is in the lover, on account of the presence of the beloved object, whereby the pleasure of the lover is strengthened, or at least maintained.

VII. HATRED is pain, accompanied by the idea of an external cause.

Explanation.— These observations are easily grasped after what has been said in the explanation of the preceding definition (*cf.* also III. xiii. note).

VIII. INCLINATION is pleasure accompanied by the idea of something which is accidentally a cause of pleasure.

IX. AVERSION is pain, accompanied by the idea of something which is accidentally the cause of pain (*cf.* III. xv. note).

X. DEVOTION is love toward one whom we admire.

Explanation.— Wonder (*admiratio*) arises (as we have shown, III. lii.) from the novelty of a thing. If, therefore, it happens that the object of our wonder is often conceived by us, we shall cease to wonder at it; thus we see, that the emotion of devotion readily degenerates into simple love.

XI. DERISION is pleasure arising from our conceiving the presence of a quality, which we despise, in an object which we hate.

Explanation.— In so far as we despise a thing which we hate, we deny existence thereof (III. lii. note), and to that extent rejoice (III. xx.). But since we assume that man hates that which he derides, it follows that the pleasure in question is not without alloy (*cf.* III. xlvii. note).

XII. HOPE is an inconstant pleasure, arising from the idea of something past or future, whereof we to a certain extent doubt the issue.

XIII. FEAR is an inconstant pain arising from the idea of something past or future, whereof we to a certain extent doubt the issue (*cf.* III. xviii. note).

Explanation.— From these definitions it follows, that there is no hope unmingled with fear, and no fear unmingled with hope. For he, who depends on hope and doubts concerning the issue of anything, is assumed to conceive something, which excludes the existence of the said thing in the future; therefore he, to this extent, feels pain (*cf.* III. xix.); consequently while dependent on hope, he fears for the issue. Contrariwise he, who fears, in other words doubts, concerning the issue of something which he hates, also conceives something which excludes the existence of the thing in question; to this extent he feels pleasure, and consequently to this extent he hopes that it will turn out as he desires (III. xx.).

XIV. CONFIDENCE is pleasure arising from the idea of something past or future, wherefrom all cause of doubt has been removed.

XV. DESPAIR is pain arising from the idea of something past or future, wherefrom all cause of doubt has been removed.

Explanation.— Thus confidence springs from hope, and despair from fear, when all cause for doubt as to the issue of an event has been removed: this comes to pass, because man conceives something past or future as present and regards it as such, or else because he conceives other things, which exclude the existence of the causes of his doubt. For, although we can never be absolutely certain of the issue of any particular event (II. xxxi. Coroll.), it may nevertheless happen that we feel no doubt concerning it. For we have shown, that to feel no doubt concerning a thing is not the same as to be quite certain of it (II. xlix. note). Thus it may happen that we are affected by the same emotion of pleasure or pain concerning a thing past or future, as concerning the conception of a thing present; this I have already shown in III. xviii. to which, with its note, I refer the reader.

XVI. JOY is pleasure accompanied by the idea of something past, which has had an issue beyond our hope.

XVII. DISAPPOINTMENT is pain accompanied by the idea of something past, which has had an issue contrary to our hope.

XVIII. PITY is pain accompanied by the idea of evil, which has befallen some one else whom we conceive to be like ourselves (*cf.* III. xxii. note, and III. xxvii. note).

Explanation.— Between pity and sympathy (*misericordia*)

there seems to be no difference, unless perhaps that the former term is used in reference to a particular action, and the latter in reference to a disposition.

XIX. APPROVAL is love toward one who has done good to another.

XX. INDIGNATION is hatred toward one who has done evil to another.

Explanation.— I am aware that these terms are employed in senses somewhat different from those usually assigned. But my purpose is to explain, not the meaning of words, but the nature of things. I therefore make use of such terms, as may convey my meaning without any violent departure from their ordinary signification. One statement of my method will suffice. As for the cause of the above named emotions see III, xxvii. Coroll. i., and III. xxii. note.

XXI. PARTIALITY is thinking too highly of any one because of the love we bear him.

XXII. DISPARAGEMENT is thinking too meanly of any one, because we hate him.

Explanation.— Thus partiality is an effect of love and disparagement an effect of hatred: so that PARTIALITY may also be defined as love, in so far as it induces a man to think too highly of a beloved object. Contrariwise, DISPARAGEMENT may be defined as hatred, in so far as it induces a man to think too meanly of a hated object. *cf.* III. xxvi. note.

XXIII. ENVY is hatred, in so far as it induces a man to be pained by another's good fortune, and to rejoice in another's evil fortune.

Explanation.— Envy is generally opposed to sympathy, which, by doing some violence to the meaning of the word, may therefore be thus defined:

XXIV. SYMPATHY (*misericordia*) is love, in so far as it induces a man to feel pleasure at another's good fortune, and pain at another's evil fortune.

Explanation.— Concerning envy see the notes to III. xxiv. and xxxii. These emotions also arise from pleasure or pain accompanied by the idea of something external, as cause either in itself or accidentally. I now pass on to other emotions, which are accompanied by the idea of something within as a cause.

XXV. Self-approval is pleasure arising from a man's contemplation of himself and his own power of action.

XXVI. Humility is pain arising from a man's contemplation of his own weakness of body or mind.

Explanation.—Self-complacency is opposed to humility, in so far as we thereby mean pleasure arising from a contemplation of our own power of action; but, in so far as we mean thereby pleasure accompanied by the idea of any action which we believe we have performed by the free decision of our mind, it is opposed to repentance, which we may thus define:

XXVII. Repentance is pain accompanied by the idea of some action, which we believe we have performed by the free decision of our mind.

Explanation.—The causes of these emotions we have set forth in III. li. note, and in III. liii. liv. lv. and note. Concerning the free decision of the mind, see II. xxxv. note. This is perhaps the place to call attention to the fact that it is nothing wonderful that all those actions, which are commonly called wrong, are followed by pain, and all those, which are called right, are followed by pleasure. We can easily gather, from what has been said, that this depends in great measure on education. Parents, by reprobating the former class of actions, and by frequently chiding their children because of them, and also by persuading to and praising the latter class, have brought it about that the former should be associated with pain and the latter with pleasure. This is confirmed by experience. For custom and religion are not the same among all men, but that which some consider sacred others consider profane, and what some consider honorable others consider disgraceful. According as each man has been educated, he feels repentance for a given action or glories therein.

XXVIII. Pride is thinking too highly of one's self from self-love.

Explanation.—Thus pride is different from partiality, for the latter term is used in reference to an external object, but pride is used of a man thinking too highly of himself. However, as partiality is the effect of love, so is pride the effect or property of SELF-LOVE, which may therefore be thus defined, LOVE OF SELF OR SELF-APPROVAL, IN SO FAR AS IT LEADS A MAN TO THINK TOO HIGHLY OF HIMSELF. To this emotion there is no contrary. For no one thinks too meanly of himself because of self-hatred; I say that no one thinks too meanly of himself, in so far as he conceives that he is incapable of doing this or that. For whatsoever a man imagines that he is incapable of doing, he imagines this of necessity, and by that notion he is so disposed, that he really cannot do that which he conceives that he cannot do. For, so long as he conceives that he cannot do it, so long is he not determined to do it, and consequently so long is it impossible for him to do it. However, if we consider such matters as only depend on opinion, we shall find it conceivable that a man may think too meanly of himself; for it may happen, that a man, sorrowfully regarding his own weakness, should imagine that he is despised by all men, while the rest of the world are thinking of nothing less than of despising him. Again, a man may think too meanly of himself, if he deny of himself in the present something in relation to a future time of which he is uncertain. As, for instance, if he should say that he is unable to form any clear conceptions, or that he can desire and do nothing but what is wicked and base, etc. We may also say, that a man thinks too meanly of himself, when we see him from excessive fear of shame refusing to do things which others, his equals, venture. We can, therefore, set down as a contrary to pride an emotion which I will call self-abasement, for as from self-complacency springs pride, so from humility springs self-abasement, which I will accordingly, thus define:

XXIX. SELF-ABASEMENT is thinking too meanly of one's self by reason of pain.

Explanation.—We are nevertheless generally accustomed to oppose pride to humility, but in that case we pay more attention to the effect of either emotion than to its nature. We are wont to call PROUD the man who boasts too much (III, xxx. note), who talks of nothing but his own virtues and other people's faults, who wishes to be first; and lastly who goes through life with a style and pomp suitable to those far above him in station. On the other hand, we call HUMBLE the man who too often blushes, who confesses his faults, who sets forth other men's virtues, and who, lastly, walks with bent head and is negligent of his attire. However, these emotions, humility and self-abasement, are extremely rare. For human nature, considered in itself, strives against them as much as it can (see III. xiii. liv.); hence those, who are believed to be most self-abased and humble, are generally in reality the most ambitious and envious.

XXX. HONOR is pleasure accompanied by the idea of some action of our own, which we believe to be praised by others.

XXXI. SHAME is pain accompanied by the idea of some action of our own, which we believe to be blamed by others.

Explanation. — On this subject see the note to III. xxx. But we should here remark the difference which exists between shame and modesty. Shame is the pain following the deed whereof we are ashamed. Modesty is the fear or dread of shame, which restrains a man from committing a base action. Modesty is usually opposed to shamelessness, but the latter is not an emotion, as I will duly show; however, the names of the emotions (as I have remarked already) have regard rather to their exercise than to their nature.

I have now fulfilled my task of explaining the emotions arising from pleasure and pain. I therefore proceed to treat of those which I refer to desire.

XXXII. REGRET is the desire or appetite to possess something, kept alive by the remembrance of the said thing, and at the same time constrained by the remembrance of other things which exclude the existence of it.

Explanation. — When we remember a thing, we are by that very fact, as I have already said more than once, disposed to contemplate it with the same emotion as if it were something present; but this disposition or endeavor, while we are awake, is generally checked by the images of things which exclude the existence of that which we remember. Thus when we remember something which affected us with a certain pleasure, we by that very fact endeavor to regard it with the same emotion of pleasure as though it were present, but this endeavor is at once checked by the remembrance of things which exclude the existence of the thing in question. Wherefore, regret is, strictly speaking, a pain opposed to that pleasure, which arises from the absence of something we hate (*cf.* III. xlvii. note). But, as the name regret seems to refer to desire, I set this emotion down, among the emotions springing from desire.

XXXIII. EMULATION is the desire of something, engendered in us by our conception that others have the same desire.

Explanation.— He who runs away, because he sees others running away, or he who fears, because he sees others in fear; or again, he who, on seeing that another man has burnt his hand, draws toward him his own hand, and moves his body as though his own hand were burnt; such an one can be said to imitate another's emotion, but not to emulate him; not because the causes of emulation and imitation are different, but because it has become customary to speak of emulation only in him, who imitates that which we deem to be honorable, useful, or pleasant. As to the cause of emulation, *cf.* III. xxvii. and note. The reason why this emotion is generally coupled with envy may be seen from III. xxxii. and note.

XXXIV. THANKFULNESS or GRATITUDE is the desire or zeal springing from love, whereby we endeavor to benefit him, who with similar feelings of love has conferred a benefit on us. *Cf.* III. xxxix. note and xl.

XXXV. BENEVOLENCE is the desire of benefiting one whom we pity. *Cf.* III. xxvii. note.

XXXVI. ANGER is the desire, whereby through hatred we are induced to injure one whom we hate, III. xxxix.

XXXVII. REVENGE is the desire whereby we are induced, through mutual hatred, to injure one who, with similar feelings, has injured us. (See III. xl. Coroll. ii. and note.)

XXXVIII. CRUELTY or SAVAGENESS is the desire, whereby a man is impelled to injure one whom we love or pity.

Explanation.— To cruelty is opposed clemency, which is not a passive state of the mind, but a power whereby man restrains his anger and revenge.

XXXIX. TIMIDITY is the desire to avoid a greater evil, which we dread, by undergoing a lesser evil. *Cf.* III. xxxix. note.

XL. DARING, is the desire, whereby a man is set on to do something dangerous which his equals fear to attempt.

XLI. COWARDICE is attributed to one, whose desire is checked by the fear of some danger which his equals dare to encounter.

Explanation.— Cowardice is, therefore, nothing else but the fear of some evil, which most men are wont not to fear; hence I do not reckon it among the emotions springing from desire. Nevertheless, I have chosen to explain it here, because, in so far as we look to the desire, it is truly opposed to the emotion of daring.

XLII. CONSTERNATION is attributed to one, whose desire of avoiding evil is checked by amazement at the evil which he fears.

Explanation.— Consternation is, therefore, a species of cowardice. But, inasmuch as consternation arises from a double fear, it may be more conveniently defined as a fear which keeps a man so bewildered and wavering, that he is not able to remove the evil. I say bewildered, in so far as we understand his desire of removing the evil to be constrained by his amazement. I say wavering, in so far as we understand the said desire to be constrained by the fear of another evil, which equally torments him: whence it comes to pass that he knows not, which he may avert of the two. On this subject, see III. xxxix. note, and III. lii. note. Concerning cowardice and daring, see III. li. note.

XLIII. COURTESY, or DEFERENCE (*humanitas seu modestia*), is the desire of acting in a way that should please men, and refraining from that which should displease them.

XLIV. AMBITION is the immoderate desire of power.

Explanation.—Ambition is the desire, whereby all the emotions (*cf.* III. xxvii. and xxxi.) are fostered and strengthened; therefore this emotion can with difficulty be overcome. For, so long as a man is bound by any desire, he is at the same time necessarily bound by this. "The best men," says Cicero, "are especially led by honor. Even philosophers, when they write a book contemning honor, sign their names thereto," and so on.

XLV. LUXURY is excessive desire, or even love of living sumptuously.

XLVI. INTEMPERANCE is the excessive desire and love of drinking.

XLVII. AVARICE is the excessive desire and love of riches.

XLVIII. LUST is desire and love in the matter of sexual intercourse.

Explanation.— Whether this desire be excessive or not, it is still called lust. These last five emotions (as I have shown in III. lvi.) have no contraries. For deference is a species of ambition. *Cf.* III. xxix. note.

Again, I have already pointed out, that temperance, sobriety and chastity indicate rather a power than a passivity of the mind. It may, nevertheless, happen, that an avaricious, an ambitious, or a timid man may abstain from excess in eating, drinking, or sexual indulgence, yet avarice, ambition, and fear are not contraries to luxury, drunkenness, and debauchery. For an avaricious man is often glad to gorge himself with food and drink at another man's expense. An ambitious man will restrain himself in nothing, so long as he thinks his indulgences are secret; and if he lives among drunkards and debauchees, he will, from the mere fact of being ambitious, be more prone to those vices. Lastly, a timid man does that which he would not. For though an avaricious man should, for the sake of avoiding death, cast his riches into the sea, he will none the less remain avaricious; so, also, if a lustful man is downcast, because he cannot follow his bent, he does not, on the ground of abstention, cease to be lustful. In fact, these emotions are not so much concerned with the actual feasting, drinking, etc., as with the appetite and love of such. Nothing, therefore, can be opposed to these emotions, but high-mindedness and valor, whereof I will speak presently.

The definitions of jealousy and other waverings of the mind I pass over in silence, first, because they arise from the compounding of the emotions already described; secondly, because many of them have no distinctive names, which shows that it is sufficient for practical purposes to have merely a general knowledge of them. However, it is established from the definitions of the emotions, which we have set forth, that they all spring from desire, pleasure, or pain, or rather, that there is nothing besides these three; wherefore each is wont to be called by a variety of names in accordance with its various relations and extrinsic tokens. If we now direct our attention to these primitive emotions, and to what has been said concerning the nature of the mind, we shall be able thus to define the emotions, in so far as they are referred to the mind only.

General Definition of the Emotions.

Emotion, which is called a passivity of the soul, is a confused idea, whereby the mind affirms concerning its body, or any part thereof, a force for existence (*existendi vis*) greater or less than before, and by the presence of which the mind is determined to think of one thing rather than another.

Explanation. — I say, first, that emotion or passion of the soul is A CONFUSED IDEA. For we have shown that the mind is only passive, in so far as it has inadequate or confused ideas. (III. iii.) I say, further, WHEREBY THE MIND AFFIRMS CONCERNING ITS BODY OR ANY PART THEREOF A FORCE FOR EXISTENCE GREATER THAN BEFORE. For all the ideas of bodies, which we possess, denote rather the actual disposition of our own body (II. xvi. Coroll. ii.) than the nature of an external body. But the idea which constitutes the reality of an emotion must denote or express the disposition of the body, or of some part thereof, which is possessed by the body, or some part thereof, because its power of action or force for existence is increased or diminished, helped or hindered. But it must be noted that, when I say A GREATER OR LESS FORCE FOR EXISTENCE than before, I do not mean that the mind compares the present with the past disposition of the body, but that the idea which constitutes the reality of an emotion affirms something of the body, which, in fact, involves more or less of reality than before.

And inasmuch as the essence of mind consists in the fact (II. xi. xiii.), that it affirms the actual existence of its own body, and inasmuch as we understand by perfection the very essence of a thing, it follows that the mind passes to greater or less perfection, when it happens to affirm concerning its own body, or any part thereof, something involving more or less reality than before.

When, therefore, I said above that the power of the mind is increased or diminished, I merely meant that the mind had formed of its own body, or of some part thereof, an idea involving more or less of reality, than it had already affirmed concerning its own body. For the excellence of ideas, and the actual power of thinking are measured by the excellence of the object. Lastly, I have added BY THE PRESENCE OF WHICH THE MIND IS DETERMINED TO THINK OF ONE THING RATHER THAN ANOTHER, so that, besides the nature of pleasure and pain, which the first part of the definition explains, I might also express the nature of desire.

PART IV.

OF HUMAN BONDAGE, OR THE STRENGTH OF THE EMOTIONS.

Preface.

Human infirmity in moderating and checking the emotions I name bondage; for, when a man is a prey to his emotions, he is not his own master, but lies at the mercy of fortune: so much so, that he is often compelled, while seeing that which is better for him, to follow that which is worse. Why this is so, and what is good or evil in the emotions, I propose to show in this part of my treatise. But, before I begin, it would be well to make a few prefatory observations on perfection and imperfection, good and evil.

When a man has purposed to make a given thing, and has brought it to perfection, his work will be pronounced perfect, not only by himself, but by everyone who rightly knows, or thinks that he knows, the intention and aim of its author. For instance, suppose anyone sees a work (which I assume to be not yet completed) and knows that the aim of the author of that work is to build a house, he will call the work imperfect; he will, on the other hand, call it perfect, as soon as he sees that it is carried through to the end, which its author had purposed for it. But if a man sees a work, the like whereof he has never seen before, and if he knows not the intention of the artificer, he plainly cannot know, whether that work be perfect or imperfect. Such seems to be the primary meaning of these terms.

But, after men began to form general ideas, to think out types of houses, buildings, towers, etc., and to prefer certain types to others, it came about, that each man called perfect that which he saw agree with the general idea he had formed of the thing in question, and called imperfect that which he saw agree less with his own preconceived type, even though it had evidently been completed in acordance with the idea of its artificer. This seems to be the only reason for calling natural phenomena, which, indeed, are not made with human hands, perfect or imperfect: for men are wont to form general ideas of things natural, no less than of things artificial, and such ideas they hold as types, believing that Nature (who they think does nothing without an object) has them in view, and has set them as types before herself. Therefore, when they behold something in Nature, which does not wholly conform to the preconceived type which they have formed of the thing in question, they say that Nature has fallen short or has blundered, and has left her work incomplete. Thus we see that men are wont to style natural phenomena perfect or imperfect rather from their own prejudices, than from true knowledge of what they pronounce upon.

Now we showed in the appendix to Part I., that nature does not work with an end in view. For the eternal and infinite being, which we call God or nature, acts by the same necessity as that whereby it exists. For we have shown that by the same necessity of its nature, whereby it exists, it likewise works (I. xvi.). The reason or cause why God or nature exists, and the reason why he acts, are one and the same. Therefore, as he does not exist for the sake of an end, so neither does he act for the sake of an end; of his existence and of his action there is neither origin nor end. Wherefore, a cause which is called final is nothing else but human desire, in so far as it is considered as the origin or cause of anything. For example, when we say that to be inhabited is the final cause of this or that house, we mean nothing more than that a man, conceiving the convenience of household life, had a desire to build a house. Wherefore, the being inhabited, in so far as it is regarded as a final cause, is nothing else but this particular desire, which is really the efficient cause; it is regarded as the primary cause, because men are generally ignorant of the causes of their desires. They are, as I have often said already, conscious of their own actions and appetites, but ignorant of the causes whereby they are determined to any particular desire. Therefore, the common saying that nature sometimes falls short, or blunders, and produces things which are imperfect, I set down among the glosses treated of in the appendix to Part I. Perfection and imperfection, then, are in reality merely modes of thinking, or notions which we form from a comparison among one another of individuals of the same species; hence I said above (II. Def. vi.), that by reality and perfection I mean the same thing. For we are wont to refer all the individual things in nature to one genus, which is called the highest genus, namely, to the category of being, whereto absolutely all individuals in nature belong. Thus, in so far as we refer the individuals in nature to this category, and comparing them one with another, find that some possess more of being or reality than others, we, to this extent, say that some are more perfect than others. Again, in so far as we attribute to them anything implying negation — as term, end, infirmity, etc., — we, to this extent, call them imperfect, because they do not affect our mind so much as the things which we call perfect, not because they have any intrinsic deficiency, or because nature has blundered. For nothing lies within the scope of a thing's nature, save that which follows from the necessity of the nature of its efficient cause, and whatsoever follows from the necessity of the nature of its efficient cause necessarily comes to pass.

As for the terms GOOD and BAD, they indicate no positive quality in things regarded in themselves, but are merely modes of thinking, or notions which we form from the comparison of things one with another. Thus one and the same thing can be at the same time good, bad, and indifferent. For instance, music is good for him that is melancholy, bad for him that mourns; for him that is deaf, it is neither good nor bad.

Nevertheless, though this be so, the terms should still be retained. For, inasmuch as we desire to form an idea of man as a type of human nature which we may hold in view, it will be useful for us to retain the terms in question, in the sense I have indicated.

In what follows, then, I shall mean by "good" that which we certainly know to be a means of approaching more nearly to the type of human nature, which we have set before ourselves; by "bad," that which we certainly know to be a hindrance to us in approaching the said type. Again, we shall say that men are more perfect, or more imperfect, in proportion as they approach more or less nearly to the said type. For it must be specially remarked that, when I say that a man passes from a lesser to a greater perfection, or *vice versâ*, I do not mean that he is changed from one essence or reality to another; for instance, a horse would be as completely destroyed by being changed into a man, as by being changed into an insect. What I mean is, that we conceive the thing's power of action, in so far as this is understood by its nature, to be increased or diminished. Lastly, by perfection in general I shall, as I have said, mean reality—in other words, each thing's essence, in so far as it exists, and operates in a particular manner, and without paying any regard to its duration. For no given thing can be said to be more perfect, because it has passed a longer time in existence. The duration of things cannot be determined by their essence, for the essence of things involves no fixed and definite period of existence; but everything, whether it be more perfect or less perfect, will always be able to persist in existence with the same force wherewith it began to exist; wherefore, in this respect, all things are equal.

DEFINITIONS.

I. By GOOD I mean that which we certainly know to be useful to us.

II. By EVIL I mean that which we certainly know to be a hindrance to us in the attainment of any good.

(Concerning these terms see the foregoing preface toward the end.)

III. Particular things I call CONTINGENT in so far as, while regarding their essence only, we find nothing therein, which necessarily asserts their existence or excludes it.

IV. Particular things I call POSSIBLE in so far as, while regarding the causes whereby they must be produced, we know not, whether such causes be determined for producing them.

(In I. xxxiii. note i., I drew no distinction between possible and contingent, because there was in that place no need to distinguish them accurately.)

V. By CONFLICTING EMOTIONS I mean those which draw a man in different directions, though they are of the same kind, such as luxury and avarice, which are both species of love, and are contraries, not by nature, but by accident.

VI. What I mean by emotion felt toward a thing, future, present, and past, I explained in III. xviii., notes i. and ii., which see.

(But I should here also remark, that we can only distinctly conceive distance of space or time up to a certain definite limit; that is, all objects distant from us more than two hundred feet, or whose distance from the place where we are exceeds that which we can distinctly conceive, seem to be an equal distance from us, and all in the same plane; so also objects, whose time of existing is conceived as removed from the present by a longer interval than we can distinctly conceive, seem to be all equally distant from the present, and are set down, as it were, to the same moment of time.)

VII. By an END, for the sake of which we do something, I mean a desire.

VIII. By VIRTUE (*virtus*) and POWER I mean the same thing; that is (III. vii.), virtue, in so far as it is referred to man, is a man's nature or essence, in so far as it has the power of effecting what can only be understood by the laws of that nature.

Axiom.

There is no individual thing in nature, than which there is not another more powerful and strong. Whatsoever thing be given, there is something stronger whereby it can be destroyed.

Prop. I. No positive quality possessed by a false idea is removed by the presence of what is true, in virtue of its being true.

Proof.—Falsity consists solely in the privation of knowledge which inadequate ideas involve (II. xxxv.), nor have they any positive quality on account of which they are called false (II. xxxiii.); contrariwise, in so far as they are referred to God, they are true (II. xxxii.). Wherefore, if the positive quality possessed by a false idea were removed by the presence of what is true, in virtue of its being true, a true idea would then be removed by itself, which (IV. iii.) is absurd. Therefore, no positive quality possessed by a false idea, etc. Q.E.D.

Note.—This proposition is more clearly understood from II. xvi. Coroll. ii. For imagination is an idea, which indicates rather the present disposition of the human body than the nature of the external body; not indeed distinctly, but confusedly; whence it comes to pass, that the mind is said to err. For instance, when we look at the sun, we conceive that it is distant from us about two hundred feet; in this judgment we err, so long as we are in ignorance of its true distance; when its true distance is known, the error is removed, but not the imagination; or, in other words, the idea of the sun, which only explains the nature of that luminary, in so far as the body is affected thereby: wherefore, though we know the real distance, we shall still nevertheless imagine the sun to be near us. For, as we said in II. xxxv. note, we do not imagine the sun to be so near us, because we are ignorant of its true distance, but because the mind conceives the magnitude of the sun to the extent that the body is affected thereby. Thus, when the rays of the sun falling on the surface of water are reflected into our eyes, we imagine the sun as if it were in the water, though we are aware of its real position; and similarly other imaginations, wherein the mind is deceived, whether they indicate the natural disposition of the body, or that its power of activity is increased or diminished, are not contrary to the truth, and do not vanish at its presence. It happens indeed that, when we mistakenly fear an evil, the fear vanishes when we hear the true tidings; but the contrary also happens, namely, that we fear an evil which will certainly come, and our fear vanishes when we hear false tidings; thus imaginations do not vanish at the presence of the truth, in virtue of its being true but because other imaginations, stronger than the first, supervene and exclude the present existence of that which we imagined, as I have shown in II. xvii.

PROP. II. We are only passive, in so far as we are a part of Nature, which cannot be conceived by itself without other parts.

Proof.—We are said to be passive, when something arises in us, whereof we are only a partial cause (III. Def. ii.), that is (III. Def. i.), something which cannot be deduced solely from the laws of our nature. We are passive therefore, in so far as we are a part of Nature, which cannot be conceived by itself without other parts. Q.E.D.

PROP. III. The force whereby a man persists in existing is limited, and is infinitely surpassed by the power of external causes.

Proof.—This is evident from the axiom of this part. For, when man is given, there is something else—say A —more powerful; when A is given, there is something else—say B—more powerful than A, and so on to infinity; thus the power of man is limited by the power of some other thing, and is infinitely surpassed by the power of external causes. Q.E.D.

PROP. IV. It is impossible, that man should not be a part of Nature, or that he should be capable of undergoing no changes, save such as can be understood through his nature only as their adequate cause.

Proof.—The power, whereby each particular thing, and consequently man, preserves his being, is the power of

God or of Nature (I. xxiv. Coroll.); not in so far as it is
infinite, but in so far as it can be explained by the actual
human essence (III. vii.). Thus the power of man, in so
far as it is explained through his own actual essence, is
a part of the infinite power of God or Nature, in other
words, of the essence thereof (I. xxxiv.). This was our
first point. Again, if it were possible, that man should
undergo no changes save such as can be understood
solely through the nature of man, it would follow that
he would not be able to die, but would always necessarily
exist; this would be the necessary consequence of a cause
whose power was either finite or infinite; namely, either
of man's power only, inasmuch as he would be capable
of removing from himself all changes which could spring
from external causes or of the infinite power of Nature,
whereby all individual things would be so ordered, that
man should be incapable of undergoing any changes save
such as tended toward his own preservation. But the
first alternative is absurd (by the last Prop., the proof
of which is universal, and can be applied to all individual things). Therefore, if it be possible, that man
should not be capable of undergoing any changes, save
such as can be explained solely through his own nature,
and consequently that he must always (as we have shown)
necessarily exist; such a result must follow from the infinite power of God, and consequently (I. xvi.) from the
necessity of the divine nature, in so far as it is regarded
as affected by the idea of any given man, the whole
order of nature as conceived under the attributes of extension and thought must be deducible. It would therefore follow (I. xxi.) that man is infinite, which (by the
first part of this proof) is absurd. It is, therefore, impossible that man should not undergo any changes save
those whereof he is the adequate cause. Q.E.D.

Corollary.—Hence it follows, that man is necessarily
always a prey to his passions, that he follows and obeys
the general order of nature, and that he accommodates
himself thereto, as much as the nature of things demands.

PROP. V. The power and increase of every passion, and
its persistence in existing are not defined by the power,

whereby we ourselves endeavor to persist in existing, but by the power of an external cause compared with our own.

Proof.— The essence of a passion cannot be explained through our essence alone (III. Def. i. and ii.), that is (III. vii.), the power of a passion cannot be defined by the power, whereby we ourselves endeavor to persist in existing, but (as is shown in II. xvi.) must necessarily be defined by the power of an external cause compared with our own. Q. E. D.

Prop. VI. The force of any passion or emotion can overcome the rest of a man's activities or power, so that the emotion becomes obstinately fixed to him.

Proof.— The force and increase of any passion and its persistence in existing are defined by the power of an external cause compared with our own (by the foregoing Prop.); therefore (IV. iii.) it can overcome a man's power, etc. Q. E. D.

Prop. VII. An emotion can only be controlled or destroyed by another emotion contrary thereto, and with more power for controlling emotion.

Proof.— Emotion, in so far as it is referred to the mind, is an idea, whereby the mind affirms of its body a greater or less force of existence than before (*cf.* the General Definition of the Emotions at the end of Part III.). When, therefore, the mind is assailed by any emotion, the body is at the same time affected with a modification whereby its power of activity is increased or diminished. Now, this modification of the body (IV. v.) receives from its cause the force for persistence in its being; which force can only be checked or destroyed by a bodily cause (II. vi.), in virtue of the body being affected with a modification contrary to (III. v.) and stronger than itself (IV. Ax.); wherefore (II. xii.) the mind is affected by the idea of a modification contrary to and stronger than the former modification, in other words (by the General Definition of the Emotions) the mind will be affected by an emotion contrary to and stronger than the former emotion, which will exclude or destroy the existence of the former emotion; thus an emotion cannot be destroyed nor controlled except by a contrary and stronger emotion. Q. E. D.

Corollary.—An emotion, in so far as it is referred to the mind, can only be controlled or destroyed through an idea of a modification of the body contrary to, and stronger than, that which we are undergoing. For the emotion which we undergo can only be checked or destroyed by an emotion contrary to, and stronger than, itself; in other words (by the General Definition of the Emotions), only by an idea of a modification of the body contrary to, and stronger than, the modification which we undergo.

PROP. VIII. The knowledge of good and evil is nothing else but the emotions of pleasure or pain, in so far as we are conscious thereof.

Proof.—We call a thing good or evil, when it is of service or the reverse in preserving our being (IV. Def. i. and ii.), that is (III. vii.), when it increases or diminishes, helps or hinders, our power of activity. Thus, in so far as we perceive that a thing affects us with pleasure or pain, we call it good or evil; wherefore the knowledge of good and evil is nothing else but the idea of the pleasure or pain, which necessarily follows from that pleasurable or painful emotion (II. xxii.). But this idea is united to the emotion in the same way as mind is united to body (II. xxi.); that is, there is no real distinction between this idea and the emotion or idea of the modification of the body, save in conception only. Therefore the knowledge of good and evil is nothing else but the emotion, in so far as we are conscious thereof. Q.E.D.

PROP. IX. An emotion whereof we conceive the cause to be with us at the present time, is stronger than if we did not conceive the cause to be with us.

Proof.—Imagination or conception is the idea, by which the mind regards a thing as present (II. xvii. note), but which indicates the disposition of the mind rather than the nature of the external thing (II. xvi. Coroll. ii.). An emotion is therefore a conception, in so far as it indicates the disposition of the body. But a conception (by II. xvii.) is stronger, so long as we conceive nothing which excludes the present existence of the external object; wherefore an emotion is also stronger or more intense, when we conceive the cause to be with us at the present time, than when we do not conceive the cause to be with us. Q.E.D.

Note.—When I said above in III. xviii. that we are affected by the image of what is past or future with the same emotion as if the thing conceived were present, I expressly stated that this is only true in so far as we look solely to the image of the thing in question itself; for the thing's nature is unchanged, whether we have conceived it or not; I did not deny that the image becomes weaker, when we regard as present to us other things which exclude the present existence of the future object; I did not expressly call attention to the fact, because I purposed to treat of the strength of the emotions in this part of my work.

Corollary.—The image of something past or future, that is, of a thing which we regard as in relation to time past or time future, to the exclusion of time present, is, when other conditions are equal, weaker than the image of something present; consequently an emotion felt toward what is past or future is less intense, other conditions being equal, than an emotion felt toward something present.

Prop. X. Toward something future, which we conceive as close at hand, we are affected more intensely, than if we conceive that its time for existence is separated from the present by a longer interval; so too by the remembrance of what we conceive to have not long passed away we are affected more intensely, than if we conceive that it has long passed away.

Proof.—In so far as we conceive a thing as close at hand, or not long passed away, we conceive that which excludes the presence of the object less, than if its period of future existence were more distant from the present, or if it had long passed away (this is obvious); therefore (by the foregoing Prop.) we are, so far, more intensely affected toward it. Q.E.D.

Corollary.—From the remarks made in Def. vi. of this part it follows that, if objects are separated from the present by a longer period than we can define in conception, though their dates of occurrence be widely separated one from the other, they all affect us equally faintly.

PROP. XI. An emotion toward that which we conceive as necessary is, when other conditions are equal, more intense than an emotion toward that which is possible, or contingent, or non-necessary.

Proof.—In so far as we conceive a thing to be necessary, we, to that extent, affirm its existence; on the other hand we deny a thing's existence, in so far as we conceive it not to be necessary (I. xxxiii. note i.); wherefore (IV. ix.) an emotion toward that which is necessary is, other conditions being equal, more intense than an emotion toward that which is non-necessary. Q. E. D.

PROP. XII. An emotion toward a thing, which we know not to exist at the present time, and which we conceive as possible, is more intense, other conditions being equal, than an emotion toward a thing contingent.

Proof.—In so far as we conceive a thing as contingent, we are affected by the conception of some further thing, which would assert the existence of the former (IV. Def. iii.); but, on the other hand, we (by hypothesis) conceive certain things which exclude its present existence. But, in so far as we conceive a thing to be possible in the future, we thereby conceive things which assert its existence (IV. iv.), that is (III. xviii.), things which promote hope or fear: wherefore an emotion toward something possible is more vehement. Q. E. D.

Corollary.—An emotion toward a thing, which we know not to exist in the present, and which we conceive as contingent, is far fainter than if we conceive the thing to be present with us.

Proof.—Emotion toward a thing, which we conceive to exist, is more intense than it would be, if we conceived the thing as future (IV. ix. Coroll.), and is much more vehement, than if the future time be conceived as far distant from the present (IV. x.). Therefore an emotion toward a thing, whose period of existence we conceive to be far distant from the present, is far fainter, than if we conceive the thing as present; it is, nevertheless, more intense, than if we conceived the thing as contingent, wherefore an emotion toward a thing, which we regard as contingent, will be far fainter, than if we conceived the thing to be present with us. Q.E.D.

PROP. XIII. Emotion toward a thing contingent, which we know not to exist in the present, is, other conditions being equal, fainter than an emotion toward a thing past.

Proof.—In so far as we conceive a thing as contingent, we are not affected by the image of any other thing, which asserts the existence of the said thing (IV. Def. iii.), but, on the other hand (by hypothesis), we conceive certain things excluding its present existence. But, in so far as we conceive it in relation to time past, we are assumed to conceive something, which recalls the thing to memory, or excites the image thereof (II. xviii. and note), which is so far the same as regarding it as present (II. xvii. Coroll.). Therefore (IV. ix.) an emotion toward a thing contingent, which we know does not exist in the present, is fainter, other conditions being equal, than an emotion toward a thing past. Q.E.D.

PROP. XIV. A true knowledge of good and evil cannot check any emotion by virtue of being true, but only in so far as it is considered as an emotion.

Proof.—An emotion is an idea, whereby the mind affirms of its body a greater or less force of existing than before (by the General Definition of the Emotions); therefore it has no positive quality, which can be destroyed by the presence of what is true; consequently the knowledge of good and evil cannot, by virtue of being true, restrain any emotion. But, in so far as such knowledge is an emotion (IV. viii.), if it have more strength for restraining emotion, it will to that extent be able to restrain the given emotion. Q.E.D.

PROP. XV. Desire arising from the knowledge of good and bad can be quenched or checked by many of the other desires arising from the emotions whereby we are assailed.

Proof.— From the true knowledge of good and evil, in so far as it is an emotion, necessarily arises desire (Def. of the Emotions, i.), the strength of which is proportioned to the strength of the emotion wherefrom it arises (III. xxxvii.). But, inasmuch as this desire arises (by hypothesis) from the fact of our truly understanding anything, it follows that it is also present with us, in so far as we are active (III. i.), and must therefore be understood through our essence only (III. Def. ii.); consequently (III. vii.) its force and increase can be defined solely by human power. Again, the desires arising from the emotions whereby we are assailed are stronger, in proportion as the said emotions are more vehement; wherefore their force and increase must be defined solely by the power of external causes, which, when compared with our own power, indefinitely surpass it (IV. iii.); hence the desires arising from like emotions may be more vehement, than the desire which arises from a true knowledge of good and evil, and may, consequently, control or quench it. Q. E. D.

PROP. XVI. Desire arising from the knowledge of good and evil, in so far as such knowledge regards what is future, may be more easily controlled or quenched, than the desire for what is agreeable at the present moment.

Proof.— Emotion toward a thing, which we conceive as future, is fainter than emotion toward a thing that is present (IV. ix. Coroll.). But desire, which arises from the true knowledge of good and evil, though it be concerned with things which are good at the moment, can be quenched or controlled by any headstrong desire (by the last Prop., the proof whereof is of universal application). Wherefore desire arising from such knowledge, when concerned with the future, can be more easily controlled or quenched, etc. Q. E. D.

PROP. XVII. Desire arising from the true knowledge of good and evil, in so far as such knowledge is concerned with what is contingent, can be controlled far more easily still, than desire for things that are present.

Proof.— This proposition is proved in the same way as the last proposition from IV. xii. Coroll.

Note.—I think I have now shown the reason, why men are moved by opinion more readily than by true reason, why it is that the true knowledge of good and evil stirs up conflicts in the soul, and often yields to every kind of passion. This state of things gave rise to the exclamation of the poet:—

> «The better path I gaze at and approve,
> The worse—I follow.»

Ecclesiastes seems to have had the same thought in his mind, when he says, " He who increaseth knowledge increaseth sorrow." I have not written the above with the object of drawing the conclusion, that ignorance is more excellent than knowledge, or that a wise man is on a par with a fool in controlling his emotions, but because it is necessary to know the power and the infirmity of our nature, before we can determine what reason can do in restraining the emotions, and what is beyond her power. I have said, that in the present part I shall merely treat of human infirmity. The power of reason over the emotions I have settled to treat separately.

Prop. XVIII. Desire arising from pleasure is, other conditions being equal, stronger than desire arising from pain.

Proof.—Desire is the essence of a man (Def. of the Emotions, i.), that is, the endeavor whereby a man endeavors to persist in his own being. Wherefore desire arising from pleasure is, by the fact of pleasure being felt, increased or helped; on the contrary, desire arising from pain is, by the fact of pain being felt, diminished or hindered; hence the force of desire arising from pleasure must be defined by human power together with the power of an external cause, whereas desire arising from pain must be defined by human power only. Thus the former is the stronger of the two. Q. E. D.

Note.—In these few remarks I have explained the causes of human infirmity and inconstancy, and shown why men do not abide by the precepts of reason. It now remains for me to show what course is marked out for us by reason, which of the emotions are in harmony with the rules of human reason, and which of them are contrary thereto. But, before I begin to prove my propositions in detailed geometrical fashion, it is advisable to sketch them briefly in advance, so that every one may more readily grasp my meaning.

As reason makes no demands contrary to nature, it demands that every man should love himself, should seek that which is useful to him — I mean, that which is really useful to him, should desire everything which really brings man to greater perfection, and should, each for himself, endeavor as far as he can to preserve his own being. This is as necessarily true, as that a whole is greater than its part. (*Cf.* III. iv.)

Again, as virtue is nothing else but action in accordance with the laws of one's own nature (IV. Def. viii.), and as no one endeavors to preserve his own being, except in accordance with the laws of his own nature, it follows, FIRST, that the foundation of virtue is the endeavor to preserve one's own being, and that happiness consists in man's power of preserving his own being; SECONDLY, that virtue is to be desired for its own sake, and that there is nothing more excellent or more useful to us, for the sake of which we should desire it; THIRDLY and lastly, that suicides are weak-minded, and are overcome by external causes repugnant to their nature. Further, it follows from Postulate iv, Part II., that we can never arrive at doing without all external things for the preservation of our being or living, so as to have no relations with things which are outside ourselves. Again, if we consider our mind, we see that our intellect would be more imperfect, if mind were alone, and could understand nothing besides itself. There are, then, many things outside ourselves, which are useful to us, and are, therefore, to be desired. Of such none can be discerned more excellent, than those which are in entire agreement with our nature. For if, for example, two individuals of entirely the same nature are united, they form a combination twice as powerful as either of them singly.

Therefore, to man there is nothing more useful than man — nothing, I repeat, more excellent for preserving their being can be wished for by men, than that all should

so in all points agree, that the minds and bodies of all
should form, as it were, one single mind and one single
body, and that all should, with one consent, as far as they
are able, endeavor to preserve their being, and all with
one consent seek what is useful to them all.   Hence, men
who are governed by reason—that is, who seek what is
useful to them in accordance with reason—desire for
themselves nothing, which they do not also desire for the
rest of mankind, and, consequently, are just, faithful, and
honorable in their conduct.

Such are the dictates of reason, which I purposed thus
briefly to indicate, before beginning to prove them in
greater detail.   I have taken this course in order, if possible, to gain the attention of those who believe, that the
principle that every man is bound to seek what is useful
for himself is the foundation of impiety, rather than of
piety and virtue.

Therefore, after briefly showing that the contrary is the
case, I go on to prove it by the same method, as that
whereby I have hitherto proceeded.

PROP. XIX. Every man, by the laws of his nature,
necessarily desires or shrinks from that which he deems
to be good or bad.

Proof.—The knowledge of good and evil is (IV. viii.)
the emotion of pleasure or pain, in so far as we are conscious thereof; therefore, every man necessarily desires
what he thinks good, and shrinks from what he thinks
bad.   Now this appetite is nothing else but man's nature
or essence (*cf.* the Def. of Appetite, III. ix. note, and
Def. of the Emotions, i.).   Therefore, every man, solely
by the laws of his nature, desires the one, and shrinks
from the other, etc.   Q.E.D.

PROP. XX. The more every man endeavors, and is able
to seek what is useful to him—in other words, to preserve his own being—the more is he endowed with virtue; on the contrary, in proportion as a man neglects to
seek what is useful to him, that is, to preserve his own
being, he is wanting in power.

Proof.—Virtue is human power, which is defined solely
by man's essence (IV. Def. viii.), that is, which is defined

solely by the endeavor made by man to persist in his own being. Wherefore, the more a man endeavors, and is able to preserve his own being, the more is he endowed with virtue, and, consequently (III. iv. and vi.), in so far as a man neglects to preserve his own being, he is wanting in power. Q.E.D.

Note.—No one, therefore, neglects seeking his own good or preserving his own being, unless he be overcome by causes external and foreign to his nature. No one, I say, from the necessity of his own nature, or otherwise than under compulsion from external causes, shrinks from food, or kills himself; which latter may be done in a variety of ways. A man, for instance, kills himself under the compulsion of another man, who twists round his right hand, wherewith he happened to have taken up a sword, and forces him to turn the blade against his own heart; or, again, he may be compelled, like Seneca, by a tyrant's command, to open his own veins—that is, to escape a greater evil by incurring a lesser; or, lastly, latent external causes may so disorder his imagination, and so affect his body, that it may assume a nature contrary to its former one, and whereof the idea cannot exist in the mind (III. x.). But that a man, from the necessity of his own nature, should endeavor to become non-existent, is as impossible as that something should be made out of nothing, as every one will see for himself, after a little reflection.

PROP. XXI. No one can desire to be blessed, to act rightly and to live rightly, without at the same time wishing to be, to act, and to live—in other words, to actually exist.

Proof.—The proof of this proposition, or rather the proposition itself, is self-evident, and is also plain from the definition of desire. For the desire of living, acting, etc., blessedly or rightly, is (Def. of the Emotions, i.) the essence of man—that is (III. vii.), the endeavor made by every one to preserve his own being. Therefore, no one can desire, etc. Q.E.D.

PROP. XXII. No virtue can be conceived as prior to this endeavor to preserve one's own being.

Proof.—The effort for self-preservation is the essence of a thing (III. vii.); therefore, if any virtue could be conceived as prior thereto, the essence of a thing would have to be conceived as prior to itself, which is obviously absurd. Therefore no virtue, etc. Q.E.D.

Corollary.—The effort for self-preservation is the first and only foundation of virtue. For prior to this principle nothing can be conceived, and without it no virtue can be conceived.

PROP. XXIII. Man, in so far as he is determined to a particular action because he has inadequate ideas, cannot be absolutely said to act in obedience to virtue; he can only be so described, in so far as he is determined for the action because he understands.

Proof.—In so far as a man is determined to an action through having inadequate ideas, he is passive (III. i.), that is (III. Def. i. and iii.), he does something, which cannot be perceived solely through his essence, that is (by IV. Def. viii.), which does not follow from his virtue. But, in so far as he is determined for an action because he understands, he is active; that is, he does something, which is perceived through his essence alone, or which adequately follows from his virtue. Q.E.D.

PROP. XXIV. To act absolutely in obedience to virtue is in us the same thing as to act, to live, or to preserve one's being (these three terms are identical in meaning) in accordance with the dictates of reason on the basis of seeking what is useful to one's self.

Proof.—To act absolutely in obedience to virtue is nothing else but to act according to the laws of one's own nature. But we only act, in so far as we understand (III. iii.): therefore to act in obedience to virtue is in us nothing else but to act, to live, or to preserve one's being in obedience to reason, and that on the basis of seeking what is useful for us (IV. xxii. Coroll.). Q.E.D.

PROP. XXV. No one wishes to preserve his being for the sake of anything else.

Proof.—The endeavor, wherewith everything endeavors to persist in its being, is defined solely by the essence of the thing itself (III. vii.); from this alone, and not

from the essence of anything else, it necessarily follows
(III. vi.) that everyone endeavors to preserve his being.
Moreover, this proposition is plain from IV. xxii. Coroll.,
for if a man should endeavor to preserve his being for
the sake of anything else, the last-named thing would
obviously be the basis of virtue, which, by the foregoing
corollary, is absurd. Therefore no one, etc. Q.E.D.

PROP. XXVI. Whatsoever we endeavor in obedience to
reason is nothing further than to understand; neither
does the mind, in so far as it makes use of reason, judge
anything to be useful to it, save such things as are conducive to understanding.

Proof.— The effort for self-preservation is nothing else
but the essence of the thing in question (III. vii.),
which, in so far as it exists such as it is, is conceived to
have force for continuing in existence (III. vi.) and
doing such things as necessarily follow from its given
nature (see the Def. of Appetite, III. ix. note). But
the essence of reason is naught else but our mind, in
so far as it clearly and distinctly understands (see the
definition in II. xl. note ii.); therefore (II. xl.) whatsoever we endeavor in obedience to reason is nothing else
but to understand. Again, since this effort of the mind
wherewith the mind endeavors, in so far as it reasons,
to preserve its own being is nothing else but understanding; this effort at understanding is (IV. xxii.
Coroll.) the first and single basis of virtue, nor shall we
endeavor to understand things for the sake of any
ulterior object (IV. xxv.); on the other hand, the mind,
in so far as it reasons, will not be able to conceive any
good for itself, save such things as are conducive to
understanding.

PROP. XXVII. We know nothing to be certainly good
or evil, save such things as really conduce to understanding, or such as are able to hinder us from understanding.

Proof.— The mind, in so far as it reasons, desires nothing
beyond understanding, and judges nothing to be useful
to itself, save such things as conduce to understanding
(by the foregoing Prop.). But the mind (II. xli. xliii.
and note) cannot possess certainty concerning anything,

except in so far as it has adequate ideas, or (what by II. xl. note, is the same thing) in so far as it reasons. Therefore we know nothing to be good or evil save such things as really conduce, etc. Q.E.D.

PROP. XXVIII. The mind's highest good is the knowledge of God, and the mind's highest virtue is to know God.

Proof.—The mind is not capable of understanding anything higher than God, that is (I. Def. vi.), than a Being absolutely infinite, and without which (I. xv.) nothing can either be or be conceived; therefore (IV. xxvi. and xxvii.), the mind's highest utility or (IV. Def. i.) good is the knowledge of God. Again, the mind is active only in so far as it understands, and only to the same extent can it be said absolutely to act virtuously. The mind's absolute virtue is therefore to understand. Now, as we have already shown, the highest that the mind can understand is God; therefore the highest virtue of the mind is to understand or to know God. Q.E.D.

PROP. XXIX. No individual thing, which is entirely different from our own nature, can help or check our power of activity, and absolutely nothing can do us good or harm, unless it has something in common with our nature.

Proof.—The power of every individual thing, and consequently the power of man, whereby he exists and operates, can only be determined by an individual thing (I. xxviii.), whose nature (II. vi.) must be understood through the same nature as that, through which human nature is conceived. Therefore our power of activity, however it be conceived, can be determined and consequently helped or hindered by the power of any other individual thing, which has something in common with us, but not by the power of anything, of which the nature is entirely different from our own; and since we call good or evil that which is the cause of pleasure or pain (IV. viii.), that is (III. xi. note), which increases or diminishes, helps or hinders, our power of activity; therefore, that which is entirely different from our nature can neither be to us good nor bad. Q.E.D.

Prop. XXX. A thing cannot be bad for us through the quality which it has in common with our nature, but it is bad for us in so far as it is contrary to our nature.

Proof.—We call a thing bad when it is the cause of pain (IV. viii.), that is (by the Def., which see in III. xi. note), when it diminishes or checks our power of action. Therefore, if anything were bad for us through that quality which it has in common with our nature, it would be able itself to diminish or check that which it has in common with our nature, which (III. iv.) is absurd. Wherefore nothing can be bad for us through that quality which it has in common with us, but, on the other hand, in so far as it is bad for us, that is (as we have just shown), in so far as it can diminish or check our power of action, it is contrary to our nature. Q. E. D.

Prop. XXXI. In so far as a thing is in harmony with our nature, it is necessarily good.

Proof.—In so far as a thing is in harmony with our nature, it cannot be bad for it. It will therefore necessarily be either good or indifferent. If it be assumed that it be neither good nor bad, nothing will follow from its nature (IV. Def. i.), which tends to the preservation of our nature, that is (by the hypothesis), which tends to the preservation of the thing itself; but this (III. vi.) is absurd; therefore, in so far as a thing is in harmony with our nature, it is necessarily good. Q. E. D.

Corollary.—Hence it follows, that, in proportion as a thing is in harmony with our nature, so is it more useful or better for us, and *vice versâ*, in proportion as a thing is more useful for us, so is it more in harmony with our nature. For, in so far as it is not in harmony with our nature, it will necessarily be different therefrom or contrary thereto. If different, it can neither be good nor bad (IV. xxix.); if contrary, it will be contrary to that which is in harmony with our nature, that is, contrary to what is good—in short, bad. Nothing, therefore, can be good, except in so far as it is in harmony with our nature; and hence a thing is useful, in proportion as it is in harmony with our nature, and *vice versâ*. Q.E.D.

PROP. XXXII. In so far as men are a prey to passion, they cannot, in that respect, be said to be naturally in harmony.

Proof.—Things, which are said to be in harmony naturally, are understood to agree in power (III. vii.), not in want of power or negation, and consequently not in passion (III. iii. note); wherefore men, in so far as they are a prey to their passions, cannot be said to be naturally in harmony. Q.E.D.

Note.—This is also self-evident; for, if we say that white and black agree only in the fact that neither is red, we absolutely affirm that they do not agree in any respect. So, if we say that a man and a stone agree only in the fact that both are finite—wanting in power, not existing by the necessity of their own nature, or, lastly, indefinitely surpassed by the power of external causes—we should certainly affirm that a man and a stone are in no respect alike; therefore, things which agree only in negation, or in qualities which neither possess, really agree in no respect.

PROP. XXXIII. Men can differ in nature, in so far as they are assailed by those emotions, which are passions, or passive states; and to this extent one and the same man is variable and inconstant.

Proof.—The nature or essence of the emotions cannot be explained solely through our essence or nature (III. Def. i. ii.), but it must be defined by the power, that is (III. vii.), by the nature of external causes in comparison with our own; hence it follows, that there are as many kinds of each emotion as there are external objects whereby we are affected (III. lvi.), and that men may be differently affected by one and the same object (III. li.), and to this extent differ in nature; lastly, that one and the same man may be differently affected toward the same object, and may therefore be variable and inconstant. Q.E.D.

PROP. XXXIV. In so far as men are assailed by emotions which are passions, they can be contrary one to another.

Proof.—A man, for instance Peter, can be the cause of Paul's feeling pain, because he (Peter) possesses something similar to that which Paul hates (III. xvi.), or because Peter has sole possession of a thing which Paul also loves (III. xxxii. and note), or for other causes (of which the chief are enumerated in III. lv. note); it may therefore happen that Paul should hate Peter (Def. of Emotions, vii.), consequently it may easily happen also, that Peter should hate Paul in return, and that each should endeavor to do the other an injury (III. xxxix.), that is (IV. xxx.), that they should be contrary one to another. But the emotion of pain is always a passion or passive state (III. lix.); hence men, in so far as they are assailed by emotions which are passions, can be contrary one to another. Q. E. D.

Note.—I said that Paul may hate Peter, because he conceives that Peter possesses something which he (Paul) also loves; from this it seems at first sight, to follow, that these two men, through both loving the same thing, and, consequently, through agreement of their respective natures, stand in one another's way; if this were so, Props. xxx. and xxxi. of this Part would be untrue. But if we give the matter our unbiased attention, we shall see that the discrepancy vanishes. For the two men are not in one another's way in virtue of the agreement of their natures, that is, through both loving the same thing, but in virtue of one differing from the other. For, in so far as each loves the same thing, the love of each is fostered thereby (III. xxxi.) that is (Def. of the Emotions, vi.) the pleasure of each is fostered thereby. Wherefore it is far from being the case, that they are at variance through both loving the same thing, and through the agreement in their natures. The cause for their opposition lies, as I have said, solely in the fact that they are assumed to differ. For we assume that Peter has the idea of the loved object as already in his possession, while Paul has the idea of the loved object as lost. Hence the one man will be affected with pleasure, the other will be affected with pain, and thus they will be at variance one with another. We can easily show in like manner, that all other causes of hatred depend solely on differences, and not on the agreement between men's natures.

PROP. XXXV. In so far only as men live in obedience to reason, do they always necessarily agree in nature.

Proof.— In so far as men are assailed by emotions that are passions, they can be different in nature (IV. xxxiii.), and at variance one with another. But men are only said to be active, in so far as they act in obedience to reason (III. iii.); therefore, whatsoever follows from human nature in so far as it is defined by reason must (III. Def. ii.) be understood solely through human nature as its proximate cause. But, since every man by the laws of his nature desires that which he deems good, and endeavors to remove that which he deems bad (IV. xix.); and further, since that which we, in accordance with reason, deem good or bad, necessarily is good or bad (II. xli.); it follows that men, in so far as they live in obedience to reason, necessarily do only such things as are necessarily good for human nature, and consequently for each individual man (IV. xxxi. Coroll.); in other words, such things as are in harmony with each man's nature. Therefore, men in so far as they live in obedience to reason, necessarily live always in harmony one with another. Q.E.D.

Corollary I.— There is no individual thing in nature, which is more useful to man, than a man who lives in obedience to reason. For that thing is to man most useful, which is most in harmony with his nature (IV. xxxi. Coroll.); that is, obviously, man. But man acts absolutely according to the laws of his nature, when he lives in obedience to reason (III. Def. ii.), and to this extent only is always necessarily in harmony with the nature of another man (by the last Prop.); wherefore among individual things nothing is more useful to man, than a man who lives in obedience to reason. Q.E.D.

Corollary II.— As every man seeks most that which is useful to him, so are men most useful one to another. For the more a man seeks what is useful to him and endeavors to preserve himself, the more is he endowed with virtue (IV. xx.), or, what is the same thing (IV. Def. viii.), the more is he endowed with power to act according to the laws of his own nature, that is to live in obedience to reason. But men are most in natural harmony, when they live in obedience to reason (by the last Prop.); therefore (by the foregoing Coroll.) men will be most useful one to another, when each seeks most that which is useful to him. Q.E.D.

Note.—What we have just shown is attested by experience so conspicuously, that it is in the mouth of nearly everyone: "Man is to man a God." Yet it rarely happens that men live in obedience to reason, for things are so ordered among them, that they are generally envious and troublesome one to another. Nevertheless they are scarcely able to lead a solitary life, so that the definition of man as a social animal has met with general assent; in fact, men do derive from social life much more convenience than injury. Let satirists then laugh their fill at human affairs, let theologians rail, and let misanthropes praise to their utmost the life of untutored rusticity, let them heap contempt on men and praises on beasts; when all is said, they will find that men can provide for their wants much more easily by mutual help, and that only by uniting their forces can they escape from the dangers that on every side beset them: not to say how much more excellent and worthy of our knowledge it is, to study the actions of men than the actions of beasts. But I will treat of this more at length elsewhere.

PROP. XXXVI. The highest good of those who follow virtue is common to all, and therefore all can equally rejoice therein.

Proof.—To act virtuously is to act in obedience with reason (IV. xxiv.), and whatsoever we endeavor to do in obedience to reason is to understand (IV. xxvi.); therefore (IV. xxviii.) the highest good for those who follow after virtue is to know God; that is (II. xlvii. and note) a good which is common to all and can be possessed by all men equally, in so far as they are of the same nature. Q.E.D.

Note.—Some one may ask how it would be, if the highest good of those who follow after virtue were not common to all? Would it not then follow, as above (IV. xxxiv.), that men living in obedience to reason, that is (IV. xxxv.), men in so far as they agree in nature, would be at variance one with another? To such an inquiry I make answer, that it follows not accidentally but from the very nature of reason, that man's highest good is common to all, inasmuch as it is deduced from the very essence of man, in so far as defined by reason; and that a man could neither be, nor be conceived without the power of taking pleasure in this highest good. For it belongs to the essence of the human mind (II. xlvii.), to have an adequate knowledge of the eternal and infinite essence of God.

Prop. XXXVII. The good which every man, who follows after virtue, desires for himself he will also desire for other men, and so much the more, in proportion as he has a greater knowledge of God.

Proof. — Men, in so far as they live in obedience to reason, are most useful to their fellow men (IV. xxxv., Coroll. i.); therefore (IV. xix.), we shall in obedience to reason necessarily endeavor to bring about that men should live in obedience to reason. But the good which every man, in so far as he is guided by reason, or, in other words, follows after virtue, desires for himself, is to understand (IV. xxvi.); wherefore the good, which each follower of virtue seeks for himself, he will desire also for others. Again, desire, in so far as it is referred to the mind, is the very essence of the mind (Def. of the Emotions, i.); now the essence of the mind consists in knowledge (II. xi.), which involves the knowledge of God (II. xlvii.) and without it (I. xv.), can neither be, nor be conceived; therefore, in proportion as the mind's essence involves a greater knowledge of God, so also will be greater the desire of the follower of virtue, that other men should possess that which he seeks as good for himself. Q. E. D.

Another Proof.—The good, which a man desires for himself and loves, he will love more constantly, if he sees that

others love it also (III. xxxi.); he will therefore endeavor
that others should love it also; and as the good in question
is common to all, and therefore all can rejoice therein, he
will endeavor, for the same reason, to bring about that
all should rejoice therein, and this he will do the more
(III. xxxvii.), in proportion as his own enjoyment of the
good is greater.

Note I.— He who, guided by emotion only, endeavors to
cause others to love what he loves himself, and to make
the rest of the world live according to his own fancy, acts
solely by impulse, and is, therefore, hateful, especially to
those who take delight in something different, and accordingly study and, by similar impulse, endeavor to make
men live in accordance with what pleases themselves.
Again, as the highest good sought by men under the
guidance of emotion is often such, that it can only be
possessed by a single individual, it follows that those who
love it are not consistent in their intentions, but, while they
delight to sing its praises, fear to be believed. But he, who
endeavors to lead men by reason, does not act by impulse
but courteously and kindly, and his intention is always
consistent. Again, whatsoever we desire and do, whereof
we are the cause in so far as we possess the idea of God, or
know God, I set down to RELIGION. The desire of well-
doing, which is engendered by a life according to reason, I
call PIETY. Further, the desire, whereby a man living
according to reason is bound to associate others with himself in friendship, I call HONOR; by HONORABLE I mean that
which is praised by men living according to reason, and by
BASE I mean that which is repugnant to the gaining of
friendship. I have also shown in addition what are the
foundations of a state; and the difference between true
virtue and infirmity may be readily gathered from what I
have said; namely, that true virtue is nothing else but
living in accordance with reason; while infirmity is nothing else but man's allowing himself to be led by things
which are external to himself, and to be by them determined to act in a manner demanded by the general disposition of things rather than by his own nature considered
solely in itself.

Such are the matters which I engaged to prove in Prop. xviii. of this Part, whereby it is plain that the law against the slaughtering of animals is founded rather on vain superstition and womanish pity than on sound reason. The rational quest of what is useful to us further teaches us the necessity of associating ourselves with our fellowmen, but not with beasts, or things, whose nature is different from our own; we have the same rights in respect to them as they have in respect to us. Nay, as everyone's right is defined by his virtue, or power, men have far greater rights over beasts than beasts have over men. Still I no not deny that beasts feel: what I deny is, that we may not consult our own advantage and use them as we please, treating them in the way which best suits us; for their nature is not like ours, and their emotions are naturally different from human emotions (III. lvii. note). It remains for me to explain what I mean by just and unjust, sin and merit. On these points see the following note.

Note II.— In the Appendix to Part I. I undertook to explain praise and blame, merit and sin, justice and injustice.

Concerning praise and blame I have spoken in III. xxix. note; the time has now come to treat of the remaining terms. But I must first say a few words concerning man in the state of nature and in society.

Even man exists by sovereign natural right, and, consequently, by sovereign natural right performs those actions which follow from the necessity of his own nature; therefore by sovereign natural right every man judges what is good and what is bad, takes care of his own advantage according to his own disposition (IV. xix. and xx.), avenges the wrongs done to him (III. xl. Coroll. ii.), and endeavors to preserve that which he loves and to destroy that which he hates (III. xxviii.). Now, if men lived under the guidance of reason, everyone would remain in possession of this his right, without any injury being done to his neighbor (IV. xxxv. Coroll. i.). But seeing that they are a prey to their emotions, which far surpass human power or virtue (IV. vi.), they are often drawn in different directions, and being at variance one with another (IV. xxxiii. xxxiv.), stand in need of mutual help (IV. xxxv. note). Wherefore, in order that men may live together in harmony, and may aid one another, it is necessary that they should forego their natural right, and, for the sake of security, refrain from all actions which can injure their fellow-men. The way in which this end can be attained, so that men who are necessarily a prey to their emotions (IV. iv. Coroll.), inconstant, and diverse, should be able to render each other mutually secure, and feel mutual trust, is evident from IV. vii. and III. xxxix. It is there shown, that an emotion can only be restrained by an emotion stronger than, and contrary to itself, and that men avoid inflicting injury through fear of incurring a greater injury themselves.

On this law society can be established, so long as it keeps in its own hand the right, possessed by everyone, of avenging injury, and pronouncing on good and evil; and provided it also possesses the power to lay down a general rule of conduct, and to pass laws sanctioned, not by reason, which is powerless in restraining emotion, but by threats (IV. xvii. note). Such a society established with laws and the power of preserving itself is called a STATE, while those who live under its protection are called CITIZENS. We may readily understand that there is in the state of nature nothing, which by universal consent is pronounced good or bad; for in the state of nature every one thinks solely of his own advantage, and according to his disposition, with reference only to his individual advantage, decides what is good or bad, being bound by no law to anyone besides himself.

In the state of nature, therefore, sin is inconceivable; it can only exist in a state, where good and evil are pronounced on by common consent, and where everyone is bound to obey the State authority. SIN, then, is nothing else but disobedience, which is therefore punished by the right of the State only. Obedience, on the other hand, is set down as MERIT, inasmuch as a man is thought worthy of merit, if he takes delight in the advantages which a State provides.

Again, in the state of nature, no one is by common consent master of anything, nor is there anything in nature, which can be said to belong to one man rather than another: all things are common to all. Hence, in the state of nature, we can conceive no wish to render to every man his own, or to deprive a man of that which belongs to him; in other words, there is nothing in the state of nature answering to justice and injustice. Such ideas are only possible in a social state, when it is decreed by common consent what belongs to one man and what to another.

From all these considerations it is evident, that justice and injustice, sin and merit, are extrinsic ideas, and not attributes which display the nature of the mind. But I have said enough.

Prop. XXXVIII. Whatsoever disposes the human body, so as to render it capable of being affected in an increased number of ways, or of affecting external bodies in an increased number of ways, is useful to man; and is so, in proportion as the body is thereby rendered more capable of being affected or affecting other bodies in an increased number of ways; contrariwise, whatsoever renders the body less capable in this respect is hurtful to man.

Proof.— Whatsoever thus increases the capabilities of the body increases also the mind's capability of perception (II. xiv.); therefore, whatsoever thus disposes the body and thus renders it capable, is necessarily good or useful (IV. xxvi. xxvii.); and is so in proportion to the extent to which it can render the body capable; contrariwise (II. xiv., IV. xxvi. xxvii.), it is hurtful, if it renders the body in this respect less capable. Q.E.D.

Prop. XXXIX. Whatsoever brings about the preservation of the proportion of motion and rest, which the parts of the human body mutually possess, is good; contrariwise, whatsoever causes a change in such proportion is bad.

Proof.— The human body needs many other bodies for its preservation (II. Post. iv.). But that which constitutes the specific reality (*forma*) of a human body is, that its parts communicate their several motions one to

another in a certain fixed proportion (Def. before Lemma
iv. after II. xiii.). Therefore, whatsoever brings about
the preservation of the proportion between motion and
rest, which the parts of the human body mutually possess, preserves the specific reality of the human body,
and consequently renders the human body capable of being
affected in many ways and of affecting external bodies in
many ways; consequently it is good (by the last Prop.).
Again, whatsoever brings about a change in the aforesaid
proportion causes the human body to assume another
specific character, in other words (see Preface to this
Part toward the end, though the point is indeed self-
evident), to be destroyed, and consequently totally incapable of being affected in an increased number of ways;
therefore it is bad. Q.E.D.

Note.— The extent to which such causes can injure or
be of service to the mind will be explained in the Fifth
Part.   But I would here remark that I consider that a body
undergoes death, when the proportion of motion and rest
which obtained mutually among its several parts is changed.
For I do not venture to deny that a human body, while
keeping the circulation of the blood and other properties,
wherein the life of the body is thought to consist, may
none the less be changed into another nature totally different from its own.   There is no reason, which compels me
to maintain that a body does not die, unless it becomes a
corpse; nay, experience would seem to point to the opposite conclusion.   It sometimes happens, that a man undergoes such changes, that I could hardly call him the same.
As I have heard tell of a certain Spanish poet, who had
been seized with sickness, and though he recovered therefrom yet remained so oblivious of his past life, that he
would not believe the plays and tragedies he had written to be his own: indeed, he might have been taken
for a grown-up child, if he had also forgotten his native
tongue.   If this instance seems incredible, what shall we
say of infants?   A man of ripe age deems their nature
so unlike his own, that he can only be persuaded that he too
has been an infant by the analogy of other men.   However, I prefer to leave such questions undiscussed, lest I

should give ground to the superstitious for raising new issues.

PROP. XL. Whatsoever conduces to man's social life, or causes men to live together in harmony, is useful, whereas whatsoever brings discord into a State is bad.

Proof.— For whatsoever causes men to live together in harmony also causes them to live according to reason (IV. xxxv.), and is therefore (IV. xxvi. and xxvii.) good, and (for the same reason) whatsoever brings about discord is bad. Q.E.D.

PROP. XLI. Pleasure in itself is not bad but good: contrariwise, pain in itself is bad.

Proof.— Pleasure (III. xi. and note) is emotion, whereby the body's power of activity is increased or helped; pain is emotion, whereby the body's power of activity is diminished or checked; therefore (IV. xxxviii.) pleasure in itself is good, etc. Q.E.D.

PROP. XLII. Mirth cannot be excessive, but is always good; contrariwise, Melancholy is always bad.

Proof.— Mirth (see its Def. in III. xi. note) is pleasure, which, in so far as it is referred to the body, consists in all parts of the body being affected equally: that is (III. xi.), the body's power of activity is increased or aided in such a manner, that the several parts maintain their former proportion of motion and rest; therefore Mirth is always good (IV. xxxix.), and cannot be excessive. But Melancholy (see its Def. in the same note to III. xi.) is pain, which, in so far as it is referred to the body, consists in the absolute decrease or hindrance of the body's power of activity; therefore (IV. xxxviii.) it is always bad. Q.E.D.

PROP. XLIII. Stimulation may be excessive and bad; on the other hand, grief may be good, in so far as stimulation or pleasure is bad.

Proof.— Localized pleasure or stimulation (*titillatio*) is pleasure, which, in so far as it is referred to the body, consists in one or some of its parts being affected more than the rest (see its Def., III. xi. note); the power of this emotion may be sufficient to overcome other actions of the body (IV. vi.), and may remain obstinately fixed therein, thus rendering it incapable of being affected in a variety of other ways: therefore (IV. xxxviii.) it may be bad. Again, grief, which is pain, cannot as such be good (IV. xli.). But, as its force and increase is defined by the power of an external cause compared with our own (IV. v.), we can conceive infinite degrees and modes of strength in this emotion (IV. iii.); we can, therefore, conceive it as capable of restraining stimulation, and preventing its becoming excessive, and hindering the body's capabilities; thus, to this extent, it will be good. Q.E.D.

PROP. XLIV. Love and desire may be excessive.

Proof.— Love is pleasure, accompanied by the idea of an external cause (Def. of Emotions, vi.); therefore stimulation, accompanied by the idea of an external cause is love (III. xi. note); hence love may be excessive. Again, the strength of desire varies in proportion to the emotion from which it arises (III. xxxvii.). Now emotion may overcome all the rest of men's actions (IV. vi.); so, therefore, can desire, which arises from the same emotion, overcome all other desires, and become excessive, as we showed in the last proposition concerning stimulation.

Note.— Mirth, which I have stated to be good, can be conceived more easily than it can be observed. For the emotions, whereby we are daily assailed, are generally referred to some part of the body which is affected more than the rest; hence the emotions are generally excessive, and so fix the mind in the contemplation of one object, that it is unable to think of others; and although men, as a rule, are a prey to many emotions — and very few are found who are always assailed by one and the same — yet there are cases, where one and the same emotion remains obstinately fixed. We sometimes see men so absorbed in one object, that, although it be not present, they think they have it before them; when this is the case with a man who is not asleep, we say he is delirious or mad; nor are those persons who are inflamed with love, and who dream all night and all day about nothing but their mistress, or some woman, considered as less mad,

for they are made objects of ridicule. But when a miser
thinks of nothing but gain or money, or when an ambitious man thinks of nothing but glory, they are not
reckoned to be mad, because they are generally harmful,
and are thought worthy of being hated. But, in reality,
Avarice, Ambition, Lust, etc., are species of madness,
though they may not be reckoned among diseases.

PROP. XLV. Hatred can never be good.

Proof.— When we hate a man, we endeavor to destroy
him (III. xxxix.), that is (IV. xxxvii.), we endeavor to
do something that is bad. Therefore, etc. Q. E. D.

N.B. Here, and in what follows, I mean by hatred
only hatred toward men.

Corollary. I.— Envy, derision, contempt, anger, revenge,
and other emotions attributable to hatred, or arising therefrom, are bad; this is evident from III. xxxix. and IV.
xxxvii.

Corollary II.— Whatsoever we desire from motives of
hatred is base, and in a state unjust. This also is evident from III. xxxix., and from the definitions of base-
ness and injustice in IV. xxxvii. note.

Note.— Between derision (which I have in Coroll. I.
stated to be bad) and laughter I recognize a great difference. For laughter, as also jocularity, is merely pleasure; therefore, so long as it be not excessive, it is in
itself good (IV. xli.). Assuredly, nothing forbids man to
enjoy himself, save grim and gloomy superstition. For
why is it more lawful to satiate one's hunger and thirst
than to drive away one's melancholy? I reason, and have
convinced myself as follows: No deity, nor any one else,
save the envious, takes pleasure in my infirmity and dis-
comfort, nor sets down to my virtue the tears, sobs, fear,
and the like, which are signs of infirmity of spirit; on
the contrary, the greater the pleasure wherewith we are
affected, the greater the perfection whereto we pass; in
other words, the more must we necessarily partake of
the divine nature. Therefore, to make use of what comes
in our way, and to enjoy it as much as possible (not to
the point of satiety, for that would not be enjoyment)
is the part of a wise man. I say it is the part of a wise

man to refresh and recreate himself with moderate and pleasant food and drink, and also with perfumes, with the soft beauty of growing plants, with dress, with music, with many sports, with theaters, and the like, such as every man may make use of without injury to his neighbor. For the human body is composed of very numerous parts, of diverse nature, which continually stand in need of fresh and varied nourishment, so that the whole body may be equally capable of performing all the actions, which follow from the necessity of its own nature; and, consequently, so that the mind may also be equally capable of understanding many things simultaneously. This way of life, then, agrees best with our principles, and also with general practice; therefore, if there be any question of another plan, the plan we have mentioned is the best, and in every way to be commended. There is no need for me to set forth the matter more clearly or in more detail.

PROP. XLVI. He who lives under the guidance of reason, endeavors, as far as possible, to render back love, or kindness, for other men's hatred, anger, contempt, etc., toward him.

Proof.—All emotions of hatred are bad (IV. xlv. Coroll. i.); therefore he who lives under the guidance of reason will endeavor, as far as possible, to avoid being assailed by such emotions (IV. xix.); consequently, he will also endeavor to prevent others being so assailed (IV. xxxvii.). But hatred is increased by being reciprocated, and can be quenched by love (III. xliii.), so that hatred may pass into love (III. xliv.); therefore he who lives under the guidance of reason will endeavor to repay hatred with love, that is, with kindness. Q.E.D.

Note.—He who chooses to avenge wrongs with hatred is assuredly wretched. But he, who strives to conquer hatred with love, fights his battle in joy and confidence; he withstands many as easily as one, and has very little need of fortune's aid. Those whom he vanquishes yield joyfully, not through failure, but through increase in their powers; all these consequences follow so plainly from the mere definitions of love and understanding, that I have no need to prove them in detail.

PROP. XLVII. Emotions of hope and fear cannot be in themselves good.

Proof.—Emotions of hope and fear cannot exist without pain. For fear is pain (Def. of the Emotions, xiii.), and hope (Def. of the Emotions, Explanation xii. and xiii.) cannot exist without fear; therefore (IV. xli.) these emotions cannot be good in themselves, but only in so far as they can restrain excessive pleasure (IV. xliii.). Q.E.D.

Note.—We may add, that these emotions show defective knowledge and an absence of power in the mind; for the same reason confidence, despair, joy, and disappointment are signs of a want of mental power. For although confidence and joy are pleasurable emotions, they nevertheless imply a preceding pain, namely, hope and fear. Wherefore the more we endeavor to be guided by reason, the less do we depend on hope; we endeavor to free ourselves from fear, and, as far as we can, to dominate fortune, directing our actions by the sure counsels of wisdom.

PROP. XLVIII. The emotions of over-esteem and disparagement are always bad.

Proof.—These emotions (see Def. of the Emotions, xxi. xxii.) are repugnant to reason; and are therefore (IV. xxvi. xxvii.) bad. Q.E.D.

PROP. XLIX. Over-esteem is apt to render its object proud.

Proof.—If we see that anyone rates us too highly, for love's sake, we are apt to become elated (III xli.), or to be pleasurably affected (Def. of the Emotions, xxx.); the good which we hear of ourselves we readily believe (III. xxv.); and therefore, for love's sake, rate ourselves too highly; in other words, we are apt to become proud. Q.E.D.

PROP. L. Pity, in a man who lives under the guidance of reason, is in itself bad and useless.

Proof.—Pity (Def. of the Emotions, xviii.) is a pain, and therefore (IV. xli.) is in itself bad. The good effect which follows, namely, our endeavor to free the object of our pity from misery, is an action which we desire to do solely at the dictation of reason (IV. xxxvii.); only at the dictation of reason are we able to perform any action, which we know for certain to be good (IV. xxvii.); thus, in a man who lives under the guidance of reason, pity in itself is useless and bad. Q.E.D.

Note.— He who rightly realizes that all things follow from the necessity of the divine nature, and come to pass in accordance with the eternal laws and rules of nature, will not find anything worthy of hatred, derision, or contempt, nor will he bestow pity on anything, but to the utmost extent of human virtue he will endeavor to do well, as the saying is, and to rejoice. We may add, that he, who is easily touched with compassion, and is moved by another's sorrow or tears, often does something which he afterward regrets; partly because we can never be sure that an action caused by emotion is good, partly because we are easily deceived by false tears. I am in this place expressly speaking of a man living under the guidance of reason. He who is moved to help others neither by reason nor by compassion, is rightly styled inhuman, for (III. xxvii.) he seems unlike a man.

PROP. LI. Approval is not repugnant to reason, but can agree therewith and arise therefrom.

Proof.— Approval is love toward one who has done good to another (Def. of the Emotions, xix.); therefore it may be referred to the mind, in so far as the latter is active (III. lix.), that is (III. iii.) in so far as it understands; therefore, it is in agreement with reason, etc. Q.E.D.

Another Proof.— He who lives under the guidance of reason, desires for others the good which he seeks for himself (IV. xxxvii.); wherefore from seeing someone doing good to his fellow his own endeavor to do good is aided; in other words he will feel pleasure (III. xi. note) accompanied by the idea of the benefactor. Therefore he approves of him. Q.E.D.

Note.— Indignation as we defined it (Def. of the Emotions, xx.) is necessarily evil (IV. xlv.); we may, however, remark that, when the sovereign power for the sake of preserving peace punishes a citizen who has injured another, it should not be said to be indignant with the criminal, for it is not incited by hatred to ruin him, it is led by a sense of duty to punish him.

Prop. LII. Self-approval may arise from reason, and that which arises from reason is the highest possible.

Proof.— Self-approval is pleasure arising from a man's contemplation of himself and his own power of action (Def. of the Emotions, xxv.). But a man's true power of action or virtue is reason herself (III. iii.), as the said man clearly and distinctly contemplates her (II. xl. xliii.); therefore self-approval arises from reason. Again, when a man is contemplating himself, he only perceives clearly and distinctly or adequately, such things as follow from his power of action (III. Def. ii.), that is (III. iii.), from his power of understanding; therefore in such contemplation alone does the highest possible self-approval arise. Q.E.D.

Note.— Self-approval is in reality the highest object for which we can hope. For (as we showed in IV. xxv.) no one endeavors to preserve his being for the sake of any ulterior object, and, as this approval is more and more fostered and strengthened by praise (III. liii. Coroll.), and on the contrary (III. lv. Coroll.) is more and more disturbed by blame, fame becomes the most powerful of incitements to action, and life under disgrace is almost unendurable.

Prop. LIII. Humility is not a virtue, or does not arise from reason.

Proof.— Humility is pain arising from a man's contemplation of his own infirmities (Def. of the Emotions, xxvi.). But, in so far as a man knows himself by true reason, he is assumed to understand his essence, that is, his power (III. vii.). Wherefore, if a man in self-contemplation perceives any infirmity in himself, it is not by virtue of his understanding himself, but (III. lv.) by virtue of his power of activity being checked. But, if we assume that a man perceives his own infirmity by virtue of understanding something stronger than himself, by the knowledge of which he determines his own power of activity, this is the same as saying that we conceive that a man understands himself distinctly (IV. xxvi.), because his power of activity is aided. Wherefore humility, or the pain which arises from a man's contemplation of his own infirmity, does not arise from the contemplation or reason, and is not a virtue but a passion. Q.E.D.

PROP. LIV. Repentance is not a virtue, or does not arise from reason; but he who repents of an action is doubly wretched or infirm.

Proof.—The first part of this proposition is proved like the foregoing one. The second part is proved from the mere definition of the emotion in question (Def. of the Emotions, xxvii.). For the man allows himself to be overcome, first, by evil desires; secondly, by pain.

Note.—As men seldom live under the guidance of reason, these two emotions, namely, Humility and Repentance, as also Hope and Fear, bring more good than harm; hence, as we must sin, we had better sin in that direction. For, if all men who are a prey to emotion were all equally proud, they would shrink from nothing, and would fear nothing; how then could they be joined or linked together in bonds of union? The crowd plays the tyrant, when it is not in fear; hence we need not wonder that the prophets, who consulted the good, not of a few, but of all, so strenuously commended Humility, Repentance, and Reverence. Indeed, those who are a prey to these emotions may be led much more easily than others to live under the guidance of reason, that is, to become free and to enjoy the life of the blessed.

PROP. LV. Extreme pride or dejection indicates extreme ignorance of self.

Proof.—This is evident from Def. of the Emotions, xxviii. and xxix.

PROP. LVI. Extreme pride or dejection indicates extreme infirmity of spirit.

Proof.—The first foundation of virtue is self-preservation (IV. xxii. Coroll.) under the guidance of reason (IV. xxiv.). He, therefore, who is ignorant of himself, is ignorant of the foundation of all virtues, and consequently of all virtues. Again, to act virtuously is merely to act under the guidance of reason (IV. xxiv.): now he, that acts under the guidance of reason, must necessarily know that he so acts (II. xliii.). Therefore, he who is in extreme ignorance of himself, and consequently of all virtues, acts least in obedience to virtue; in other words (IV. Def. viii.), is most infirm of spirit. Thus extreme pride or dejection indicates extreme infirmity of spirit. Q.E.D.

Corollary.— Hence it most clearly follows, that the proud and the dejected specially fall a prey to the emotions.

Note.— Yet dejection can be more easily corrected than pride; for the latter being a pleasurable emotion, and the former a painful emotion, the pleasurable is stronger than the painful (IV. xviii.).

PROP. LVII. The proud man delights in the company of flatterers and parasites, but hates the company of the high-minded.

Proof.— Pride is pleasure arising from a man's over-estimation of himself (Def. of the Emotions, xxviii. and vi.); this estimation the proud man will endeavor to foster by all the means in his power (III. xiii. note); he will therefore delight in the company of flatterers and parasites (whose character is too well known to need definition here), and will avoid the company of high-minded men, who value him according to his deserts. Q.E.D.

Note.— It would be too long a task to enumerate here all the evil results of pride, inasmuch as the proud are a prey to all the emotions, though to none of them less than to love and pity. I cannot, however, pass over in silence the fact, that a man may be called proud from his under-estimation of other people; and, therefore, pride in this sense may be defined as pleasure arising from the false opinion, whereby a man may consider himself superior to his fellows. The dejection, which is the opposite quality to this sort of pride, may be defined as pain arising from the false opinion, whereby a man may think himself inferior to his fellows. Such being the case, we can easily see that a proud man is necessarily

envious (III. xli. note), and only takes pleasure in the
company, who fool his weak mind to the top of his bent,
and make him insane instead of merely foolish.

Though dejection is the emotion contrary to pride, yet
is the dejected man very near akin to the proud man.
For, inasmuch as his pain arises from a comparison between his own infirmity and other men's power or virtue,
it will be removed, or, in other words, he will feel pleasure, if his imagination be occupied in contemplating
other men's faults; whence arises the proverb, "The unhappy are comforted by finding fellow-sufferers." Contrariwise, he will be the more pained in proportion as
he thinks himself inferior to others; hence none are so
prone to envy as the dejected, they are specially keen
in observing men's actions, with a view to fault-finding
rather than correction, in order to reserve their praises
for dejection, and to glory therein, though all the time
with a dejected air. These effects follow as necessarily
from the said emotion, as it follows from the nature of
a triangle, that the three angles are equal to two right
angles. I have already said that I call these and similar
emotions bad, solely in respect to what is useful to man.
The laws of nature have regard to nature's general order, whereof man is but a part. I mention this, in passing, lest any should think that I have wished to set forth
the faults and irrational deeds of men rather than the
nature and properties of things. For, as I said in the
preface to the third Part, I regard human emotions and
their properties as on the same footing with other natural phenomena. Assuredly human emotions indicate
the power and ingenuity of nature, if not of human
nature, quite as fully as other things which we admire,
and which we delight to contemplate. But I pass on to
note those qualities in the emotions, which bring advantage to man, or inflict injury upon him.

PROP. LVIII. Honor (*gloria*) is not repugnant to
reason, but may arise therefrom.

Proof.— This is evident from Def. of the Emotions,
xxx., and also from the definition of an honorable man
(IV. xxxvii. note i.).

Note.— Empty honor, as it is styled, is self-approval fostered only by the good opinion of the populace; when this good opinion ceases there ceases also the self-approval, in other words, the highest object of each man's love (IV. lii. note); consequently he whose honor is rooted in popular approval must, day by day, anxiously strive, act, and scheme in order to retain his reputation. For the populace is variable and inconstant, so that, if a reputation be not kept up, it quickly withers away. Everyone wishes to catch popular applause for himself, and readily represses the fame of others. The object of the strife being estimated as the greatest of all good, each combatant is seized with a fierce desire to put down his rivals in every possible way, till he who at last comes out victorious is more proud of having done harm to others than of having done good to himself. This sort of honor, then, is really empty, being nothing.

The points to note concerning shame may easily be inferred from what was said on the subject of mercy and repentance. I will only add that shame, like compassion, though not a virtue, is yet good in so far as it shows that the feeler of shame is really imbued with the desire to live honorably; in the same way as suffering is good, as showing that the injured part is not mortified. Therefore, though a man who feels shame is sorrowful, he is yet more perfect than he, who is shameless, and has no desire to live honorably.

Such are the points which I undertook to remark upon concerning the emotions of pleasure and pain; as for the desires, they are good or bad according as they spring from good or evil emotions. But all, in so far as they are engendered in us by emotions wherein the mind is passive, are blind (as is evident from what was said in IV. xliv. note), and would be useless, if men could easily be induced to live by the guidance of reason only, as I will now briefly show.

PROP. LIX. To all the actions, whereto we are determined by emotion wherein the mind is passive, we can be determined without emotion by reason.

Proof.—To act rationally is nothing else (III. iii. and

Def. ii.) but to perform those actions, which follow from the necessity of our nature considered in itself alone. But pain is bad, in so far as it diminishes or checks the power of action (IV. xli.); wherefore we cannot by pain be determined to any action, which we should be unable to perform under the guidance of reason. Again, pleasure is bad only in so far as it hinders a man's capability for action (IV. xli. xliii.); therefore to this extent we could not be determined by it to any action, which we could not perform under the guidance of reason. Lastly, pleasure, in so far as it is good, is in harmony with reason (for it consists in the fact that a man's capability for action is increased or aided); nor is the mind passive therein, except in so far as a man's power of action is not increased to the extent of affording him an adequate conception of himself and his actions (III. iii. and note).

Wherefore, if a man who is pleasurably affected be brought to such a state of perfection that he gains an adequate conception of himself and his own actions, he will be equally, nay more, capable of those actions, to which he is determined by emotion wherein the mind is passive. But all emotions are attributable to pleasure, to pain, or to desire (Def. of the Emotions, iv. explanation); and desire (Def. of the Emotions, i.) is nothing else but the attempt to act; therefore, to all actions, etc. Q. E. D.

Another Proof.— A given action is called bad, in so far as it arises from one being affected by hatred or any evil emotion. But no action, considered in itself alone, is either good or bad (as we pointed out in the preface to Part iv.), one and the same action being sometimes good, sometimes bad; wherefore to the action which is sometimes bad, or arises from some evil emotion, we may be led by reason (IV. xix.). Q. E. D.

Note.—An example will put this point in a clearer light. The action of striking, in so far as it is considered physically, and in so far as we merely look to the fact that a man raises his arm, clenches his fist, and moves his whole arm violently downward, is a virtue or excellence which is conceived as proper to the structure of the human body. If, then, a man, moved by anger or hatred, is led to clench his fist or to move his arm, this result takes place (as we showed in Part II.), because one and the same action can be associated with various mental images of things; therefore we may be determined to the performance of one and the same action by confused ideas, or by clear and distinct ideas. Hence it is evident that every desire which springs from emotion, wherein the mind is passive, would become useless, if men could be guided by reason. Let us now see why desire which arises from emotion, wherein the mind is passive is called by us blind.

Prop. LX. Desire arising from a pleasure or pain, that is not attributable to the whole body, but only to one or certain parts thereof, is without utility in respect to a man as a whole.

Proof.—Let it be assumed, for instance, that A, a part of a body, is so strengthened by some external cause, that it prevails over the remaining parts (IV. vi.). This part will not endeavor to do away with its own powers, in order that the other parts of the body may perform its office; for this it would be necessary for it to have a force or power of doing away with its own powers, which (III. vi.) is absurd. The said part, and, consequently, the mind also, will endeavor to preserve its condition. Wherefore desire arising from a pleasure of the kind aforesaid has no utility in reference to a man as a whole. If it be assumed, on the other hand, that the part, A, be checked so that the remaining parts prevail, it may be proved in the same manner that desire arising from pain has no utility in respect to a man as a whole. Q.E.D.

Note.—As pleasure is generally (IV. xliv. note) attributed to one part of the body, we generally desire to preserve our being without taking into consideration our health as a whole: to which it may be added, that the desires which have most hold over us (IV. ix.) take account of the present and not of the future.

Prop. LXI. Desire which springs from reason cannot be excessive.

Proof.—Desire (Def. of the Emotions, i.) considered absolutely in the actual essence of man, in so far as it is conceived as in any way determined to a particular activity by some given modification of itself. Hence desire, which arises from reason, that is, (III. iii.), which is engendered in us in so far as we act, is the actual essence or nature of man, in so far as it is conceived as determined to such activites as are adequately conceived through man's essence only (III. Def. ii.). Now, if such desire could be excessive, human nature considered in itself alone would be able to exceed itself, or would be able to do more than it can, a manifest contradiction. Therefore, such desire cannot be excessive. Q.E.D.

Prop. LXII. In so far as the mind conceives a thing under the dictates of reason, it is affected equally, whether the idea be of a thing future, past, or present.

Proof.—Whatsoever the mind conceives under the guidance of reason, it conceives under the form of eternity or necessity (II. xliv. Coroll. ii.), and is therefore affected with the same certitude (II. xliii. and note). Wherefore, whether the thing be present, past, or future, the mind conceives it under the same necessity and is affected with the same certitude; and whether the idea be of something present, past, or future, it will in all cases be equally true (II. xli.); that is, it will always possess the same properties of an adequate idea (II. Def. iv.); therefore, in so far as the mind conceives things under the dictates of reason, it is affected in the same manner, whether the idea be of a thing future, past, or present. Q.E.D.

Note.—If we could possess an adequate knowledge of the duration of things, and could determine by reason their periods of existence, we should contemplate things future with the same emotion as things present; and the mind would desire as though it were present the good which it conceived as future; consequently it would necessarily neglect a lesser good in the present for the sake of a greater good in the future, and would in no wise desire that which is good in the present but a source of evil in the future, as we shall presently show. However, we can have but a very inadequate knowledge of the duration of things (II. xxxi.); and the periods of their existence (II. xliv. note) we can only determine by imagination, which is not so powerfully affected by the future as by the present. Hence such true knowledge of good and evil as we possess is merely abstract or general, and the judgment which we pass on the order of things and the connection of causes, with a view to determining what is good or bad for us in the present, is rather imaginary than real. Therefore it is nothing wonderful, if the desire arising from such knowledge of good and evil, in so far as it looks on into the future, be more readily checked than the desire of things which are agreeable at the present time. (*Cf.* IV. xvi.)

PROP. LXIII. He who is led by fear, and does good in order to escape evil, is not led by reason.

Proof.—All the emotions which are attributable to the mind as active, or in other words to reason, are emotions of pleasure and desire (III. lix.); therefore, he who is led by fear, and does good in order to escape evil, is not led by reason.

Note.—Superstitious persons, who know better how to rail at vice than how to teach virtue, and who strive not to guide men by reason, but so to restrain them that they would rather escape evil than love virtue, have no other aim but to make others as wretched as themselves; wherefore it is nothing wonderful, if they be generally troublesome and odious to their fellow-men.

Corollary.—Under desire which springs from reason, we seek good directly, and shun evil indirectly.

Proof.—Desire which springs from reason can only spring from a pleasurable emotion, wherein the mind is not passive (III. lix.), in other words, from a pleasure which cannot be excessive (IV. lxi.), and not from pain; wherefore this desire springs from the knowledge of good, not of evil (IV. viii.); hence, under the guidance of reason we seek good directly and only by implication shun evil. Q.E.D.

Note.—This Corollary may be illustrated by the example of a sick and a healthy man. The sick man through fear of death eats what he naturally shrinks from, but the healthy man takes pleasure in his food, and thus gets a better enjoyment out of life, than if he were in fear of death, and desired directly to avoid it. So a judge, who condemns a criminal to death, not from hatred or anger, but from love of the public well-being, is guided solely by reason.

PROP. LXIV. The knowledge of evil is an inadequate knowledge.

Proof.— The knowledge of evil (IV. viii.) is pain, in so far as we are conscious thereof. Now pain is the transition to a lesser perfection (Def. of the Emotions, iii.), and therefore cannot be understood through man's nature (III. vi. and vii.); therefore it is a passive state (III. Def. ii.) which (III. iii.) depends on inadequate ideas; consequently the knowledge thereof (II. xxix.), namely, the knowlege of evil, is inadequate. Q.E.D.

Corollary.— Hence it follows that, if the human mind possessed only adequate ideas, it would form no conception of evil.

PROP. LXV. Under the guidance of reason we should pursue the greater of two good and the lesser of two evils.

Proof.— A good which prevents our enjoyment of a greater good is in reality an evil; for we apply the terms good and bad to things, in so far as we compare them one with another (see Preface to this Part); therefore, evil is in reality a lesser good; hence under the guidance of reason we seek or pursue only the greater good and the lesser evil. Q.E.D.

Corollary.— We may, under the guidance of reason, pursue the lesser evil as though it were the greater good, and we may shun the lesser good, which would be the cause of the greater evil. For the evil, which is here called the lesser, is really good, and the lesser good is really evil, wherefore we may seek the former and shun the latter. Q.E.D.

PROP. LXVI. We may, under the guidance of reason, seek a greater good in the future in preference to a lesser good in the present, and we may seek a lesser evil in the present in preference to a greater evil in the future.

Proof.— If the mind could have an adequate knowledge of things future, it would be affected toward what is future in the same way as toward what is present (IV. lxii.); wherefore, looking merely to reason, as in this proposition we are assumed to do, there is no difference, whether the greater good or evil be assumed as present, or assumed as future; hence (IV. lxv.) we may seek a greater good in the future in preference to a lesser good in the present, etc. Q.E.D.

Corollary.— We may, under the guidance of reason, seek a lesser evil in the present, because it is the cause of a greater good in the future, and we may shun a lesser good in the present, because it is the cause of a greater evil in the future. This Corollary is related to the foregoing Proposition as the Corollary to IV. lxv. is related to the said IV. lxv.

Note.— If these statements be compared with what we have pointed out concerning the strength of the emotions in this Part up to Prop. xviii., we shall readily see the difference between a man, who is led solely by emotion or opinion, and a man, who is led by reason. The former, whether he will or no, performs actions whereof he is utterly ignorant; the latter is his own master and only performs such actions, as he knows are of primary importance in life, and therefore chiefly desires; wherefore I call the former a slave, and the latter a free man, concerning whose disposition and manner of life it will be well to make a few observations.

PROP. LXVII. A free man thinks of death least of all things; and his wisdom is a meditation not of death but of life.

Proof.— A free man is one who lives under the guidance of reason, who is not led by fear (IV. lxiii.), but who directly desires that which is good (IV. lxiii. Coroll.), in other words (IV. xxiv.), who strives to act, to live, and to preserve his being on the basis of seeking his own true advantage; wherefore such an one thinks of nothing less than of death, but his wisdom is a meditation of life. Q.E.D.

PROP. LXVIII. If men were born free, they would, so

long as they remained free, form no conception of good and evil.

Proof.—I call free him who is led solely by reason; he, therefore, who is born free, and who remains free, has only adequate ideas; therefore (IV. lxiv. Coroll.), he has no conception of evil, or consequently (good and evil being correlative) of good. Q.E.D.

Note.—It is evident, from IV. iv., that the hypothesis of this Proposition is false and inconceivable, except in so far as we look solely to the nature of man, or rather to God; not in so far as the latter is infinite, but only in so far as he is the cause of man's existence.

This, and other matters which we have already proved, seem to have been signified by Moses in the history of the first man. For in that narrative no other power of God is conceived, save that whereby he created man, that is, the power wherewith he provided solely for man's advantage; it is stated that God forbade man, being free, to eat of the tree of the knowledge of good and evil, and that, as soon as man should have eaten of it, he would straightway fear death rather than desire to live. Further, it is written that when man had found a wife, who was in entire harmony with his nature, he knew that there could be nothing in nature which could be more useful to him; but that after he believed the beasts to be like himself, he straightway began to imitate their emotions (III. xxvii.), and to lose his freedom; this freedom was afterward recovered by the patriarchs, led by the spirit of Christ; that is, by the idea of God, whereon alone it depends, that man may be free, and desire for others the good which he desires for himself, as we have shown above (IV. xxxvii.).

Prop. LXIX. The virtue of a free man is seen to be as great, when it declines dangers, as when it overcomes them.

Proof.—Emotion can only be checked or removed by an emotion contrary to itself, and possessing more power in restraining emotion (IV. vii.). But blind daring and fear are emotions, which can be conceived as equally great (IV. v. and iii.): hence, no less virtue or firmness is required in checking daring than in checking fear (III. lix. note); in other words (Def. of the Emotions, xl. and xli.), the free man shows as much virtue, when he declines dangers, as when he strives to overcome them. Q.E.D.

Corollary.—The free man is as courageous in timely retreat as in combat; or, a free man shows equal courage or presence of mind, whether he elect to give battle or to retreat.

Note.—What courage (*animositas*) is, and what I mean thereby, I explained in III. lix. note. By danger I mean everything, which can give rise to any evil, such as pain, hatred, discord, etc.

PROP. LXX. The free man, who lives among the ignorant, strives, as far as he can, to avoid receiving favors from them.

Proof.—Everyone judges what is good according to his disposition (III. xxxix. note); wherefore an ignorant man, who has conferred a benefit on another, puts his own estimate upon it, and, if it appears to be estimated less highly by the receiver, will feel pain (III. xlii.). But the free man only desires to join other men to him in friendship (IV. xxxvii.), not repaying their benefits with others reckoned as of like value, but guiding himself and others by the free decision of reason, and doing only such things as he knows to be of primary importance. Therefore the free man, lest he should become hateful to the ignorant, or follow their desires rather than reason, will endeavor, as far as he can, to avoid receiving their favors.

Note.—I say, AS FAR AS HE CAN. For though men be ignorant, yet are they men, and in cases of necessity could afford us human aid, the most excellent of all things: therefore it is often necessary to accept favors from them, and consequently to repay such favors in kind; we must, therefore, exercise caution in declining favors, lest we should have the appearance of despising those who bestow them, or of being, from avaricious motives, unwilling to requite them, and so give ground for offense by the very fact of striving to avoid it. Thus, in declining favors, we must look to the requirements of utility and courtesy.

Prop. LXXI. Only free men are thoroughly grateful one to another.

Proof.—Only free men are thoroughly useful one to another, and associated among themselves by the closest necessity of friendship (IV. xxxv. and Coroll. i.) only such men endeavor, with mutual zeal of love, to confer benefits on each other (IV. xxxvii.), and, therefore, only they are thoroughly grateful one to another. Q.E.D.

Note.—The good will, which men who are led by blind desire have for one another, is generally a bargaining or enticement, rather than pure good will. Moreover, ingratitude is not an emotion. Yet it is base, inasmuch as it generally shows, that a man is affected by excessive hatred, anger, pride, avarice, etc. He who, by reason of his folly, knows not how to return benefits, is not ungrateful, much less he who is not gained over by the gifts of a courtesan to serve her lust, or by a thief to conceal his thefts, or by any similar persons. Contrariwise, such an one shows a constant mind, inasmuch as he cannot by any gifts be corrupted, to his own or the general hurt.

Prop. LXXII. The free man never acts fraudulently, but always in good faith.

Proof—If it be asked: What should a man's conduct be in a case where he could by breaking faith free himself from the danger of present death? Would not his plan of self-preservation completely persuade him to deceive? this may be answered by pointing out that, if reason persuaded him to act thus, it would persuade all men to act in a similar manner, in which case reason would persuade men not to agree in good faith to unite their forces, or to have laws in common, that is, not to have any general laws, which is absurd.

Prop. LXXIII. The man who is guided by reason, is more free in a State, where he lives under a general system of law, than in solitude, where he is independent.

Proof.—The man who is guided by reason, does not obey through fear (IV. lxiii.): but, in so far as he endeavors to preserve his being according to the dictates of reason, that is (IV. lxvi. note), in so far as he endeavors to live in freedom, he desires to order his life according to the general good (IV. xxxvii.), and consequently (as we showed in IV. xxxvii. note ii.), to live according to the laws of his country. Therefore the free man, in order to enjoy greater freedom, desires to possess the general rights of citizenship. Q.E.D.

Note.— These and similar observations, which we have made on man's true freedom, may be referred to strength, that is, to courage and nobility of character (III. lix. note). I do not think it worth while to prove separately all the properties of strength; much less need I show, that he that is strong hates no man, is angry with no man, envies no man, is indignant with no man, despises no man, and least of all things is proud. These propositions, and all that relate to the true way of life and religion, are easily proved from IV. xxxvii. and xlvi.; namely, that hatred should be overcome with love, and that every man should desire for others the good which he seeks for himself. We may also repeat what we drew attention to in the note to IV. l., and in other places; namely, that the strong man has ever first in his thoughts, that all things follow from the necessity of the divine nature; so that whatsoever he deems to be hurtful and evil, and whatsoever, accordingly, seems to him impious, horrible, unjust, and base, assumes that appearance owing his own disordered, fragmentary, and confused view of the universe. Wherefore he strives before all things to conceive things as they really are, and to remove the hindrances to true knowledge, such as are hatred, anger, envy, derision, pride, and similar emotions, which I have mentioned above. Thus he endeavors, as we said before, as far as in him lies, to do good, and to go on his way rejoicing. How far human virtue if capable of attaining to such a condition, and what its powers may be, I will prove in the following Part.

APPENDIX.

WHAT I have said in this Part concerning the right way of life has not been arranged, so as to admit of being seen at one view, but has been set forth piecemeal, according as I thought each proposition could most readily be deduced from what preceded it. I propose, therefore, to rearrange my remarks and to bring them under leading heads.

I. All our endeavors or desires so follow from the necessity of our nature, that they can be understood either through it alone, as their proximate cause, or by virtue of our being a part of nature, which cannot be adequately conceived through itself without other individuals.

II. Desires, which follow from our nature in such a manner, that they can be understood through it alone, are those which are referred to the mind, in so far as the latter is conceived to consist of adequate ideas: the remaining desires are only referred to the mind, in so far as it conceives things inadequately, and their force and increase are generally defined not by the power of man, but by the power of things external to us: wherefore the former are rightly called actions, the latter passions, for the former always indicate our power, the latter, on the other hand, show our infirmity and fragmentary knowledge.

III. Our actions, that is, those desires which are defined by man's power or reason, are always good. The rest may be either good or bad.

IV. Thus in life it is before all things useful to perfect the understanding, or reason, as far as we can, and in this alone man's highest happiness or blessedness consists, indeed blessedness is nothing else but the contentment of spirit, which arises from the intuitive knowledge of God: now, to perfect the understanding is nothing else but to understand God, God's attributes, and the actions which follow from the necessity of his nature. Wherefore of a man, who is led by reason, the ultimate aim or highest desire, whereby he seeks to govern all his fellows, is that whereby he is brought to the adequate conception of himself and of all things within the scope of his intelligence.

V. Therefore, without intelligence there is not rational life: and things are only good in so far as they aid man in his enjoyment of the intellectual life, which is defined by intelligence. Contrariwise, whatsoever things hinder man's perfecting of his reason, and capability to enjoy the rational life, are alone called evil.

VI. As all things whereof man is the efficient cause are necessarily good, no evil can befall man except through external causes; namely, by virtue of man being a part of universal nature, whose laws human nature is compelled to obey, and to conform to in almost infinite ways.

VII. It is impossible, that man should not be a part of nature, or that he should not follow her general order; but if he be thrown among individuals whose nature is in harmony with his own, his power of action will thereby be aided and fostered, whereas, if he be thrown among such as are but very little in harmony with his nature, he will hardly be able to accommodate himself to them without undergoing a great change himself.

VIII. Whatsoever in nature we deem to be evil, or to be capable of injuring our faculty for existing and enjoying the rational life, we may endeavor to remove in whatever way seems safest to us; on the other hand, whatsoever we deem to be good or useful for preserving our being, and enabling us to enjoy the rational life, we may appropriate to our use and employ as we think best. Every one without exception may, by sovereign right of nature, do whatsoever he thinks will advance his own interest.

IX. Nothing can be in more harmony with the nature of any given thing than other individuals of the same species; therefore (*cf.* vii.) for man in the preservation of his being and the enjoyment of the rational life there is nothing more useful than his fellow-man who is led by reason. Further, as we know not anything among individual things which is more excellent than a man led by reason, no man can better display the power of his skill and disposition, than in so training men, that they come at last to live under the dominion of their own reason.

X. In so far as men are influenced by envy or any kind of hatred, one toward another, they are at variance, and are therefore to be feared in proportion, as they are more powerful than their fellows.

XI. Yet minds are not conquered by force, but by love and high-mindedness.

XII. It is before all things useful to men to associate their ways of life, to bind themselves together with such bonds as they think most fitted to gather them all into unity, and generally to do whatsoever serves to strengthen friendship.

XIII. But for this there is need of skill and watchfulness. For men are diverse (seeing that those who live under the guidance of reason are few), yet are they generally envious and more prone to revenge than to sympathy. No small force of character is therefore required to take every one as he is, and to restrain one's self from imitating the emotions of others. But those who carp at mankind, and are more skilled in railing at vice than in instilling virtue, and who break rather than strengthen men's dispositions, are hurtful both to themselves and others. Thus many from too great impatience of spirit, or from misguided religious zeal, have preferred to live among brutes rather than among men; as boys or youths, who cannot peaceably endure the chidings of their parents, will enlist as soldiers and choose the hardships of war and the despotic discipline in preference to the comforts of home and the admonitions of their father: suffering any burden to be put upon them, so long as they may spite their parents.

XIV. Therefore, although men are generally governed in everything by their own lusts, yet their association in common brings many more advantages than drawbacks. Wherefore it is better to bear patiently the wrongs they may do us, and to strive to promote whatsoever serves to bring about harmony and friendship.

XV. Those things, which beget harmony, are such as are attributable to justice, equity, and honorable living. For men brook ill not only what is unjust or iniquitous, but also what is reckoned disgraceful, or that a man should slight the received customs of their society. For winning love those qualities are especially necessary which have regard to religion and piety (*cf.* IV. xxxvii. notes, i. ii.; xlvi. note; and lxxiii. note).

XVI. Further, harmony is often the result of fear; but such harmony is insecure. Further, fear arises from infirmity of spirit, and moreover belongs not to the exercise of reason: the same is true of compassion, though this latter seems to bear a certain resemblance to piety.

XVII. Men are also gained over by liberality, especially such as have not the means to buy what is necessary to sustain life. However, to give aid to every poor man is far beyond the power and the advantage of any private person. For the riches of any private person are wholly inadequate to meet such a call. Again, an individual man's resources of character are too limited for him to be able to make all men his friends. Hence providing for the poor is a duty, which falls on the State as a whole, and has regard only to the general advantage.

XVIII. In accepting favors, and in returning gratitude our duty must be wholly different (*cf.* IV. lxx. note; lxxi. note).

XIX. Again, meretricious love, that is, the lust of generation arising from bodily beauty, and generally every sort of love, which owns anything save freedom of soul as its cause, readily passes into hate; unless indeed, what is worse, it is a species of madness; and then it promotes discord rather than harmony (*cf.* III. xxxi. Coroll.).

XX. As concerning marriage, it is certain that this is in harmony with reason, if the desire for physical union be not engendered solely by bodily beauty, but also by the desire to beget children and to train them up wisely; and moreover, if the love of both, to wit, of the man and of the woman, is not caused by bodily beauty only, but also by freedom of soul.

XXI. Furthermore, flattery begets harmony; but only by means of the vile offense of slavishness or treachery. None are more readily taken with flattery than the proud, who wish to be first, but are not.

XXII. There is in abasement a spurious appearance of piety and religion. Although abasement is the opposite to pride, yet is he that abases himself most akin to the proud (IV. lvii. note).

XXIII. Shame also brings about harmony, but only in such matters as cannot be hid. Further, as shame is a species of pain, it does not concern the exercise of reason.

XXIV. The remaining emotions of pain toward men are directly opposed to justice, equity, honor, piety, and religion; and, although indignation seems to bear a certain resemblance to equity, yet is life but lawless, where every man may pass judgment on another's deeds, and vindicate his own or other men's rights.

XXV. Correctness of conduct (*modestia*), that is, the desire of pleasing men which is determined by reason, is attributable to piety (as we said in IV. xxxvii, note i.). But, if it spring from emotion, it is ambition, or the desire whereby men, under the false cloak of piety, generally stir up discords and seditions. For he who desires to aid his fellows either in word or in deed so that they may together enjoy the highest good, he, I say, will before all things, strive to win them over with love: not to draw them into admiration, so that a system may be called after his name, nor to give any cause for envy. Further, in his conversation, he will shrink from talking of men's faults, and will be careful to speak but sparingly of human infirmity; but he will dwell at length on human virtue or power, and the way whereby it may be perfected. Thus will men be stirred not by fear, nor by aversion, but only by the emotion of joy, to endeavor, so far as in them lies, to live in obedience to reason.

XXVI. Besides men, we know of no particular thing in nature in whose mind we may rejoice, and whom we can associate with ourselves in friendship or any sort of fellowship; therefore, whatsoever there be in nature besides man, a regard for our advantage does not call on us to preserve, but to preserve or destroy according to its various capabilities, and to adapt to our use as best we may.

XXVII. The advantage which we derive from things external to us, besides the experience and knowledge which we acquire from observing them, and from recombining their elements in different forms, is principally the preservation of the body; from this point of view, those things are most useful which can so feed and nourish the body, that all its parts may rightly fulfil their functions. For, in proportion as the body is capable of being affected in a greater variety of ways, and of affecting external bodies in a great number of ways, so much the more is the mind capable of thinking (IV. xxxviii. xxxix.). But there seem to be very few things of this kind in nature; wherefore for the due nourishment of the body we must use many foods of diverse nature. For the human body is composed of very many parts of different nature, which stand in continual need of varied nourishment, so that the whole body may be equally capable of doing everything that can follow from its own nature, and consequently that the mind also may be equally capable of forming many perceptions.

XXVIII. Now for providing these nourishments the strength of each individual would hardly suffice, if men did not lend one another mutual aid. But money has furnished us with a token for everything: hence it is with the notion of money, that the mind of the multitude is chiefly engrossed: nay, it can hardly conceive any kind of pleasure, which is not accompanied with the idea of money as cause.

XXIX. This result is the fault only of those, who seek money, not from poverty or to supply their necessary wants, but because they have learned the arts of gain, wherewith they bring themselves to great splendor. Certainly they nourish their bodies, according to custom, but scantily, believing that they lose as much of their wealth as they spend on the preservation of their body. But they who know the true use of money, and who fix the measure of wealth solely with regard to their actual needs, live content with little.

XXX. As, therefore, those things are good which assist the various parts of the body, and enable them to perform their functions; and as pleasure consists in an increase of, or aid to, man's power, in so far as he is composed of mind and body; it follows that all those things which bring pleasure are good. But seeing that things do not work with the object of giving us pleasure, and that their power of action is not tempered to suit our advantage, and lastly, that pleasure is generally referred to one part of the body more than to the other parts; therefore most emotions of pleasure (unless reason and watchfulness be at hand), and consequently the desires arising therefrom, may become excessive. Moreover we may add that emotion leads us to pay most regard to what is agreeable in the present, nor can we estimate what is future with emotions equally vivid. (IV. xliv. note, and lx. note.)

XXXI. Superstition, on the other hand, seems to account as good all that brings pain, and as bad all that brings pleasure. However, as we have said above (IV. xlv. note), none but the envious take delight in my infirmity and trouble. For the greater the pleasure whereby we are affected, the greater is the perfection whereto we pass, and consequently the more do we partake of the divine nature; no pleasure can ever be evil, which is regulated by a true regard for our advantage. But contrariwise he, who is led by fear and does good only to avoid evil, is not guided by reason.

XXXII. But human power is extremely limited, and is infinitely surpassed by the power of external causes; we have not, therefore, an absolute power of shaping to our use those things which are without us. Nevertheless, we shall bear with an equal mind all that happens to us in contravention to the claims of our own advantage, so long as we are conscious, that we have done our duty, and that the power which we possess is not sufficient to enable us to protect ourselves completely; remembering that we are a part of universal nature, and that we follow her order. If we have a clear and distinct understanding of this, that part of our nature which is defined by intelligence, in other words the better part of ourselves, will assuredly acquiesce in what befalls us, and in such acquiescence will endeavor to persist. For, in so far as we are intelligent beings, we cannot desire anything save that which is necessary, nor yield absolute acquiescence to anything, save to that which is true; wherefore, in so far as we have a right understanding of these things, the endeavor of the better part of ourselves is in harmony with the order of nature as a whole.

PART V.

OF THE POWER OF THE UNDERSTANDING, OR OF HUMAN FREEDOM.

PREFACE.

AT LENGTH I pass to the remaining portion of my Ethics, which is concerned with the way leading to freedom, I shall therefore treat therein of the power of the reason, showing how far the reason can control ·the emotions, and what is the nature of Mental Freedom or Blessedness; we shall then be able to see, how much more powerful the wise man is than the ignorant. It is no part of my design to point out the method and the means whereby the understanding may be perfected, nor to show the skill whereby the body may be so tended as to be capable of the due performance of its functions. The latter question lies in the province of Medicine, the former in the province of Logic. Here, therefore, I repeat, I shall treat only of the power of the mind, or of reason; and I shall mainly show the extent and nature of its dominion over the emotions, for their control and moderation. That we do not possess absolute dominion over them, I have already shown. Yet the Stoics have thought, that the emotions depended absolutely on our will, and that we could absolutely govern them. But these philosophers were compelled, by the protest of experience, not from their own principles, to confess, that no slight practice and zeal is needed to control and moderate them: and this someone endeavored to illustrate by the example (if I remember rightly) of two dogs, the one a house dog and the other a hunting dog. For by long training it could be brought about, that the house dog should become accustomed to hunt, and the hunting dog to cease from running after hares. To this opinion Descartes not a little inclines. For he maintained, that the soul or mind is specially united to a particular part of the brain, namely, to that part called the pineal gland, by the aid of which the mind is enabled to feel all the movements which are set going in the body, and also external objects, and which the mind by a simple act of volition can put in motion in various ways. He asserted, that this gland is so suspended in the midst of the brain, that it could be moved by the slightest motion of the animal spirits: further, that this gland is suspended in the midst of the brain in as many different manners, as the animal spirits can impinge thereon ; and, again, that as many different marks are impressed on the said gland, as there are different external objects which impel the animal spirits toward it; whence it follows, that if the will of the soul suspends the gland in a position, wherein it has already been suspended once before by the animal spirits driven in one way or another, the gland in its turn reacts on the said spirits, driving and determining them to the condition wherein they were, when repulsed before by a similar position of the gland. He further asserted, that every act of mental volition is united in nature to a certain given motion of the gland. For instance, whenever anyone desires to look at a remote object, the act of volition causes the pupil of the eye to dilate, whereas, if the person in question had only thought of the dilatation of the pupil, the mere wish to dilate it would not have brought about the result, inasmuch as the motion of the gland, which serves to impel the animal spirits toward the optic nerve in a way which would dilate or contract the pupil, is not associated in nature with the wish to dilate or contract the pupil, but with the wish to look at remote or very near objects. Lastly, he maintained that, although every motion of the aforesaid gland seems to have been united by nature to one particular thought out of the whole number of our thoughts from the very beginning of our life, yet it can nevertheless become through habituation associated with other thoughts; this he endeavors to prove in the " Passions de l'âme," I. 50.

He thence concludes, that there is no soul so weak, that it
cannot, under proper directions, acquire absolute power
over its passions. For passions as defined by him are
"perceptions, or feelings, or disturbances of the soul,
which are referred to the soul as species, and which (mark
the expression) are produced, preserved, and strengthened
through some movement of the spirits." ("Passions de
l'âme," I. 27.) But seeing that we can join any motion
of the gland, or consequently of the spirits, to any volition, the determination of the will depends entirely on
our own powers; if, therefore, we determine our will
with sure and firm decisions in the direction to which
we wish our actions to tend, and associate the motions of the
passions which we wish to acquire with the said decisions,
we shall acquire an absolute dominion over our passions.
Such is the doctrine of this illustrious philosopher (in so
far as I gather it from his own words); it is one which,
had it been less ingenious, I could hardly believe to
have proceeded from so great a man. Indeed, I am
lost in wonder, that a philosopher, who had stoutly asserted, that he would draw no conclusions which do not
follow from self-evident premises, and would affirm nothing which he did not clearly and distinctly perceive, and
who had so often taken to task the scholastics for wishing
to explain obscurities through occult qualities, could
maintain a hypothesis, beside which occult qualities are
commonplace. What does he understand, I ask, by the
union of the mind and the body? What clear and distinct conception has he got of thought in most intimate
union with a certain particle of extended matter? Truly
I should like him to explain this union through its proximate cause. But he had so distinct a conception of
mind being distinct from body, that he could not assign
any particular cause of the union between the two, or
of the mind itself, but was obliged to have recourse to the
cause of the whole universe, that is to God. Further, I
should much like to know what degree of motion the mind
can impart to this pineal gland and with what force can it
hold it suspended? For I am in ignorance, whether this
gland can be agitated more slowly or more quickly by

the mind than by the animal spirits, and whether the
motions of the passions, which we have closely united
with firm decisions, cannot be again disjoined therefrom
by physical causes; in which case it would follow that,
although the mind firmly intended to face a given danger,
and had united to this decision the motions of boldness,
yet at the sight of the danger the gland might become
suspended in a way, which would preclude the mind
thinking of anything except turning away. In truth, as
there is no common standard of volition and motion, so
is there no comparison possible between the powers of
the mind and the power or strength of the body; consequently the strength of one cannot in anywise be determined by the strength of the other. We may also add,
that there is no gland discoverable in the midst of the
brain, so placed that it can thus easily be set in motion
in so many ways, and also that all the nerves are not
prolonged so far as the cavities of the brain. Lastly, I
omit all the assertions which he makes concerning the will
and its freedom, inasmuch as I have abundantly proved
that his premises are false. Therefore, since the power
of the mind, as I have shown above, is defined by the
understanding only, we shall determine solely by the
knowledge of the mind the remedies against the emotions, which I believe all have had experience of, but
do not accurately observe or distinctly see, and from the
same basis we shall deduce all those conclusions, which
have regard to the mind's blessedness.

Axioms.

I. If two contrary actions be started in the same subject, a change must necessarily take place, either in both,
or in one of the two, and continue until they cease to
be contrary.

II. The power of an affect is defined by the power of
its cause, in so far as its essence is explained or defined
by the essence of its cause.

(This axiom is evident from III. vii.)

Prop. I. Even as thoughts and the ideas of things are
arranged and associated in the mind, so are the modifi-

cations of the body or the images of things precisely in the same way arranged and associated in the body.

Proof.— The order and connection of ideas is the same (II. vii.) as the order and connection of things, and *vice versâ* the order and connection of things is the same (II. vi. Coroll. and vii.) as the order and connection of ideas. Wherefore, even as the order and connection of ideas in the mind takes place according to the order and association of modifications of the body (II. xviii.), so *vice versâ* (III. ii.) the order and connection of modifications of the body takes place in accordance with the manner, in which thoughts and the ideas of things are arranged and associated in the mind. Q. E. D.

PROP. II. If we remove a disturbance of the spirit, or emotion, from the thought of an external cause, and unite it to the other thoughts, then will the love or hatred toward that external cause, and also the vacillations of spirit which arise from these emotions, be destroyed.

Proof.— That, which constitutes the reality of love or hatred, is pleasure or pain, accompanied by the idea of an external cause (Def. of the Emotions, vi. vii.); wherefore, when this cause is removed, the reality of love or hatred is removed with it; therefore these emotions and those which arise therefrom are destroyed. Q. E. D.

PROP. III. An emotion, which is a passion, ceases to be a passion, as soon as we form a clear and distinct idea thereof.

Proof.— An emotion, which is a passion, is a confused idea (by the general Def. of the Emotions.). If, therefore, we form a clear and distinct idea of a given emotion, that idea will only be distinguished from the emotion, in so far as it is referred to the mind only, by reason (II. xxi. and note); therefore (III. iii.) the emotion will cease to be a passion. Q. E. D.

Corollary.— An emotion therefore, becomes more under our control, and the mind is less passive in respect to it, in proportion as it is more known to us.

PROP. IV. There is no modification of the body, whereof we cannot form some clear and distinct conception.

Proof.—Properties which are common to all things can only be conceived adeqately (II. xxxviii.); therefore (II. xii. and Lemma ii. after II. xiii.) there is no modification of the body, whereof we cannot form some clear and distinct conception. Q. E. D.

Corollary.— Hence it follows that there is no emotion, whereof we cannot form some clear and distinct conception. For an emotion is the idea of a modification of the body (by the general Def. of the Emotions), and must therefore (by the preceding Prop.) involve some clear and distinct conception.

Note.—Seeing that there is nothing which is not followed by an effect (I. xxxvi.), and that we clearly and distinctly understand whatever follows from an idea, which in us is adequate (II. xl.), it follows that everyone has the power of clearly and distinctly understanding himself and his emotions, if not absolutely, at any rate in part, and consequently of bringing it about, that he should become less subject to them. To attain this result, therefore, we must chiefly direct our efforts to acquiring, as far as possible, a clear and distinct knowledge of every emotion, in order that the mind may thus, through emotion, be determined to think of those things which it clearly and distinctly perceives, and wherein it fully acquiesces: and thus that the emotion itself may be separated from the thought of an external cause, and may be associated with true thoughts; whence it will come to pass, not only that love, hatred, etc., will be destroyed (V. ii.), but also that the appetites or desires, which are wont to arise from such emotion, will become incapable of being excessive (IV. lxi.). For it must be especially remarked, that the appetite through which a man is said to be active, and that through which he is said to be passive is one and the same. For instance, we have shown that human nature is so constituted, that everyone desires his fellow-men to live after his own fashion (III. xxxi. note); in a man, who is not guided by reason, this appetite is a passion which is called ambition, and does not greatly differ from pride; whereas in a man, who lives by the dictates of reason, it is an activity or virtue which is called piety (IV. xxxvii. note i. and second proof). In like manner all appetites or desires are only passions, in so far as they spring from inadequate ideas; the same results are accredited to virtue, when they are aroused or generated by adequate ideas. For all desires, whereby we are determined to any given action, may arise as much from adequate as from inadequate ideas (IV. lix.). Than this remedy for the emotions (to return to the point from which I started), which consists in a true knowledge thereof, nothing more excellent, being within our power, can be devised. For the mind has no other power save that of thinking and of forming adequate ideas, as we have shown above (III. iii.).

PROP. V. An emotion toward a thing, which we conceive simply, and not as necessary, or as contingent, or as possible, is, other conditions being equal, greater than any other emotion.

Proof.—An emotion toward a thing, which we conceive to be free, is greater than one toward what we conceive to be necessary (III. xlix.), and, consequently, still greater than one toward what we conceive as possible, or contingent (IV. xi.). But to conceive a thing as free can be nothing else than to conceive it simply, while we are in ignorance of the causes whereby it has been determined to action (II. xxxv. note); therefore, an emotion toward a thing which we conceive simply is, other conditions being equal, greater than one, which we feel toward what is necessary, possible, or contingent, and, consequently, it is the greatest of all. Q.E.D.

PROP. VI. The mind has greater power over the emotions and is less subject thereto, in so far as it understands all things as necessary.

Proof.—The mind understands all things to be necessary (I. xxix.) and to be determined to existence and operation by an infinite chain of causes; therefore (by the foregoing Proposition), it thus far brings it about, that it is less subject to the emotions arising therefrom, and (III. xlviii.) feels less emotion toward the things themselves. Q.E.D.

Note.—The more this knowledge, that things are necessary, is applied to particular things, which we conceive more distinctly and vividly, the greater is the power of the mind over the emotions, as experience also testifies. For we see, that the pain arising from the loss of any good is mitigated, as soon as the man who has lost it perceives, that it could not by any means have been preserved. So also we see that no one pities an infant, because it cannot speak, walk, or reason, or lastly, because it passes so many years, as it were, in unconsciousness. Whereas, if most people were born full-grown and only one here and there as an infant, every one would pity the infants; because infancy would not then be looked on as a state natural and necessary, but as a fault or delinquency in Nature; and we may note several other instances of the same sort.

Prop. VII. Emotions which are aroused or spring from reason, if we take account of time, are stronger than those, which are attributable to particular objects that we regard as absent.

Proof.—We do not regard a thing as absent, by reason of the emotion wherewith we conceive it, but by reason of the body being affected by another emotion excluding the existence of the said thing (II. xvii.). Wherefore, the emotion, which is referred to the thing which we regard as absent, is not of a nature to overcome the rest of a man's activities and power (IV. vi.), but is, on the contrary, of a nature to be in some sort controlled by the emotions, which exclude the existence of its external cause (IV. ix.). But an emotion which springs from reason is necessarily referred to the common properties of things (see the Def. of Reason in II. xl. note ii.), which we always regard as present (for there can be nothing to exclude their present existence), and which we always conceive in the same manner (II. xxxviii.). Wherefore an emotion of this kind always remains the same; and consequently (V. Ax. i.) emotions, which are contrary thereto and are not kept going by their external causes, will be obliged to adapt themselves to it more and more until they are no longer contrary to it; to this extent the emotion which springs from reason is more powerful. Q.E.D.

PROP. VIII. An emotion is stronger in proportion to the number of simultaneous concurrent causes whereby it is aroused.

Proof.— Many simultaneous causes are more powerful than a few (III. vii.): therefore (IV. v.), in proportion to the increased number of simultaneous causes whereby it is aroused, an emotion becomes stronger. Q.E.D.

Note.— This proposition is also evident from V. Ax. ii.

PROP. IX. An emotion, which is attributable to many and diverse causes which the mind regards as simultaneous with the emotion itself, is less hurtful, and we are less subject thereto and less affected toward each of its causes, than if it were a different and equally powerful emotion attributable to fewer causes or to a single cause.

Proof.— An emotion is only bad or hurtful, in so far as it hinders the mind from being able to think (IV. xxvi. xxvii.); therefore, an emotion, whereby the mind is determined to the contemplation of several things at once, is less hurtful than another equally powerful emotion, which so engrosses the mind in the single contemplation of a few objects or of one, that it is unable to think of anything else; this was our first point. Again, as the mind's essence in other words, its power (III. vii.), consists solely in thought (II. xi.), the mind is less passive in respect to an emotion, which causes it to think of several things at once, than in regard to an equally strong emotion, which keeps it engrossed in the contemplation of a few or of a single object: this was our second point. Lastly, this emotion (III. xlviii.), in so far as it is attributable to several causes, is less powerful in regard to each of them. Q.E.D.

PROP. X. So long as we are not assailed by emotions contrary to our nature, we have the power of arranging and associating the modifications of our body according to the intellectual order.

Proof.— The emotions, which are contrary to our nature, that is (IV. xxx.), which are bad, are bad in so far as they impede the mind from understanding (IV. xxvii.).

So long, therefore, as we are not assailed by emotions contrary to our nature, the mind's power, whereby it endeavors to understand things (IV. xxvi.), is not impeded, and therefore it is able to form clear and distinct ideas and to deduce them one from another (II. xl. note ii. and xlvii. note); consequently we have in such cases the power of arranging and associating the modifications of the body according to the intellectual order. Q.E.D.

Note. — By this power of rightly arranging and associating the bodily modifications we can guard ourselves from being easily affected by evil emotions. For (V. vii.) a greater force is needed for controlling the emotions, when they are arranged and associated according to the intellectual order, than when they are uncertain and unsettled. The best we can do, therefore, so long as we do not possess a perfect knowledge of our emotions, is to frame a system of right conduct, or fixed practical precepts, to commit it to memory, and to apply it forthwith to the particular circumstances which now and again meet us in life, so that our imagination may become fully imbued therewith, and that it may be always ready to our hand. For instance, we have laid down among the rules of life (IV. xlvi. and note), that hatred should be overcome with love or high-mindedness, and not requited with hatred in return. Now, that this precept of reason may be always ready to our hand in time of need, we should often think over and reflect upon the wrongs generally committed by men, and in what manner and way they may be best warded off by high-mindedness: we shall thus associate the idea of wrong with the idea of this precept, which accordingly will always be ready for use when a wrong is done to us (II. xviii.). If we keep also in readiness the notion of our true advantage, and of the good which follows from mutual friendships, and common fellowships; further, if we remember that complete acquiescence is the result of the right way of life (IV. lii.), and that men, no less than everything else, act by the necessity of their nature: in such case I say the wrong, or the hatred, which commonly arises therefrom, will engross a very small part of our imagination and will be easily overcome; or, if the anger which springs from a grievous wrong be not overcome easily, it will nevertheless be overcome, though not without a spiritual conflict, far sooner than if we had not thus reflected on the subject beforehand. As is indeed evident from V. vi. vii. viii. We should, in the same way, reflect on courage as a means of overcoming fear; the ordinary dangers of life should frequently be brought to mind and imagined, together with the means whereby through readiness of resource and strength of mind we can avoid and overcome them. But we must note, that in arranging our thoughts and conceptions we should always bear in mind that which is good in every individual thing (IV. lxiii. Coroll. and III. lix.), in order that we may always be determined to action by an emotion of pleasure. For instance, if a man sees that he is too keen in the pursuit of honor, let him think over its right use, the end for which it should be pursued, and the means whereby he may attain it. Let him not think of its misuse, and its emptiness, and the fickleness of mankind, and the like, whereof no man thinks except through a morbidness of disposition; with thoughts like these do the most ambitious most torment themselves, when they despair of gaining the distinctions they hanker after, and in thus giving vent to their anger would fain appear wise. Wherefore it is certain that those, who cry out the loudest against the misuse of honor and the vanity of the world, are those who most greedily covet it. This is not peculiar to the ambitious, but is common to all who are ill-used by fortune, and who are infirm in spirit. For a poor man also, who is miserly, will talk incessantly of the misuse of wealth and of the vices of the rich; whereby he merely torments himself, and shows the world that he is intolerant, not only of his own poverty, but also of other people's riches. So, again, those who have been ill received by a woman they love think of nothing but the inconstancy, treachery and other stock faults of the fair sex; all of which they consign to oblivion, directly they are again taken into favor by their sweetheart. Thus he who would govern his emotions and appetite solely by the love of freedom strives, as far as he can, to gain a knowledge of the virtues and their causes, and to fill his spirit with the joy which arises from the true knowledge of them: he will in no wise desire to dwell on men's faults, or to carp at his fellows, or to revel in a false show of freedom. Whosoever will diligently observe and practice these precepts (which indeed are not difficult) will verily, in a short space of time, be able for the most part to direct his actions according to the commandments of reason.

PROP. XI. In proportion as a mental image is referred to more objects, so is it more frequent, or more often vivid, and occupies the mind more.

Proof.—In proportion as a mental image or an emotion is referred to more objects, so are there more causes whereby it can be aroused and fostered, all of which (by hypothesis) the mind contemplates simultaneously in association with the given emotion; therefore the emotion is more frequent, or is more often in full vigor, and (V. viii.) occupies the mind more. Q.E.D.

PROP. XII. The mental images of things are more easily associated with the images referred to things which we clearly and distinctly understand, than with others.

Proof.—Things, which we clearly and distinctly understand, are either the common properties of things or deductions therefrom (see Def. of Reason, II. xl. note ii.), and are consequently (by the last Prop.) more often aroused in us. Wherefore it may more readily happen, that we should contemplate other things in conjunction with these than in conjunction with something else, and consequently (II. xviii.) that the images of the said things should be more often associated with the images of these than with the images of something else. Q.E.D.

PROP. XIII. A mental image is more often vivid, in proportion as it is associated with a greater number of other images.

Proof. — In proportion as an image is associated with a greater number of other images, so (II. xviii.)

are there more causes whereby it can be aroused.
Q. E. D.

PROP. XIV. The mind can bring it about, that all
bodily modifications or images of things may be referred
to the idea of God.

Proof.— There is no modification of the body, whereof
the mind may not form some clear and distinct conception (V. iv.); wherefore it can bring it about, that they
should all be referred to the idea of God (I. xv.). Q. E. D.

PROP. XV. He who clearly and distinctly understands
himself and his emotions loves God, and so much the
more in proportion as he more understands himself and
his emotions.

Proof.— He who clearly and distinctly understands himself and his emotions feels pleasure (III. liii.), and this
pleasure is (by the last Prop.) accompanied by the idea
of God; therefore (Def. of the Emotions, vi.) such an one
loves God, and (for the same reason) so much the more
in proportion as he more understands himself and his
emotions. Q. E. D.

PROP. XVI. This love toward God must hold the chief
place in the mind.

Proof.— For this love is associated with all the modifications of the body (V. xiv.) and is fostered by them all
(V. xv.); therefore (V. xi.), it must hold the chief place
in the mind. Q. E. D.

PROP. XVII. God is without passions, neither is he
affected by any emotion of pleasure or pain.

Proof.— All ideas, in so far as they are referred to God,
are true (II. xxxii.), that is (II. Def. iv.) adequate; and
therefore (by the General Def. of the Emotions) God is
without passions. Again, God cannot pass either to a
greater or to a lesser perfection (I. xx. Coroll. ii.); therefore (by Def. of the Emotions. ii. iii.), he is not affected
by any emotion of pleasure or pain.

Corollary.— Strictly speaking, God does not love or hate
anyone. For God (by the foregoing Prop.) is not affected
by any emotion of pleasure or pain, consequently (Def. of
the Emotions, vi. vii.) he does not love or hate anyone.

PROP. XVIII. No one can hate God.

Proof.— The idea of God which is in us is adequate and perfect (II. xlvi. xlvii.); wherefore, in so far as we contemplate God, we are active (III. iii.); consequently (III. lix.) there can be no pain accompanied by the idea of God, in other words (Def. of the Emotions, vii.), no one can hate God. Q. E. D.

Corollary.— Love toward God cannot be turned into hate.

Note.— It may be objected that, as we understand God as the cause of all things, we by that very fact regard God as the cause of pain. But I make answer, that, in so far as we understand the causes of pain, it to that extent (V. iii) ceases to be a passion, that is, it ceases to be pain (III. lix.); therefore, in so far as we understand God to be the cause of pain, we to that extent feel pleasure.

Prop. XIX. He, who loves God, cannot endeavor that God should love him in return.

Proof.— For if a man should so endeavor, he would desire (V. xvii. Coroll.) that God, whom he loves, should not be God, and consequently he would desire to feel pain (III. xix.); which is absurd (III. xxviii.). Therefore, he who loves God, etc. Q. E. D.

Prop. XX. This love toward God cannot be stained by by the emotion of envy or jealousy: contrariwise, it is the more fostered, in proportion as we conceive a greater number of men to be joined to God by the same bond of love.

Proof.— This love toward God is the highest good which we can seek for under the guidance of reason (IV. xxviii.), it is common to all men (IV. xxxvi.), and we desire that all should rejoice therein (IV. xxxvii.); therefore (Def. of the Emotions, xxiii.), it cannot be stained by the emotion of envy, nor by the emotion of jealousy (V. xviii. see Def. of Jealousy, III. xxxv. note); but, contrariwise, it must needs be the more fostered, in proportion as we conceive a greater number of men to rejoice therein. Q. E. D.

Note.— We can in the same way show, that there is no emotion directly contrary to this love, whereby this love can be destroyed; therefore we may conclude, that this love toward God is the most constant of all the emotions, and that, in so far as it is referred to the body, it cannot be destroyed unless the body be destroyed also. As to its nature, in so far as it is referred to the mind only, we shall presently inquire.

I have now gone through all the remedies against the emotions, or all that the mind, considered in itself alone, can do against them. Whence it appears that the mind's power over the emotions consists:

I. In the actual knowledge of the emotions (V. iv. note).

II. In the fact that it separates the emotions from the thought of an external cause, which we conceive confusedly (V. ii. and iv. note).

III. In the fact, that, in respect to time, the emotions referred to things, which we distinctly understand, surpass those referred to what we conceive in a confused and fragmentary manner (V. vii.).

IV. In the number of causes whereby those modifications* are fostered, which have regard to the common properties of things or to God (V. ix. xi.).

V. Lastly, in the order wherein the mind can arrange and associate, one with another, its own emotions (V. x. note and xii. xiii. xiv.).

But in order that this power of the mind over the emotions may be better understood, it should be specially observed that the emotions are called by us strong, when we compare the emotion of one man with the emotion of another, and see that one man is more troubled than another by the same emotion; or when we are comparing the various emotions of the same man one with another, and find that he is more affected or stirred by one emotion than by another. For the strength of every emotion is defined by a comparison of our own power with the power of an external cause. Now the power of the mind is defined by knowledge only, and its infirmity or passion is defined by the privation of knowledge only: it therefore follows, that that mind is most passive, whose greatest part is made up of inadequate ideas, so that it may

* *Affectiones.* Camerer reads *affectus*—emotions.

be characterized more readily by its passive states than by its activities: on the other hand, that mind is most active, whose greatest part is made up of adequate ideas, so that, although it may contain as many inadequate ideas as the former mind, it may yet be more easily characterized by ideas attributable to human virtue, than by ideas which tell of human infirmity. Again, it must be observed, that spiritual unhealthiness and misfortunes can generally be traced to excessive love for something which is subject to many variations, and which we can never become masters of. For no one is solicitous or anxious about anything, unless he loves it; neither do wrongs, suspicions, enmities, etc., arise, except in regard to things whereof no one can be really master.

We may thus readily conceive the power which clear and distinct knowledge, and especially that third kind of knowledge (II. xlvii. note), founded on the actual knowledge of God, possesses over the emotions; if it does not absolutely destroy them, in so far as they are passions (V. iii. and iv. note); at any rate, it causes them to occupy a very small part of the mind (V. xiv.). Further, it begets a love toward a thing immutable and eternal (V. xv.), whereof we may really enter into possession (II. xlv.); neither can it be defiled with those faults which are inherent in ordinary love; but it may grow from strength to strength, and may engross the greater part of the mind, and deeply penetrate it.

And now I have finished with all that concerns this present life; for, as I said in the beginning of this note, I have briefly described all the remedies against the emotions. And this every one may readily have seen for himself, if he has attended to what is advanced in the present note, and also to the definitions of the mind and its emotions, and, lastly to Propositions i. and iii. of Part III. It is now, therefore, time to pass on to those matters, which appertain to the duration of the mind, without relation to the body.

PROP. XXI. The mind can only imagine anything, or remember what is passed, while the body endures.

Proof.— The mind does not express the actual exist-ence of its body, nor does it imagine the modifications of the body as actual, except while the body endures (II. viii. Coroll.); and, consequently, (II. xxvi.), it does not imagine anybody as actually existing, except while its own body endures. Thus it cannot imagine anything (for Def. of Imagination, see II. xvii. note), or re-member things past, except while the body endures (see Def. of Memory, II. xviii. note). Q.E.D.

PROP. XXII. Nevertheless in God there is necessarily an idea, which expresses the essence of this or that human body under the form of eternity.

Proof.— God is the cause, not only of the existence of this or that human body, but also of its essence (I. xxv.). This essence, therefore, must necessarily be con-ceived through the very essence of God (I. Ax. iv.), and be thus conceived by a certain eternal necessity (I. xvi.); and this conception must necessarily exist in God (II. iii.). Q.E.D.

PROP. XXIII. The human mind cannot be absolutely destroyed with the body, but there remains of it some-thing which is eternal.

Proof.— There is necessarily in God a concept or idea, which expresses the essence of the human body (last Prop.), which, therefore, is necessarily something apper-taining to the essence of the human mind (II. xiii.). But we have not assigned to the human mind any duration, definable by time, except in so far as it expresses the actual existence of the body, which is explained through duration, and may be defined by time — that is (II. viii. Coroll.), we do not assign to it dura-tion, except while the body endures. Yet, as there is something, notwithstanding, which is conceived by a certain eternal necessity through the very essence of God (last Prop.); this something, which appertains to the essence of the mind, will necessarily be eternal. Q.E.D.

Note.— This idea, which expresses the essence of the body under the form of eternity, is, as we have said, a certain mode of thinking, which belongs to the essence of the mind, and is necessarily eternal. Yet it is not possible that we should remember that we existed before our body, for our body can bear no trace of such existence, neither can eternity be defined in terms of time, or have any relation to time. But, notwithstanding, we feel and know that we are eternal. For the mind feels those things that it conceives by understanding, no less than those things that it remembers. For the eyes of the mind, whereby it sees and observes things, are none other than proofs. Thus, although we do not remember that we existed before the body, yet we feel that our mind, in so far as it involves the essence of the body, under the form of eternity, is eternal, and that thus its existence cannot be defined in terms of time, or explained through duration. Thus our mind can only be said to endure, and its existence can only be defined by a fixed time, in so far as it involves the actual existence of the body. Thus far only has it the power of determining the existence of things by time, and conceiving them under the category of duration.

PROP. XXIV. The more we understand particular things, the more do we understand God.

Proof.— This is evident from I. xxv. Coroll.

PROP. XXV. The highest endeavor of the mind, and the highest virtue is to understand things by the third kind of knowledge.

Proof.— The third kind of knowledge proceeds from an adequate idea of certain attributes of God to an adequate knowledge of the essence of things (see its definition II. xl. note ii.); and, in proportion as we understand things more in this way, we better understand God (by the last Prop.); therefore (IV. xxviii.) the highest virtue of the mind, that is (IV. Def. viii.) the power, or nature, or (III. vii.) highest endeavor of the mind, is to understand things by the third kind of knowledge. Q.E.D.

PROP. XXVI. In proportion as the mind is more capable of understanding things by the third kind of knowledge, it desires more to understand things by that kind.

Proof.— This is evident. For, in so far as we conceive the mind to be capable of conceiving things by this kind of knowledge, we, to that extent, conceive it as determined thus to conceive things; and consequently (Def. of the Emotions, i.), the mind desires so to do, in proportion as it is more capable thereof. Q.E.D.

PROP. XXVII. From this third kind of knowledge arises the highest possible mental acquiescence.

Proof.—The highest virtue of the mind is to know God (IV. xxviii.), or to understand things by the third kind of knowledge (V. xxv.), and this virtue is greater in proportion as the mind knows things more by the said kind of knowledge (V. xxiv.): consequently, he who knows things by this kind of knowledge passes to the summit of human perfection, and is therefore (Def. of the Emotions, ii.) affected by the highest pleasure, such pleasure being accompanied by the idea of himself and his own virtue: thus (Def. of the Emotions, xxv.), from this kind of knowledge arises the highest possible acquiescence. Q.E.D.

PROP. XXVIII. The endeavor or desire to know things by the third kind of knowledge cannot arise from the first, but from the second kind of knowledge.

Proof.—This proposition is self-evident. For whatsoever we understand clearly and distinctly, we understand either through itself, or through that which is conceived through itself; that is, ideas which are clear and distinct in us, or which are referred to the third kind of knowledge (II. xl. note ii.) cannot follow from ideas that are fragmentary aud confused, and are referred to knowledge of the first kind, but must follow from adequate ideas, or ideas of the second and third kind of knowledge; therefore (Def. of the Emotions, i.), the desire of knowing things by the third kind of knowledge cannot arise from the first, but from the second kind. Q.E.D.

PROP. XXIX. Whatsoever the mind understands under the form of eternity, it does not understand by virtue of conceiving the present actual existence of the body, but by virtue of conceiving the essence of the body under the form of eternity.

Proof.—In so far as the mind conceives the present existence of its body, it to that extent conceives duration which can be determined by time, and to that extent only has it the power of conceiving things in relation to time (V. xxi. II. xxvi.). But eternity cannot be explained in terms of duration (I. Def. viii. and explanation). Therefore to this extent the mind has not the power of conceiving things under the form of eternity, but it possesses such power, because it is of the nature of reason to conceive things under the form of eternity (II. xliv. Coroll. ii.), and also because it is of the nature of the mind to conceive the essence of the body under the form of eternity (V. xxiii.), for besides these two there is nothing which belongs to the essence of mind (II. xiii.). Therefore this power of conceiving things under the form of eternity only belongs to the mind in virtue of the mind's conceiving the essence of the body under the form of eternity. Q.E.D.

Note.— Things are conceived by us as actual in two ways: either as existing in relation to a given time and place, or as contained in God and following from the necessity of the divine nature. Whatsoever we conceive in this second way as true or real, we conceive under the form of eternity, and their ideas involve the eternal and infinite essence of God, as we showed in II. xlv. and note, which see.

PROP. XXX. Our mind, in so far as it knows itself and the body under the form of eternity, has to that extent necessarily a knowledge of God, and knows that it is in God, and is conceived through God.

Proof.— Eternity is the very essence of God, in so far as this involves necessary existence (I. Def. viii.). Therefore to conceive things under the form of eternity, is to conceive things in so far as they are conceived through the essence of God as real entities, or in so far as they involve existence through the essence of God; wherefore our mind, in so far as it conceives itself and the body under the form of eternity, has to that extent necessarily a knowledge of God, and knows, etc. Q.E.D.

PROP. XXXI. The third kind of knowledge depends on the mind, as its formal cause, in so far as the mind itself is eternal.

Proof.—The mind does not conceive anything under the form of eternity, except in so far as it conceives its own body under the form of eternity (V. xxix.); that is, except in so far as it is eternal (V. xxi. xxiii.); therefore (by the last Prop.), in so far as it is eternal, it possesses the knowledge of God, which knowledge is necessarily adequate (II. xlvi.); hence the mind, in so far as it is eternal, is capable of knowing everything which can follow from this given knowledge of God (II. xl.), in other words, of knowing things by the third kind of knowledge (see Def. in II. xl. note ii.), whereof accordingly the mind (III. Def. i.), in so far as it is eternal, is the adequate or formal cause of such knowledge. Q. E. D.

Note.—In proportion, therefore, as a man is more potent in this kind of knowledge, he will be more completely conscious of himself and of God; in other words, he will be more perfect and blessed, as will appear more clearly in the sequel. But we must here observe that, although we are already certain that the mind is eternal, in so far as it conceives things under the form of eternity, yet, in order that what we wish to show may be more readily explained and better understood, we will consider the mind itself, as though it had just begun to exist and to understand things under the form of eternity, as indeed we have done hitherto; this we may do without any danger of error, so long as we are careful not to draw any conclusion, unless our premises are plain.

Prop. XXXII. Whatsoever we understand by the third kind of knowledge, we take delight in, and our delight is accompanied by the idea of God as cause.

Proof.—From this kind of knowledge arises the highest possible mental acquiescence, that is (Def. of the Emotions, xxv.), pleasure, and this acquiescence is accompanied by the idea of the mind itself (V. xxvii.), and consequently (V. xxx.) the idea also of God as cause. Q. E. D.

Corollary.—From the third kind of knowledge necessarily arises the intellectual love of God. From this kind of knowledge arises pleasure accompanied by the idea of

God as cause, that is (Def. of the Emotions, vi.), the love
of God; not in so far as we imagine him as present (V.
xxix.), but in so far as we understand him to be eternal;
this is what I call the intellectual love of God.

PROP. XXXIII. The intellectual love of God, which
arises from the third kind of knowledge, is eternal.

Proof.—The third kind of knowledge is eternal (V.
xxxi. I. Ax. iii.); therefore (by the same Axiom), the love
which arises therefrom is also necessarily eternal. Q.E.D.

Note.—Although this love toward God has (by the foregoing Prop.) no beginning, it yet possesses all the perfections of love, just as though it had arisen as we feigned
in the Corollary of the last Proposition. Nor is there
here any difference, except that the mind possesses as
eternal those same perfections which we feigned to accrue to it, and they are accompanied by the idea of God
as eternal cause. If pleasure consists in the transition
to a greater perfection, assuredly blessedness must consist in the mind being endowed with perfection itself.

PROP. XXXIV. The mind is, only while the body endures, subject to those emotions which are attributable to
passions.

Proof.—Imagination is the idea wherewith the mind
contemplates a thing as present (II. xvii. note); yet this
idea indicates rather the present disposition of the human
body than the nature of the external thing (II. xvi. Coroll.
ii.). Therefore emotion (see General Def. of Emotions)
is imagination, in so far as it indicates the present disposition of the body; therefore (V. xxi.) the mind is,
only while the body endures, subject to emotions which
are attributable to passions. Q.E.D.

Corollary.—Hence it follows that no love save intellectual love is eternal.

Note.—If we look to men's general opinion, we shall
see that they are indeed conscious of the eternity of
their mind, but that they confuse eternity with duration,
and ascribe it to the imagination or the memory which they
believe to remain after death.

PROP. XXXV. God loves himself with an infinite intellectual love.

Proof.—God is absolutely infinite (I. Def. vi.), that is
(II. Def. vi.), the nature of God rejoices in infinite perfection; and such rejoicing is (II. iii.) accompanied by
the idea of himself, that is (I. xi. and Def. i.), the idea
of his own cause: now this is what we have (in V. xxxii.
Coroll.) described as intellectual love.

PROP. XXXVI. The intellectual love of the mind toward
God is that very love of God whereby God loves himself,
not in so far as he is infinite, but in so far as he can
be explained through the essence of the human mind
regarded under the form of eternity; in other words, the
intellectual love of the mind toward God is part of the
infinite love wherewith God loves himself.

Proof.—This love of the mind must be referred to the
activities of the mind (V. xxxii. Coroll. and III. iii.); it
is itself, indeed, an activity whereby the mind regards
itself accompanied by the idea of God as cause (V. xxxii.
and Coroll.); that is (I. xxv. Coroll. and II. xi. Coroll.)
an activity whereby God, in so far as he can be explained
through the human mind, regards himself accompanied
by the idea of himself; therefore (by the last Prop.),
this love of the mind is part of the infinite love wherewith God loves himself. Q.E.D.

Corollary.—Hence it follows that God, in so far as he
loves himself, loves man, and consequently, that the
love of God toward men, and the intellectual love of the
mind toward God are identical.

Note.—From what has been said we clearly understand,
wherein our salvation, or blessedness, or freedom, consists: namely, in the constant and eternal love toward
God, or in God's love toward men. This love or blessedness is, in the Bible, called Glory, and not undeservedly.
For whether this love be referred to God or to the mind, it
may rightly be called acquiescence of spirit, which (Def.
of the Emotions, xxv. xxx.) is not really distinguished
from glory. In so far as it is referred to God, it is (V.
xxxv) pleasure, if we may still use that term, accompanied by the idea of itself, and, in so far as it is referred
to the mind, it is the same (V. xxvii.).

Again, since the essence of our mind consists solely in

knowledge, whereof the beginning and the foundation is God (I. xv. and II. xlvii. note), it becomes clear to us, in what manner and way our mind, as to its essence and existence, follows from the divine nature and constantly depends on God. I have thought it worth while here to call attention to this, in order to show by this example how the knowledge of particular things, which I have called intuitive or of the third kind (II. xl. note ii.), is potent, and more powerful than the universal knowledge, which I have styled knowledge of the second kind. For, although in Part I. I showed in general terms, that all things (and consequently, also, the human mind) depend as to their essence and existence on God, yet that demonstration, though legitimate and placed beyond the chances of doubt, does not affect our mind so much, as when the same conclusion is derived from the actual essence of some particular thing, which we say depends on God.

PROP. XXXVII. There is nothing in nature, which is contrary to this intellectual love, or which can take it away.

Proof.— This intellectual love follows necessarily from the nature of the mind, in so far as the latter is regarded through the nature of God as an eternal truth (V. xxxiii. and xxix.). If, therefore, there should be anything which would be contrary to this love, that thing would be contrary to that which is true; consequently, that, which should be able to take away this love, would cause that which is true to be false; an obvious absurdity. Therefore there is nothing in nature which, etc. Q.E.D.

Note.— The Axiom of Part IV. has reference to particular things, in so far as they are regarded in relation to a given time and place: of this, I think, no one can doubt.

PROP. XXXVIII. In proportion as the mind understands more things by the second and third kind of knowledge, it is less subject to those emotions which are evil, and stands in less fear of death.

Proof.— The mind's essence consists in knowledge (II. xi.); therefore, in proportion as the mind understands more things by the second and third kinds of knowledge, the greater will be the part of it that endures (V. xxix. and xxiii.), and, consequently (by the last Prop.), the greater will be the part that is not touched by the emotions, which are contrary to our nature, or in other words, evil (IV. xxx.). Thus, in proportion as the mind understands more things by the second and third kinds of knowledge, the greater will be the part of it, that remains unimpaired, and, consequently, less subject to emotions, etc. Q. E. D.

Note.—Hence we understand that point which I touched on in IV. xxxix. note, and which I promised to explain in this Part; namely, that death becomes less hurtful, in proportion as the mind's clear and distinct knowledge is greater, and, consequently, in proportion as the mind loves God more. Again, since from the third kind of knowledge arises the highest possible acquiescence (V. xxvii.), it follows that the human mind can attain to being of such a nature, that the part thereof which we have shown to perish with the body (V. xxi.) should be of little importance when compared with the part which endures. But I will soon treat of the subject at greater length.

PROP. XXXIX. He, who possesses a body capable of the greatest number of activities, possesses a mind whereof the greatest part is eternal.

Proof.—He, who possesses a body capable of the greatest number of activities, is least agitated by those emotions which are evil (IV. xxxviii.)—that is (IV. xxx.), by those emotions which are contrary to our nature; therefore (V. x.), he possesses the power of arranging and associating the modifications of the body according to the intellectual order, and, consequently, of bringing it about, that all the modifications of the body should be referred to the idea of God; whence it will come to pass that (V. xv.) he will be affected with love toward God, which (V. xvi.) must occupy or constitute the chief part of the mind; therefore (V. xxxiii.), such a man will possess a mind whereof the chief part is eternal. Q. E. D.

Note.—Since human bodies are capable of the greatest number of activities, there is no doubt but that they may be of such a nature, that they may be referred to minds possessing a great knowledge of themselves and of God, and whereof the greatest or chief part is eternal, and, therefore, that they should scarcely fear death. But, in order that this may be understood more clearly, we must here call to mind, that we live in a state of perpetual variation, and, according as we are changed for the better or the worse, we are called happy or unhappy.

For he, who, from being an infant or a child, becomes a corpse, is called unhappy; whereas it is set down to happiness, if we have been able to live through the whole period of life with a sound mind in a sound body. And, in reality, he, who, as in the case of an infant or a child, has a body capable of very few activities, and depending, for the most part, on external causes, has a mind which, considered in itself alone, is scarcely conscious of itself, or of God, or of things; whereas, he, who has a body capable of very many activities, has a mind which, considered in itself alone, is highly conscious of itself, of God, and of things. In this life, therefore, we primarily endeavor to bring it about, that the body of a child, in so far as its nature allows and conduces thereto, may be changed into something else capable of very many activities, and referable to a mind which is highly conscious of itself, of God, and of things; and we desire so to change it, that what is referred to its imagination and memory may become insignificant, in comparison with its intellect, as I have already said in the note to the last Proposition.

Prop. XL. In proportion as each thing possesses more of perfection, so is it more active, and less passive; and, *vice versâ*, in proportion as it is more active, so is it more perfect.

Proof. — In proportion as each thing is more perfect, it possesses more of reality (II. Def. vi.), and, consequently (III. iii. and note), it is to that extent more active and less passive. This demonstration may be reversed, and thus prove that, in proportion as a thing is more active, so is it more perfect. Q. E. D.

Corollary. — Hence it follows that the part of the mind which endures, be it great or small, is more perfect than the rest. For the eternal part of the mind (V. xxiii. xxix.) is the understanding, through which alone we are said to act (III. iii.); the part which we have shown to perish is the imagination (V. xxi.), through which only we are said to be passive (III. iii. and general Def. of the Emotions); therefore, the former, be it great or small, is more perfect than the latter. Q. E. D.

Note. — Such are the doctrines which I had purposed to set forth concerning the mind, in so far as it is regarded without relation to the body; whence, as also from I. xxi. and other places, it is plain that our mind, in so far as it understands, is an eternal mode of thinking, which is determined by another eternal mode of thinking, and this other by a third, and so on to infinity; so that all taken together at once constitute the eternal and infinite intellect of God.

Prop. XLI. Even if we did not know that our mind is eternal, we should still consider as of primary importance piety and religion, and generally all things which, in Part. IV., we showed to be attributable to courage and high-mindedness.

Proof. — The first and only foundation of virtue, or the rule of right living is (IV. xxii. Coroll. and xxiv.) seeking one's own true interest. Now, while we determined what reason prescribes as useful, we took no account of the mind's eternity, which has only become known to us in this Fifth Part. Although we were ignorant at that time that the mind is eternal, we nevertheless stated that the qualities attributable to courage and high-mindedness are of primary importance. Therefore, even if we were still ignorant of this doctrine, we should yet put the aforesaid precepts of reason in the first place. Q. E. D.

Note. — The general belief of the multitude seems to be different. Most people seem to believe that they are free, in so far as they may obey their lusts, and that they cede their rights, in so far as they are bound to live according to the commandments of the divine law. They therefore believe that piety, religion, and generally, all things attributable to firmness of mind, are burdens, which, after death, they hope to lay aside, and to receive the reward for their bondage, that is, for their piety and religion; it is not only by this hope, but also, and chiefly, by the fear of being horribly punished after death, that they are induced to live according to the divine commandments, so far as their feeble and infirm spirit will carry them.

If men had not this hope and this fear, but believed that the mind perishes with the body, and that no hope of prolonged life remains for the wretches who are broken down with the burden of piety, they would return to their own inclinations, controlling everything in accordance with their lusts, and desiring to obey fortune rather than themselves. Such a course appears to me not less absurd than if a man, because he does not believe that he can by wholesome food sustain his body for ever, should wish to cram himself with poisons and deadly fare; or if, because he sees that the mind is not eternal or immortal, he should prefer to be out of his mind altogether, and to live without the use of reason; these ideas are so absurd as to be scarcely worth refuting.

PROP. XLII. Blessedness is not the reward of virtue, but virtue itself; neither do we rejoice therein, because we control our lusts, but contrariwise, because we rejoice therein, we are able to control our lusts.

Proof.— Blessedness consists in love toward God (V. xxxvi. and note), which love springs from the third kind of knowledge (V. xxxii. Coroll.); therefore this love (III. iii. lix.) must be referred to the mind, in so far as the latter is active; therefore (IV. Def. viii.) it is virtue itself. This was our first point. Again, in proportion as the mind rejoices more in this divine love or blessedness, so does it the more understand (V. xxxii.); that is (V. iii. Coroll.), so much the more power has it over the emotions, and (V. xxxviii.) so much the less is it subject to those emotions which are evil; therefore, in proportion as the mind rejoices in this divine love or blessedness, so has it the power of controlling lusts. And, since human power in controlling the emotions consists solely in the understanding, it follows that no one rejoices in blessedness, because he has controlled his lusts, but, contrariwise, his power of controlling his lusts arises from this blessedness itself. Q.E.D.

Note.—I have thus completed all I wished to set forth touching the mind's power over the emotions and the mind's freedom. Whence it appears, how potent is the wise man, and how much he surpasses the ignorant man, who is driven only by his lusts. For the ignorant man is not only distracted in various ways by external causes without ever gaining the true acquiescence of his spirit, but moreover lives, as it were unwitting of himself, and of God, and of things, and as soon as he ceases to suffer, ceases also to be.

Whereas the wise man, in so far as he is regarded as such, is scarcely at all disturbed in spirit, but, being conscious of himself, and of God, and of things, by a certain eternal necessity, never ceases to be, but always possesses true acquiescence of his spirit.

If the way which I have pointed out as leading to this result seems exceedingly hard, it may nevertheless be discovered. Needs must it be hard, since it is so seldom found. How would it be possible, if salvation were ready to our hand, and could without great labor be found, that it should be by almost all men neglected? But all things excellent are as difficult as they are rare.

ORDER FORM
GREAT BOOKS IN PHILOSOPHY PAPERBACK SERIES

SPECIAL—For your library . . . The entire collection of 28 "Great Books in Philosophy" available at a savings of more than 15%. Only $142.50 (plus $5.00 postage and handling.) Please indicate "Great Books—Complete Set" on your order form.

The books listed can be obtained from your book dealer or directly from Prometheus Books. Please indicate the appropriate books. Remittance must accompany all orders from individuals. Please include $2.25 postage and handling for the first book and $.85 for each additional title (maximum $5.00). (NYS residents please include applicable sales tax.) This offer ends without notice.

Send to _____

(please print clearly)

Address _____

City _____ State _____ Zip _____

Amount enclosed _____

Charge my ☐ **VISA** ☐ **Mastercard**

Account # ☐☐☐☐☐☐☐☐☐☐☐☐☐☐☐☐☐☐☐

Exp. Date _____ / _____ Tel. # ( )_____

Signature _____

Prometheus Books
700 E. Amherst Street, Buffalo, New York 14215

Phone Orders (Outside NYS)
Call toll free: (800) 421-0351
In N.Y. State: (716) 837-2475
FAX # (716) 835-6901
Please allow 3-6 weeks for delivery